How & When to Tell Your Kids About Sex

A Lifelong Approach to Shaping Your Child's Sexual Character

STANTON L. & BRENNA B. JONES

NAVPRESS

BRINGING TRUTH TO LIFE
NavPress Publishing Group
P.O. Box 35001, Colorado Springs, Colorado 80935

© 1993 By Stanton L. and Brenna B. Jones
All rights reserved. No part of this publication may be reproduced in any form without
    written permission from NavPress, P.O. Box 35001, Colorado Springs, CO 80935.
Library of Congress Catalog Card Number: 93-22640
ISBN 08910-97511

Cover photograph: © 1993 The Stock Market/Paul Steel

Some of the anecdotal illustrations in this book are true to life and are included with the permission of the persons involved. All other illustrations are composites of real situations, and any resemblance to people living or dead is coincidental.

Unless otherwise indicated, all Scripture quotations in this publication are from the *HOLY BIBLE: NEW INTERNATIONAL VERSION®* (NIV®). Copyright © 1973, 1978, 1984, by International Bible Society. Used by permission of Zondervan Bible Publishering House. All rights reserved. The Bible verses marked RSV are from the *Revised Standard Version Bible*, copyright © 1946, 1952, 1971, by the Division of Christian Education of the National Council of the Churches of Christ in the USA, and are used by permission. All rights reserved. Another version used is the *New American Standard Bible* (NASB), © The Lockman Foundation 1960, 1962, 1963, 1968, 1971, 1972, 1973, 1975, 1977.

Poem excerpt in chapter 5 from *The Irrational Season* by Madeleine L'Engle. Copyright © 1977 by Crosswicks, Ltd. Reprinted by permission of HarperCollins Publishers.
    Thanks to Carolyn Nystrom, author of *Before I Was Born* (Westchester, IL: Crossway, 1984; illustrated by Dwight Walles), for permission to quote her work in chapter 6.

Jones, Stanton L.
    How and when to tell your kids about sex : a lifelong approach to shaping your child's sexual character / Stanton L. and Brenna B. Jones.
        p.   cm.
    ISBN 0-89109-751-1
    1. Sex instruction—Religious aspects—Christianity. 2. Parenting—Religious aspects—Christianity. 3. Sexual ethics. I. Jones, Brenna B. II. Title.
HQ57.J64   1993
649'.65—dc20   93-22640
                                                                                CIP

Printed in the United States of America

5 6 7 8 9 10 11 12 13 14 15 / 99 98 97

FOR A FREE CATALOG OF
NAVPRESS BOOKS & BIBLE STUDIES,
CALL 1-800-366-7788 (USA)
or 1-416-499-4615 (CANADA)

Contents

✠

To our parents with our love and appreciation.
Jerry and Wilma Barber
Marion and Edith Jones

Acknowledgments

✚

We would like to thank the couples who are our friends with whom we have shared the joys and travails of the journey of parenting, and from whom we have derived wonderful guidance about the ideas in this book: Miriam and Fred Antonini, Rich and Debbie Butman, Charley and Cindy Carlson, Steve and Jan Evans, Lori and Jim Hock, Lisa and Mark McMinn, Cindy and Marion Neal, Elizabeth and Bob Roberts, Linda Roberts and Lance Wilcox, Joni and John Tenery, and Jay and Janice Wood.

Our thanks go out to Carol Blauwkamp and Geraldine Carlson, Stan's secretaries at Wheaton College, who typed some of the initial material that eventually grew to fill these many pages. We would like to thank eleven generations of graduate students in Stan's Human Sexuality summer course whose insightfulness, openness, and inquisitiveness have so enriched our understanding of sexuality. Special thanks go to Elizabeth Watson, Stan's research assistant in 1989-90 who found many of the resources cited in this book. Finally, we wish to thank the staff of NavPress, especially our editor, Steve Webb, for their willingness to address the critical needs of the Church and the Christian family in the area of sexuality by publishing this book.

Introduction

✦

We hardly need to describe the magnitude of the problem for the typical parent. Teenagers are engaging in sexual intercourse, becoming "sexually active," at earlier ages than we parents did. The greatest changes in behavior have occurred for young women; a much higher percentage of teenage girls are engaging in sexual intercourse than ever before. By the time kids graduate from high school today, *almost three-fourths of them are nonvirgins.* About one-third of all births in the United States are to unwed teenage mothers. It is estimated that five hundred thousand abortions were performed on teenage girls in 1988.

Increasing sexual activity among young people is not just a moral threat; it's a threat to the very lives of our children. The rates of sexually transmitted diseases, many of them not easily detectable, are reaching epic, and epidemic, proportions. Looming in the background for everyone is the specter of AIDS. The HIV virus is steadily, undramatically becoming a disease of heterosexuals in America—of men and women who have sex with multiple partners. It has always been a heterosexual disease in most of the world. Bluntly, this means that AIDS will eventually afflict many young unmarried people—our children.

Christian parents desperately want to assist their children to make right decisions in all areas of life—decisions that honor God and will allow them to live a fulfilling and wholesome life. We are particularly concerned with their sexual decisions because of the risks involved and the great potential for wrong choices.

OUR MAIN GOAL AS PARENTAL SEX EDUCATORS

Let's pause for a second and ask, "What is it that we really want to accomplish in sex education as parents?" What is our goal? Often, the first response that leaps from our hearts to the tips of our tongues is that we want to protect our dear children, our precious little ones now growing up. We want to protect them from death and from the ruins and ravages of disease, illegitimate pregnancy, abortion, guilt, and emotional devastation. With the same intensity we feel when we lunge to pull our child back from stepping into the path of an oncoming car, we long to protect our child from the damaging consequences of the choices they might make as teenagers.

Such goals of protection are wonderful and natural for us to have as parents. But don't you want more for your children than simply protecting them from damage; than simply keeping them from illegitimate pregnancy, disease, or abortion?

As Christian parents, we *do* want more. "What good will it be for a man if he gains the whole world, yet forfeits his soul?" (Matthew 16:26). In addition to preventing our children from suffering in this life, we want to protect them from something deeper—from the ravages of immorality and the possible devastation that departing from God's ways can have for their lives of faith. The mature Christian parent is under no illusion that sexual sins are the greatest sins. But we *are* aware that sexuality is an area of great testing and great temptation in our society today, an area where our children take their spiritual lives into their hands. And so we want to protect them spiritually, because the risk of ruin is great.

But don't we also want to *give our children something positive*? Don't we really hope that building something positive for them will itself protect them from the negative physical and spiritual consequences of sex outside of marriage? Protecting our children from the physical, emotional, and spiritual damage that can result from irresponsible and inappropriate sexual choices is important. But we would argue that *our most important goal is to equip and empower our children to enter adulthood capable of living godly, wholesome, and fulfilled lives as Christian men and women, as Christian wives and husbands.*

We can see the importance of this positive goal more clearly when we realize that one way of protecting our children from the negative results that can come from bad sexual choices would be to terrify them about sexuality as children. We could build such a fearful and negative view of sexuality into our children that we could be reasonably sure we would get them through adolescence as virgins. Would this have the result that we want? Surely not, because no parent would want to send his or her child into young adulthood as a neurotic, fearful, inhibited, and damaged virgin.

And to do this would be to take God's marvelous gift of sexuality and treat it as evil and dirty. We must not do this.

If we want to equip and empower our children to live godly, wholesome, and fulfilled lives in adulthood, we need to prepare them for the best kind of marital relationships, parenting relationships, and friendships possible. The vast majority of adults will marry, and for the vast majority of adults, their marital relationship has a most powerful influence on their general life satisfaction as adults. A recent study of American marriages found that the two most powerful factors associated with highly satisfactory marriages were whether couples prayed together regularly and whether they reported a rewarding sexual life together. And the less involved the partners had been in premarital sex, the more likely they were to have a rewarding sexual relationship.[1] If we add the capacity for communication that emerges time and time again as an ever-present part of all satisfying marriages, we come up with three keys to a satisfying marriage: a spiritual union, sexual satisfaction, and rich communication.

Our goal then is not just to protect our children from death, disease, and sin. *Our goal is to protect them from these things by preparing them to become the kinds of adults who can have deep and meaningful marriages filled with spiritual, sexual, and emotional intimacy, and who can have loving and deep family relationships and friendships.* To paraphrase a recent wonderful essay, "Sex education is about nothing less than how and when our children will hand over the astonishing gift of their very selves to another. The goal is that they will be able to love and trust and believe enough to commit their whole selves and their whole futures."[2]

SEX EDUCATION AS CHARACTER FORMATION

How do we achieve this goal? We rightly want help from our churches and schools, but we cannot abdicate such an important task to them. When we think of what we are aiming at, we clearly see it is inadequate to view parental sex education as information giving. We can also see the limitations of "THE TALK," the single dramatic sex talk with the early teen. Clearly one or even several dramatic sex talks with a twelve- or fourteen-year-old cannot turn the tide. Our children are inundated with messages and "programming" about sexuality, all pointing them in the wrong direction, wherever they turn—in our neighborhoods, in the schools, from the media, from all directions. Can one talk counteract all these destructive messages?

So how do we achieve this goal? *We must strive to deliberately shape and form our children's character, with the understanding that their "sexual character" is a significant part, but only a part, of their overall character.*

We will offer core principles of family sex education throughout this book, and we would like this principle to be our first:

> **PRINCIPLE 1:** *Sexual education is the shaping of character.* Education about sexuality goes beyond providing information that is accurate and timely. We must also shape the values and attitudes of our kids, shape their worldview, practice what we preach (modeling), provide our children with the emotional strength they will need to make godly decisions, and instill in them the skills to implement the good decisions they make. Most importantly, their behavior will spring from their hearts, which will be formed by their personal relationship and devotion to God. Thus, influencing their spiritual growth must be a top priority.

WHAT THIS BOOK OFFERS

Our goal is to assist you in influencing the sexual choices your children will make as young adults by helping you to deliberately shape their sexual character as they grow. Specifically, we hope to:

1. Motivate you to this challenging task by showing you just how bad the problem is (chapter 1).
2. Help you assess your strengths and weaknesses as a sex educator and as a parent (chapter 2).
3. Provide you with a way of understanding your child's character and how it may be shaped (chapters 3 and 4).
4. Give you a Christian understanding of sexuality in general, and the resources to grapple with the hard moral issues of human sexuality. Children today are not likely to be satisfied with a response of "because God says so" to their probing questions. We will try to speak confidently wherever God speaks clearly through Scriptures, but will try to be cautious about proclamations where Scripture does not speak clearly (chapters 5, 6, 10, 15, and throughout).
5. Give you concrete suggestions of what a parent can do to shape the child's sexual character *at every age*, from birth to independence. Effective sex education in the home will start at birth and not stop until adulthood (chapters 5-20).
6. Distill twelve key principles of effective sex education with children. Many of these principles are based on the best research available on how to prevent problems in adolescence.
7. Develop a balanced understanding of how all aspects of our sexuality fit into the total picture of our lives. How do the dimensions of our sexuality that are focused on our bodies, our feelings, our beliefs, our attitudes, our relationships,

our morality, and our religious faith go together? People who understand every part of their sexuality will be able to make the best possible decisions about how to live out that sexuality.

How is this book different from the many other Christian books on sex? We feel there are generally two types of books for parents out there. Books strong on helping kids live by traditional Christian sexual morality tend to be written as if parents start talking to children about sex when they become teens. We believe that if you wait that long, you've probably lost the battle. Books strong on talking to kids about sex when they're young tend to focus on helping them feel good about their sexuality, but they're weak on raising kids to follow our historic morality. None of the books that are out there are based upon a model of how to think about your child's character. None draw on the extensive research on how to prevent problems in adolescence. And so we hope this book will be uniquely helpful.

The objectives of this book revolve around giving you, the reader, the knowledge and skills you need to instill in your child a distinctively Christian sexual character. We hope, in this way, that you will be able to equip your children to make godly and wise decisions about their sexuality in their teenage years, but just as importantly that you will lay the foundations for them to experience the blessings of God's gift of sexuality as mature and responsible adults, whether married or single. It is with that hope and prayer that this book is offered to you.

Now available:
GOD'S DESIGN FOR SEX
A new series for children edited by Stan and Brenna Jones

"God means for Christian parents to be the primary sex educators of their children," write Stan and Brenna Jones. Yet children in today's society are bombarded with destructive messages about sex and sexuality virtually from birth. That's why the best way to educate your child about *God's* design for sex is to get an early start.

This four-book series is designed to help you answer difficult or embarrassing questions about sex comfortably and truthfully, in age-appropriate terms, and encourage healthy communication between your child and you through the challenging years ahead.

Book 1: The Story of Me (ages 3-5)
Book 2: Before I Was Born (ages 5-8)
Book 3: What's the Big Deal? Why God Cares About Sex (ages 8-11)
Book 4: Facing the Facts: The Truth About Sex and You (ages 11-14)

Part One

FOUNDATIONS

1

The Battle We Are Losing

✛

*[Parents are] wasting their breath
if they simply command their teens to postpone
sexual activity because it is wrong at their age,
or dangerous, or against parental principles.
None of the above tells teenagers anything they need to know.*

How To Talk with Your Child About Sexuality
PLANNED PARENTHOOD FEDERATION OF AMERICA

A re things having to do with sex really in that much of a mess? Are the times really worse now, sexually speaking, than when we were kids, or when our parents were kids?

Yes, all the indications are that things really *are* worse.

In this chapter, we want to convince you that your kids are at risk morally, spiritually, emotionally, and physically simply because they will grow up in the 1990s and the 2000s. Their risks on all fronts are much greater than ours were. We also want to examine major influences upon your child's developing sexuality—school sex education programs, cultural attitudes, peer groups, and the media—to see if you can view any of these influences as allies in your efforts to raise your kids pure. Our conclusion is that parents have few if any truly reliable allies in this vital parenting task.

Nearly all parents need some motivation to push them past and through their discomfort in dealing with sexual matters with their children. The average Christian parent has wonderful intentions for raising his or her child to follow the traditional Christian sexual ethic or moral standard. The average Christian parent *also* has a lot of trouble talking about sex in general, and especially with her or his children. Parents frequently tell us they feel tongue-tied, inhibited, shy, intimidated or even panicked when the time comes to talk about sex. Two basic things can help you get past these inhibitions: being motivated by the vital importance of talking to your child about sex (that is the point of this chapter), and having confidence that you have something of quality to say to your child (that is what we hope to develop in the rest of this book).

WHAT ARE TEENS ACTUALLY DOING?

The best recent estimate of teenage sexual activity comes from a survey of over 1,100 high school students conducted by the U.S. Center for Disease Control (CDC).[1] The study found that 54 percent reported having had sexual intercourse at least once in their lives, and 39 percent reported having had intercourse in the last three months. Let us say it bluntly: *Most kids in high school have had sexual intercourse.*

As kids move through grades nine through twelve, the percentages increase. Boys tend to be slightly more sexually active than girls. Altogether, about 40 percent of high schoolers are already nonvirgins by the end of ninth grade. This rate goes up steadily through the senior year, by which time about 72 percent are nonvirgins. In other words, almost three-fourths of high school graduates are nonvirgins!

It is technically incorrect to say that every young person who has ever had sexual intercourse is sexually active; after all, a young person could engage in sex once or twice and then refrain from that point on. No one knows how the nonvirgin rate relates to how frequently young people are having sex and with how many partners. But the CDC asked not just whether kids had ever had sex, but also if they had had sex in the three months immediately preceding the survey. Sadly, the rates for the latter did not lag very far behind the rates for the former. In ninth grade, about 25 percent had had sex in the last three months, whereas by the senior year this percentage had grown to 55 percent. This needs our attention: *Over half of high school seniors, about 53 percent of women and 57 percent of men, have had sex in the last three months.* It is perhaps right to say that over half are "sexually active" in the truest sense of that phrase.

The greatest changes in sexual behavior over the years have occurred among young women. While the sexual activity rates among young men have edged up only a few percentage points over the last four decades, the sexual activity rates for women have increased *dramatically*. Kinsey estimated in the 1950s that less than 20 percent of young women were nonvirgins when graduating from high school. The CDC's recent estimate is 67 percent. The main result of the sexual revolution for teens has been that young women have adopted the same sexually active patterns that young men have followed for some time.

Contraceptive Use

Most studies suggest that teens are terribly unreliable in their use of contraceptives for birth control and disease prevention. The CDC reports that condom usage is slowly increasing. Their survey found that about 45 percent of high school students said they used a condom in their last experience of intercourse. This is a higher estimate than most other studies have produced. A recent report in *Newsweek* stated that "Although many adolescents say they use condoms, experts think most don't."[2] The fact that about one million adolescent girls become pregnant each year, and that the lion's share of sexually transmitted diseases (STDs) occur in people under thirty, would suggest that contraceptives are not being used frequently or correctly, and that such methods are not the answer our young people need.

Pregnancy

Here are a smattering of the most frightening facts about teen pregnancy in the United States:[3]

- "More than one million pregnancies occur each year among American teenage females, which is equivalent to one adolescent pregnancy beginning every 35 seconds."[4]
- Thirty thousand pregnancies per year occur to girls fourteen or younger.
- Four out of ten girls now at age fourteen will get pregnant during their teen years.
- About one out of five girls who have ever had sex get pregnant every year.
- About a half million babies are brought to live birth by teenage mothers each year.
- The majority of girls who get pregnant before age seventeen will get pregnant again before age nineteen.

Consider the resources devoted to dealing with this problem, including the emotional agony of families; the time, energy, and cost of medical attention to the mothers; and the legacy of difficulties faced by the child born to a teenage mother. Is it any wonder that teen pregnancy is universally regarded as an epidemic that is out of control?

Abortions

The research branch of the Planned Parenthood Federation of America estimates that 2.8 percent of all women have an abortion *each year*. But the rates are much higher than this for women under twenty: An estimated 3.1 percent of women between fifteen and seventeen are reported to have an abortion each year (about one out of every thirty-two women in this group), and 6.3 percent of women aged eighteen and nineteen are reported to have an abortion each year (about one out of every sixteen women in this group). These statistics mean that in 1985:

- 16,970 abortions were performed on women under age fifteen.
- 165,630 abortions were performed on women age fifteen to seventeen.
- 233,570 abortions were performed on women age eighteen to nineteen.[5]

Women under twenty account for over one-quarter of all abortions. At the rates reported in 1985, it is estimated that approximately one out of eleven young women will have had at least one abortion by their eighteenth birthday. It is estimated that by age twenty, almost one in six will have undergone an abortion.

The most frequent reasons given for teenagers to choose abortion include the following: "concerned about how having a baby could change her life," "is not mature enough or is too young to have a child," "can't afford a baby now," "doesn't want others to know that she has had sex or is pregnant," "has problems with relationship or wants to avoid single parenthood," and "is unready for responsibility."[6]

Sexually Transmitted Diseases (STDs)

A recent research summary reported that sexually active teenagers have a higher rate of contracting STDs than any other age group.[7] Why? There are two basic reasons. First, teenagers are more likely to have multiple sex partners. Second, they are more likely not to use contraception, and if they do attempt contraception they tend to use methods that are ineffective at preventing the spread of disease (such as withdrawal). People are most likely to use contraceptives reliably in stable, mature relationships, which teenagers are very unlikely to have. Most married couples find they must adjust to the use of a birth-control method.

In spite of numerous education programs, most teens are ignorant of contraception and believe numerous fallacies about birth-control methods. Contraceptive use seems particularly lacking among teens who have poor communication with their parents (also a risk factor for engaging in sex, unfortunately); who have friends who get pregnant; who do not have high hopes for doing well in school or in life; who are anxious; and who have low self-esteem, little hope, and a low sense of personal effectiveness. And so, these teens are at much greater risk of contracting a disease.

Once they get an STD, teens are less likely than adults to get effective treatment and are more likely to have complications from it.[8] Young women in particular are in a process of rapid physical change and development anyway, and an STD may complicate their physical development and affect them for the rest of their lives. Further, many teenagers are not aware that many of the STDs do not produce dramatic symptoms. Some diseases may thus go largely undetected, possibly causing the young woman to sustain lifelong damage to her reproductive system and resulting in other long-term medical complications. During this time, she can infect numerous other people.

Until the advent of AIDS, none of the STDs was considered life-threatening. But now AIDS is one of the most dreaded killers on the public health front. It took over nine years for the number of full-blown AIDS cases in the United States to reach one hundred thousand, spanning the years from 1981–1990. The number of AIDS cases then doubled in less than two years, rising to two hundred thousand early in 1992. Recently released statistics, reported widely in the popular press, suggest that one out of every hundred men and one out of every two hundred women are currently infected with the HIV virus and thus destined, as we currently understand it, to die of AIDS. AIDS is no longer a disease of just adults; it is currently the sixth-leading cause of death among fifteen- to twenty-four-year-olds.[9] And HIV infection is increasing much more rapidly among heterosexual young people than in any other group in our country.

Drug and Alcohol Use
Research suggests that sexual activity rates are highest for teenagers who also use alcohol or other illicit drugs. And sadly, alcohol abuse and drug use are rampant in our society and among our young people. It is reported that about one-third of all high school students have consumed five or more drinks in a row at least once in the previous two weeks. Forty-eight percent of high school seniors report having tried marijuana or some other illicit drug; 29 percent of high school seniors have tried some drug other than marijuana. The National Institute on Drug Abuse reports that "this nation's high school students and other young adults show a level of involvement with illicit drugs which is greater than can be found in any other industrialized nation in the world." Overall, there appears to have been a significant but modest decline in alcohol and illicit drug use over the last decade.[10] But these are still alarming statistics, especially when we consider that kids who use alcohol and drugs are more likely to engage in sex, and in a way more likely to result in pregnancy and transmission of diseases.

Rape
With the rise in premarital sex has come an additional and truly frightening trend, an increase in rape. Experts are clear that the most common form of rape is date rape or acquaintance rape. One study found that almost 60 percent of rapes occurred in dating relationships and about 85 percent of rape victims knew their assailants.[11] Studies of female college students on public university campuses have found that at least one in sixteen and possibly as many as one in five women report having been forced to have sexual intercourse on a date against their will. Men have apparently come

to believe that women want sex even when they say they don't, and a polite refusal is no longer enough in many relationships. A substantial number of men, especially those involved with pornography, express attitudes about sex that put them in the role of a predator and the woman as the prey. Studies of rape in high school or earlier are practically nonexistent, but most authorities believe there have been dramatic increases in this group as well.

Teenagers are engaging in a lot of behavior that is contrary to God's intended design and to the wishes of their parents. The stakes have always been high when teens have played with the fire of premarital sexual experimentation. But more teens than ever before are taking the gamble. And more teens than ever before are losing that gamble. Where can the concerned parent find an ally?

DO OUR "SOCIAL INSTITUTIONS" SUPPORT THE CHRISTIAN SEXUAL ETHIC?

It appears in some ways that our society is still quite morally conservative. For instance, one recent survey found that approximately 90 percent of the American population agrees that adultery is always or almost always wrong.[12] In fact, it appears that negative views of adultery have actually been getting stronger over the last two decades. The same survey suggested that between 70 and 80 percent of the American populace judge homosexual relations to always or almost always be wrong. This percentage seems to not be changing much.

But the public appears to take a much more "tolerant" view of premarital sexual relations. The same study found that *less than 40 percent of Americans regard premarital sexual activity to be always or almost always wrong*. Another study found that slightly over 50 percent of those surveyed agreed or strongly agreed with the statement "Sex before marriage is okay, if a couple loves each other."[13] Clearly, the opinions of most adults in our society do not support the traditional Christian sexual standard of chastity. A strong majority agreed or strongly agreed with the statement "Methods of birth control should be available to teenagers even if their parents do not approve."

While over half of the Americans in this second study described their religious beliefs as very important, Americans nevertheless are quite relativistic. Over two-thirds said there are few moral absolutes and that right or wrong varies from situation to situation. More Americans judge their own personal experience to be the most believable authority in matters of truth than those who see the teachings of Scripture in that place. Christians can no longer look to prevailing views of sexual morality for support of the chastity standard of traditional orthodox Christianity.

Media Influences

Our twelve-year-old daughter recently received an attractive flier in the mail for a new magazine for "young women like you": *Y & M: Young and Modern* magazine. The text of the card said: "If you're interested in twenty-five great make-over secrets. Twenty-three sure-fire beauty tips. Plus the best looking guys on the planet. . . . If you want to make it terrific: Your face. Your skin. . . . Your thighs. . . . Your hips. Your lips. Your derriere. . . . Then welcome to YM!" The flier artwork boasted articles with the following titles or headlines: "Don't let him read this! How to get him—insider advice from expert guy-getters"; "Love horoscope: Your love life for the next year"; "Clothes guys love: Real sexy"; "Why he won't commit to you"; "Lose 10 pounds now!"

With this book in mind, we requested the sample issue, which turned out to be more repulsive than our worst nightmares! The love horoscope included predictions about which parts of guys' bodies the girl would find "irresistible." A special feature entitled "Hot and Bothered" presented scantily clad young men who were deemed worth lusting over. Other features presented generous advice on how to make guys fall for the girl reader, and how to get out from under the thumbs of domineering parents.

This is a magazine targeted at juveniles! Someone wanted our twelve-year-old girl to buy and read this!! Unfortunately, this magazine is typical of the material in teen publications.

Television is the medium that teens are exposed to more than any other. How does television portray sexuality? Clearly the stock and trade of network television is illicit sex. Sexual relations between married partners are rarely implied or focused upon. Rather, premarital and extramarital affairs are the norm. Recently we were discussing passionate or "French" kissing with our nine-year-old boy, who is convinced that such "staying on" or "staying compressed" is unbelievably sick. We happened to see a couple engage in such passionate kissing on television, to which Brandon commented confidently that "married couples don't kiss like that." Surprised, we asked why he thought that. He replied, "Because on television, only people who have just met or who are just dating kiss like that. Married people never do." His observations are very accurate; it is everyone except the married people who have all the fun.

On July 6, 1992, while washing dishes at 8:30 p.m. on a weeknight, we turned at random to a new CBS show entitled "Grapevine." The "teaser" introduction explicitly promised to follow the sex lives of its main characters. The first bit of dialogue began with an unknown woman walking into a bar. The handsome bartender, sorting cash in his cash register, said, "What can I get you? Coffee, a drink, some money? (laughter)." The young woman looked him in the eye and said, "I want you to sleep with me tonight." From that auspicious beginning, the show within eight minutes began to explore incest, casual sex with strangers, couples videotaping their sexual exploits, and more! And this in an age of AIDS! On prime-time network television during the dinner hour!

If we think further about the sexual relations demonstrated or implied on television, we must be struck with how unrealistic they are. Negative consequences are never exhibited. The ravages of STDs, teen pregnancy, or abortion are rarely the focus of television drama. When they are, the focus is typically on an unrealistic triumph by the individual over their negative circumstances. We rarely see the young woman made sterile by the ravages of pelvic inflammatory disease, the woman still agonizing about the abortion she had eight years ago, or the desperate loneliness of the man ever on the "hunt" for a new sexual conquest but uninterested in stable monogamous relationships. The use of birth control, so commonly touted today, is hardly ever in evidence.

And what about movies? It was recently estimated that the "typical" teenager sees about fifty R-rated movies per year. And the "F-word" is used twenty-two times per film in the average R-rated movie (many more times than other less offensive profanities), which contains over ten profane references to God.[14] This is probably a minor concern compared to the frequency of explicit and immoral sexual relations that are depicted; these are the mainstay of the typical R-rated movie today.[15]

The increasingly sexually explicit material of many contemporary songs and music videos today is evident to anyone who listens to or views these materials. Watching a current music video program on cable or network television is a real antidote for parental naiveté. Images of cleavage, gyrating hips, seductive looks, shedding clothes, and of barely concealed sexual encounters are common. The lyrics of a large number of songs call for overt sexual acting out on all impulses. Our contemporary music is a source of deep concern.

The Influence of Contemporary Sex-Education Programs
The one resource many parents rely upon for help, school-based sex education, is an unreliable ally at best. We are not enemies of sex education in public schools. But we are, as parents, deeply concerned about the potential impact of *seemingly* "value-neutral" sex education that by omission or commission promotes immoral behavior.

Can sex education ever be "value-neutral"? One saying that is frequently reported in anthropological studies of sexuality is that "sex always means."[16] This saying suggests that there is no such thing as a meaningless sex act in any society. Sex always has a meaning for relationships and for society that transcends the physical acts. If you will pardon our pun, all sex acts are pregnant with meaning.

If we start with the assumption that sex always means something to a person, to his or her relationships, and to society, we can begin to discern immediately how it is impossible to ever have value-neutral sex education. The essence of sexuality is *its meaning*. At its worst, value-neutral sex education takes the most meaningful of human actions and presents it to the student stripped of its meaning. Thus, value-neutral sex education is actually *meaningless*, or meaning-removed, sex education. In actuality, sex education is never value-neutral or meaning-neutral. Rather, only certain meanings and values are removed. Every public sex education program teaches the positive values of sexual pleasure and of sexual expression as affection or an expression of closeness or caring. It is the particular moral dimensions of sexual action that are removed in value-neutral sex education.

Anyone who reads the literature of professional sexuality educators can be under no illusions that there is such a thing as value-neutral sex education. The values (for better or for worse) of those who are training others in the field of sex education are blatantly evident in their writings. For example, two leading sex educators recently spoke of their hopes for sex education in the future in the widely read *Journal of Sex Education and Therapy*.[17] They expressed their hope that sex education would knock down "the negative barriers that have been used to limit the number of sexual contacts." In other words, they support increasing our numbers of sexual partners! They also expressed their hope that teenagers could all be "rendered temporarily infertile through skin implants" of contraceptives so that they would be "free to engage in sexual activity without those fears that so inhibited their parents and grandparents." They predicted that sex education programs will someday probe sexual expression "in infancy, childhood, . . . with same-sex and other-sex partners and even cross racial and generational lines," an apparent reference to encouraging the explicit homosexual and heterosexual activity of children with adults and other children. Finally, they wished for our children to see activities that had once been called "perversions" or "abnormality" as "life-enhancing activity." In summary, their goal for sex education is for all moral judgments to be swept away in favor of indiscriminate acceptance and enjoyment.

Future public school sex educators receive their collegiate training in human sexuality using supposedly balanced college-level textbooks that are rife with value commitments and value statements. One of the most widely used textbooks discusses the influences of premarital cohabitation and sex. The authors cite research showing that such cohabitation reduces marital happiness and stability and increases divorce rates, but then dismiss this research as the biased statements of moral critics. They conclude, contrary to the existing evidence, that "although there is not enough current data, it is possible that cohabitation may actually lower the divorce rate by allowing couples a closer premarital look at each other."[18] Similarly, they cite solid research which has shown that marriages tend to be rated as more successful when premarital chastity has been maintained, and that premarital experimentation tends to be correlated with extramarital affairs. These findings support traditional Christian morality. But they dismiss these findings as well, predicting that "better designed studies might show more positive effects of premarital sex—for example better sexual communication and less sexual inhibition."[19]

A second major college textbook explicitly aims to "mainstream" homosexuality. The author does this by presenting homosexual action as a parallel option alongside all of her discussions of heterosexuality. For instance, in her chapter on techniques of sexual expression, the author presents gay sexual technique alongside the discussion of heterosexual sexual technique.[20] A third textbook argues that homosexual relationships are just like heterosexual relationships, thus ignoring the substantial disparities between heterosexual people and homosexual people in terms of numbers of sexual partners, prevalence of sexually transmitted diseases, diminished stability of relationships, increased levels of promiscuous sexual activity, and so forth.[21]

If value-neutral sex education is a myth, we must ask what effect comes from claiming that it is value-neutral when it is not. Diana Baumrind, a developmental psychology theorist, has suggested that supposedly value-neutral sexual education can cause substantial damage.[22] She argues that children are basically raised to expect value judgments from authority figures such as teachers in such vital areas as sexuality. When values are not mentioned at all, or when a string of possible different values are presented to students with no particular prioritization or emphasis ("Here are some of the many views about sex; what do you think about them?"), adolescents interpret this as an authoritative adult declaration that *no value is better than any other value*. The results of such a lesson are obviously devastating.

What are the effects of contemporary public sex education? From a diverse array of sources, we might boil down the purported goals of school-based sex education programs into the following:

> Goal 1—To increase positive adjustment to and enjoyment of mature sexual expression.
> Goal 2—To decrease the incidence of sexually transmitted diseases.
> Goal 3—To decrease rates of irresponsible sexual experimentation among teenagers.
> Goal 4—To increase utilization of contraception by teenagers.
> Goal 5—To decrease teen pregnancy and birthrates, principally through goals 3 and 4.

How is public sex education doing on these goals? The first goal is so ambiguous as to be unmeasurable. There is more sex happening, but is it better sex? Does a possible increase in physical enjoyment outweigh the devastation being wreaked in people's lives by sexually transmitted diseases, infertility, diminished capacities to form committed life unions, and the emotional turmoil of broken relationships? We don't think so. Further, contemporary handbooks on the treatment of sexual problems do not suggest that these problems are going away. If anything, researchers in this area are suggesting that contemporary sex problems are much more complicated and difficult to treat than those experienced by earlier generations. Perplexingly, in this age of sexual affirmation, deeply entrenched and hard-to-treat problems of low sexual desire are increasing rapidly.

Second, we know beyond a doubt that sexual disease rates are holding their own, with a few (for example, gonorrhea) going down and others (for example, syphilis, genital herpes) going up. Relatively stable rates for some of the less serious diseases are far outweighed by the terrifying specter of AIDS, which is increasing steadily.

Third, all of the aforementioned evidence suggests that rates of teenage sexual activity have gone up markedly over the last four decades. Irresponsible behavior is increasing rather than decreasing.

Fourth, as discussed earlier, there is very little evidence showing that contemporary sex education programs actually increase the use of contraceptive methods. Teenagers are notoriously inept and infrequent utilizers of birth-control methods.

What about the last goal of reducing teen pregnancy? This is the one area where proponents of sex education often claim success. But when asked whether school-based sex education programs actually decrease teen pregnancy, researchers often describe the results of their programs in terms of decreased "fertility rates." This is a very confusing term, because when adults think of fertility, they typically think of getting pregnant. So we are led to believe that if a program results in a decreased fertility rate, it is actually decreasing pregnancies. Nothing could be further from the truth, however.

The term *fertility rate* actually refers in the professional literature to rate of live births, of numbers of babies born alive. Thus, a sex education program is presented as a success when it decreases the live-birth rate. We can see logically, though, that to decrease the live-birth rate we could (1) decrease the rate at which teenagers engage in sex (which we know has not happened), (2) increase their use of contraceptive methods (which we know has not happened), or (3) increase teen utilization of abortion. A recent study concluded that "greater teenage involvement in family planning leads to decreased child bearing (live births) among adolescents. . . . [However,] greater teenage involvement in family planning programs appears to be associated with *higher* rather than lower, teenage pregnancy rates."[23] The authors concluded that the major effect of teenage involvement in family-planning programs is to increase teenage utilization of abortion as a method of birth control.

These authors are not alone in their conclusions. Even an article in the prestigious *American Psychologist* noted that though 80 percent of school districts offer some sort of sex education programming, "effects of these education programs are unrelated to changes in sexual behavior, such as reduced frequency of 'unsafe' sexual intercourse or lower adolescent pregnancy rates."[24] Any decreases or even stabilizations in live births to teenagers are due to increased use of abortion, not to decreased sexual activity or increased use of contraception.

Thus, only one goal of public sex education has been successfully achieved. It is the goal that is not often publicly stated: decreasing live births by increasing the utilization of abortion by teenage women.

Overall, Christian parents have very substantial grounds for feeling concerned and hesitant about sex education programs in the public schools.[25] We would argue that these findings should encourage Christian parents to do their job well—and early—in sexually educating their own children. Public school sex education programs can be a source of useful information to our children. Some schools are now beginning to use abstinence-oriented sex education materials. But we would urge all Christian parents to take this responsibility upon themselves rather than relegating it to school curricula. We should work hard to see that the schools supplement and complement what we have done at home. But school-based education in this area can never replace what a parent has to offer.

The Influence of Our Churches

If there is one place where parents would really hope for an ally, it is in the church. How are the churches doing?

It is clear that involvement in church can make a difference for our children. One study showed that teens who were involved in church were sexually active at about half the rate of those who were not.[26] The general conclusion of research is that personal religious devotion is a strong protective influence against sexual experimentation.[27]

Conservative churches are steadily getting more involved in the sex education of their young people. The effectiveness of these types of programs is as yet untested. Further, it is quite difficult to get an accurate reading of the shape these efforts are taking because of the congregational focus and independence of most evangelical congregations. Sadly, the more conservative the denomination, the less likely it will have a sexuality education curriculum; the only exception to this trend is the fine curriculum for seventh and eighth graders published by the Lutheran Church—Missouri

Synod (a very conservative Lutheran denomination).[28] Some biblically based curricula for youth are being published.[29]

But in general, we cannot say with confidence that theologically conservative congregations can be counted on to have quality sex education programs for youth. Almost none have such programs for children fourteen or younger. Often, frankly, education committees of conservative churches can be intimidated by those few parents who are most ill-disposed to any discussion about sex at all. Fearing the reactions of these parents, churches tend to veer on the side of "playing it safe," offering too little that is too vague and coming too late. There are undoubtedly many churches with fine programs, but they are probably the exception rather than the norm.

Probably the finest, most balanced religiously grounded sex education programs and curricula available on the American Christian scene today are those offered in and through the Roman Catholic Church.[30] Thorough, balanced, unequivocally abstinence-oriented, and committed to helping parent and child achieve a Christian view of their sexuality, these materials should serve to challenge Protestants as to what can be done in developing church resources.

The materials and programs offered by the mainline Protestant denominations are of very mixed quality. Some are so caught up with giving positive messages about sexuality and with avoiding the "rigidity and negativism" of moral absolutes, that they give little help to the Christian parent.

Churches do need to be much more aggressively involved in the sexual education of their young people. Unfortunately, we fear that our local churches are not always sure resources for parents to count on. If you belong to a church that has a biblical, comprehensive, thoughtful, and thorough sex education program, we hope you will count your blessings, because you have received a great gift.

The Influence of Families
How are parents doing at sex education? The majority opinion among the experts is, "not well." Very few children report having informative and comfortable interactions with their parents about sexuality. Many initially remember no sex education at all, but when prompted can recall one or two isolated instances of instruction that were so uncomfortable as to have no impact. Often, they remember moral instruction as being confusing and unconvincing, with no or inadequate justifications being offered for the principles that were taught. And the most often discussed "missing piece" that teens wanted to know about but which is hardly ever discussed was relationships, the emotional dynamics of love, attraction, and desire.

And yet parents continue to have an influence. A number of studies have suggested that one of the best predictors of sexual conservativeness in young people is closeness to one parent. Teens who report being able to talk to a parent and who feel close to that parent appear to have a solid foundation in that relationship that allows them to make better decisions and better resist peer pressure toward sexual activity.[31]

The increase in divorce has led to ever-increasing numbers of children being raised in single-parent homes. We are sad to say that growing up in a single-parent home appears to put a child at risk for earlier sexual involvement and involvement with more sexual partners.[32] Such teenagers typically enter adolescent dating with more confusion about relationships, with heightened needs for acceptance and affection from the opposite sex, and with less parental supervision and support. Raising a child after divorce or the death of a spouse is a daunting challenge. While this book is written with two-parent families in mind, we hope to make many applications for the single parent as well.

CONCLUSION: THE BENEFITS OF DOING IT GOD'S WAY

It really is bad out there. Our children today are growing up in a different sort of world than we did, a much more deadly world, a world in much less "natural accord" with Christian principles. And we have few allies in this battle. Are you ready to do what you can for your children? Are you ready to deliberately try to shape their sexual character? We hope you are, and that you are willing to start when they are young.

We agree with Tim Stafford, who recently argued that we need nothing less now than to create a Christian sexual counterculture, to sponsor a Christian "sexual revolution."[33] That is what raising a generation of pure kids will amount to. Will such a generation of kids have anything to offer to a sex-obsessed world? Yes. They will form a community that will experience, for all the world to see, the benefits of doing it God's way.

The Joy and Blessing of Obedience

The greatest benefit of conducting our sexual lives in the manner in which God urges us to, and teaching our children to do the same, is that we can know that we are doing what our Father wants us to do. Further, we are promised that in obedience our faith can be completed or perfected:

> [Jesus said,] "If you love me, you will obey what I command. . . . Whoever has my commands and obeys them, he is the one who loves me. He who loves me will be loved by my Father, and I too will love him and show myself to him. . . . If anyone loves me, he will obey my teaching. My Father will love him, and we will come to him and make our home with him. He who does not love me will not obey my teaching. These words you hear are not my own; they belong to the Father who sent me." (John 14:15,21,23-24)

We know that we have come to know him if we obey his commands. The man who says, "I know him," but does not do what he
commands is a liar, and the truth is not in him. But if anyone obeys
his word, God's love is truly made complete in him. This is how
we know we are in him: Whoever claims to live in him must walk
as Jesus did. (1 John 2:3-6)

The testimonies of Christians throughout the ages have suggested that tremendous fruits flow from diligent obedience of God's commands.

The Joy and Blessing of Safety
We live in a time of tremendous fear about sexually transmitted diseases.
Anyone who has paid any attention to the contemporary debate realizes that
most of the serious sexually transmitted diseases would be utterly wiped out
if just one or two generations of humans would all abide by God's standards.
Premarital chastity and marital monogamy are virtual safeguards against the
transmission of most sexually transmitted diseases. More broadly, obedient
Christians are also safer from the relational confusion and emotional traumas that premature sexual intimacy can foster.

The Joy and Blessing of Godly Marriage
Remaining chaste before marriage is no perfect guarantee of having a good
marriage, as many have discovered. But there is indisputable evidence that
it helps. Andrew Greeley, the Catholic priest, sociologist, and novelist, has
recently published a major sociological study of marriage written for a popular
audience.[34] Some of the major findings of the study were the following:

- In spite of the commonly expressed belief that religion has little
  impact upon day-to-day life, the single most powerful predictor
  of a good marriage was whether couples pray together regularly.
- In spite of the commonly voiced opinion that religion and sex
  don't mix, the couple able to pray together and enjoy good sex
  together was the least likely to divorce.
- In spite of the common wisdom that cohabitation is a good way
  to prepare for marriage, cohabitation before marriage approximately doubles the degree to which couples themselves believe
  that they are likely to get a divorce.
- In spite of the common wisdom that premarital sexual experimentation increases a person's capacity to enjoy sex and hence
  marriage, increased incidence of premarital sex is a predictor
  of the likelihood of marital infidelity. In the words of Greeley,
  "there is no support for the folk wisdom that premarital sex of
  one variety or another is a preparation for marital happiness."[35]

- In spite of the common cynicism about marriage and the belief that most people are unhappily married, Greeley found that the vast majority of Americans would choose to marry the same spouse if they had the chance to do it all over again.
- In contrast to the widely publicized and poor quality studies (such as the famous *Redbook* study) which have suggested that adultery is rampant, this study found that 90 percent of Americans have been sexually faithful to their partner throughout their marriage.

Understanding these benefits, which we can offer to our children with God's help through shaping their sexual character, helps us to understand the goals of godly sexual instruction in the home. So often we think primarily about the urgent, about averting the crises that we are worried will destroy our child's life. When we think of our urgent goals, we think of making sure they don't get obsessed with sex, preventing premarital pregnancy, or making sure that they don't die of AIDS. These are vital, urgent goals, but none of them should represent our ultimate goal in sex education.

Our ultimate goal, our most important goal in sex education, is to shape our child's character so that in the sexual area, as in all areas of his or her life, he or she will glorify God by the choices and actions he takes and by the very nature of the character she manifests in *all* of life. As a part of this, we must look at the child's choices in the teenage years as absolutely essential, but we must also look past the teenage years into adulthood and have a vision for what kind of adult we want the child to be.

We must think of the whole person as we do sex education. We are preparing our children not just to resist sexual temptation in the teenage years, but to be godly persons who understand and accept their sexuality and make good decisions about it in the teenage years so that they can enjoy the full fruits of what God means them to experience when they marry. Any approach to sex education that ignores the dangers of sexual expressions that are beyond the bounds of God's revealed will is in serious error. So also is any approach that so emphasizes the dangers that it cripples the child's ability to obtain the fruits that God hopes to develop in his or her life as a married adult.

Do we really want the best for our children? Are we willing to sacrifice and work hard to provide the best for them? If you said yes, then you should also be willing to work hard to shape your children's sexual character when they are young so that when they are independent they may experience the benefits and fruits that God wants to bestow upon them as a result of their good choices. And that is what this book is about.

2

Taking Stock:
Knowing Your Strengths
and Weaknesses
as a Parent

✛

nd exactly what are your qualifications for the very important job of
family sex educator? What makes you think you are fit for this position?
What makes you think you can do it right and not really foul those kids
up? Do you have any prior experience in this line of work? Do you have the
required educational background? And while we're at it, how have you handled
your own sexuality? Are you a suitable role model for your child? Are your
own attitudes Christlike? Just what do you have to offer?

Intimidating questions? You bet they are. But for better or worse, you
inherited the job. God has put you in charge of shaping the precious lives of
your children. The question is not whether you will provide sex education
for your child. The question is, Will you do it carefully, thoughtfully, and
in accord with God's desires, or will you do it poorly through neglect,
miscommunication, poor preparation, and bad timing? In fact, our second
principle of parental sex education in the Christian home is:

> **PRINCIPLE 2:** Parents *are* the principle sex educators; you will
> either have an anemic, unintentional, mixed-up, and hence nega-
> tive impact, or a powerful, deliberate, clear and positive impact.

Before we brush away those harsh questions in our opening paragraph
with a shrug, saying with a deep sigh, "Well, I'm it," let us stop briefly in
this chapter for a self-assessment. Jesus urged us to do this. We are to count

the cost of any venture we take on to see if we have what it takes to finish the job (Luke 14:28-32). Doing this in the practical areas of our lives is part of our stewardship of what God has given us, and it is also a lesson in learning to truly count what it costs to follow Christ. But the job *is* ours as parents, so when we count up our resources and find ourselves with weaknesses in some areas, we must deliberately work to build up our strengths in those areas. If we can't do that, we need to turn to others in the Body of Christ whose strengths can perhaps make up for our weaknesses.

The critical areas we ask you to look at in yourself are (1) your own commitment to Christ and the strengths and weaknesses of your personal faith; (2) your strengths and weaknesses in your overall parenting style; (3) your attitudes and feelings about sexuality in general and your own sexuality in particular, especially as influenced by the family you grew up in; (4) your level of knowledge about the facts of sexuality; (5) your ability to clearly express and defend a Christian view of sexuality and sexual ethics; and (6) your ability to talk about sex with your child with comfort and confidence.

It is our prayer that this process of self-examination, as well as the reading of this book and the long process of shaping your child's sexual character, will produce growth for you, the parent. As parents we often find that we experience spurts in our own personal growth when we are striving to nurture and teach our own children. God seems to stretch and challenge us through our parenting. In dealing with these matters of sexuality, we will be challenged to examine our own thoughts and practices. Teaching our children the values they should live by encourages us to embrace our beliefs more confidently and live more consistently with them. God can also use this process for the healing of our own past wounds and failures, teaching us and our children more valuable lessons about God's love, forgiveness, and redemption.

ASSESSING YOUR OWN PERSONAL FAITH IN CHRIST

Why put a self-examination of our personal faith as the first item of our parental self-assessment? Because at the most basic level, your children's moral choices will be determined by *their* personal faith. And we as parents cannot make our children have faith; we cannot force or cause them to follow Christ. Their faith is first God's responsibility; He calls to His sheep and they answer Him (John 10:27). Beyond God's work in calling our children to Himself, we as parents have the responsibility of shaping our family life to make it as likely as possible that our children will come to know and love the Father through us (see chapter 5).

In addition to which, our own faith can have a profound impact upon our children. Remember the old saying, "True faith isn't taught, it's caught"? How can our kids catch a living faith from us if ours is not a living faith? Thus, we have to start by heeding the call of the Apostle Paul: "Examine yourselves to see whether you are in the faith; test yourselves" (2 Corinthians 13:5).

Unfortunately, Paul does not give us a quick, five-step program for self-examination. At the most basic level, this kind of self-knowledge is a gift from God. We urge, therefore, that you ask God to give you an honest view of your own faith. We need to approach God through prayer, through study of His inspired Scriptures, through fellowship with His people. We need to do this in a spirit of openness, wanting the truth rather than struggling to protect ourselves and preserve our illusions about ourselves. We need to ask God to reveal to us what we really love, where our first allegiances lie, what we really live for. We need to read the words of Christ in the gospels, and hear His questions to His followers as questions to us: "But what about you? . . . Who do you say I am?" (Matthew 16:15); "Do you truly love me?" (John 21:15-17). We must have the courage to answer these questions in humble honesty as Peter did. Thankfully, we can ask with confidence that the same Jesus who loved His wavering and doubting followers will give us the desire to love Him more, regardless of how weak our faith may be.

Do you have a faith that serves as your life foundation, that can serve as the bedrock of your own thinking about sexuality as well as what you teach your child?

ASSESSING YOUR PARENTING STYLE:
THE FOUR PARENTING STYLES

Parenting is an extremely complex activity. Psychologists have been trying for quite some time to classify types of parents according to the most vital aspects of parenting, and to understand how each type might influence children. The best recent research in this area should prove very encouraging to Christian parents.[1] Researchers have divided parents into four types on the basis of two major factors: what the parents expect of their children and how they respond to the children emotionally. The four types of parents are neglecting, permissive, authoritarian, and authoritative. As we describe each of these styles, we urge you to examine where you are strong and where you are less strong.

Neglecting parents are unresponsive to the child, cool and aloof, or just distracted, and do not impose demands or attempt to control the child at all. They have few expectations. To these parents, the child basically does not matter. Parents can be neglecting for a variety of reasons. For instance, one parent might be neglecting simply because she does not care about the child. Perhaps the child came along at an inconvenient time in life or is associated with an unhappy prior relationship, and so the parent chooses to not invest anything in the child. A parent can also be neglecting because of personal distress such as depression or because of an all-consuming problem like alcoholism. Parents who are going through difficulties like divorce or grief over a death can, unhappily, be so consumed by their own personal grief that they have little or nothing left to give to a child. Finally, a parent can be neglecting by virtue of overinvestment in other things. When consumed by work or church, parents can believe with all their heart that their child is important but simply have so little left to give to the child that they are effectively neglecting parents.

Permissive or indulgent parents are accepting, warm, and responsive to the child. Permissive parenting is a style that parenting "experts" commended to parents in the 1960s and 1970s. As a result of the humanistic psychology movement, grounded in the belief that children are basically good, parents were led to believe that the best approach to parenting was to simply allow their child's natural tendencies and abilities to emerge. The belief was that if parents provided love and acceptance, children would naturally "blossom." Christians would say that these theorists ignored the reality of human sin. Permissive parenting can also result from guilt over disciplining your children, or as an overreaction to growing up in a rigid and authoritarian home yourself. Long-term studies of the children of indulgent parents clearly suggest that these kids do not fare well—they have very positive self-esteem and feel good, but their behavior tends to be quite immature; they tend to be more impulsive, to show more signs of social irresponsibility than others, but not as much self-reliance; and interestingly, they tend to show more aggression and hostility toward other kids.

The third type is what researchers call the *authoritarian parent.* It is our fear that too many Christian families fall into this category. For quite some time, Christian parenting books have overemphasized discipline, expectations, and control of children in response to the humanistic overemphasis on child acceptance without discipline. Researchers classify as authoritarian parents who have strong expectations of their children and attempt to control and shape their children, but do so without a significant degree of responsiveness, respect, and acceptance of them. This parenting style is all discipline and little expressed love. Authoritarian parents set up rules to which full obedience is expected. They teach the child what they believe, but often don't respect the child enough to hear what the child has to say in response.

Research has suggested that children of authoritarian parents grow up harshly judging themselves according to rigid standards. These children often have no sense of worth or value if they are not meeting up to someone's externally imposed standards. Authoritarian parents may be raising up children who have no sense of value unless they are pleasing someone else and "obeying the rules." These children tend to do reasonably well in school, to be competent and responsible, but tend to be socially withdrawn, to lack spontaneity, and to lack a sense of connection with other people. Girls who grow up in such homes are particularly noted to have trouble later on, in that they have enduring problems with being dependent upon their parents (whom they spend most of their lives trying to please) and lacking many of the attitudes and skills that allow them to achieve well in school.

Finally, the *authoritative parent* is high in both expectations for and responsiveness to the child. These parents have expectations of their children, things they want to teach them, but they combine this emphasis on discipline with warmth, communication, respect, and affection. They have rules, but they are willing to solicit and discuss their children's opinions and feelings about those rules. Research suggests that children of this type of parent tend to have the highest levels of self-esteem, self-reliance, and social competence as compared to all of the other groups of children. They tend to perform better in school, having a strong motivation to achieve. The consensus today is that this is the most effective parenting style and produces the healthiest kids.

This research reinforces our belief that parenting is a way in which we symbolize God within our families. Parents are representatives of God in the lives of their children.[2] Two of the primary facets of God's character are His righteousness and His love. A truly Christian understanding of God balances these two realities. Christian traditions that emphasize God's love to the exclusion of His righteousness lose the dimension of rigor in Christian faith. God becomes the sweet Sugar Daddy in the sky who wants nothing more than simply to accept and affirm us as we are, and Christian faith becomes simply a warmed-over spirituality with no substance, no bite. We lose the gospel emphasis of costly discipleship, of the narrow road, of bearing the cross of Christ. On the other hand, an understanding of God that is all righteousness and justice at the expense of God's love translates into a legalistic religion where we live in constant fear and trembling of an angry God who has no mercy. Our faith becomes rule keeping, "works righteousness," a pathetic attempt to appease this angry God.

We can think of parental expectations and demands as reflecting the righteousness dimension of God's character to our children. We can think of our emotional response to our children as reflecting the nature of God's love. In this way, truly authoritative parents become living symbols for their child of two of the most important dimensions of God's character. In having demands and expectations for their child, they are embodying God's character of justice and righteousness, in which He reveals His will for His people and expects them to live up to it. In being accepting and child-centered parents, they are embodying God's character of love, in which He time and again pursues His people, expressing the affection of the loving Father who pursues His wayward children until He brings them home, regardless of how they flee from Him and offend Him.

Your child's future sexual choices will be affected by the overall quality of your relationship with him or her. What are you good at in your parenting style? Are you all expectations and little love? Are you all acceptance and warmth but no discipline? Where do you need to grow as a parent?

ASSESSING YOUR ATTITUDES AND FEELINGS ABOUT SEXUALITY

Where are you starting from in your attitudes about sexuality? We are about to ask you the types of questions a counselor might ask when trying to understand how you came to have your feelings and attitudes toward sexuality. But this is not a book about how you can change your own responses, how you can grow or heal from the past. Our focus here is not change or healing for you, but rather awareness so that you can better shape the life of your child. We ask you to read these questions seriously and reflectively, asking God to reveal to you where your strengths and weaknesses may lie.

Start by asking yourself about the attitudes toward sexuality that were lived out by your parents in your home. What were the attitudes toward nudity? What did your parents seem to communicate about the human body? Were they comfortable, uncomfortable, or panic-stricken by any hint of talk about sexuality? How did they handle their own sexual relationship; were they open and comfortable with their love and affection for each other, were they cold to each other, were they secretive? How do you remember feeling about being a boy or girl: delighted, ashamed, guilty, disappointed, proud? How did your parents contribute to these feelings?

How were you taught about sex as a child in the home? What did you learn and how was it conveyed? Some kids get the right factual information, but it is delivered with an attitude of "this is filthy and I'm only talking about this because I have to." Other kids get little factual information, but experience a powerful sense of acceptance and approval from their parents. What do you, as an adult, believe your parents felt about sex back when you were a kid? If they were silent about sex, as many were, what sense do you make of that silence now? Many people whose parents were silent on the subject felt that an attitude of dangerous mystery, shame, and guilt was associated with sex, and still have these feelings in adulthood.

Did any crucial experiences shape your feelings about sex in childhood? Examples might include: an experience of sexual molestation; walking in on parents having intercourse with the results of deep embarrassment, confusion, anger, or rejection; engaging in sex play with another child and perhaps being caught or punished by parents; family traumas such as an older sister getting pregnant or having an abortion; the presence of pornography in the home. These are examples of the many experiences that can leave deep impressions, even scars, on us. You might ask yourself, "Was there a lesson that I learned from this experience?" Early experience with pornography might communicate the lesson that "Women are sex objects." An experience of abuse might teach that "Men cannot be trusted." Parental scolding might teach "Sex is a shameful and dirty part of our animal nature." What lessons did you learn?

What views about men and women were lived out and taught (not the same thing!) in your home? Was manhood esteemed, or were men characterized as animals, ignorant, untrustworthy, insensitive, uncaring, or unfeeling? Was womanhood esteemed, or were women characterized as inferior, dependent, sex objects, or driven by emotions and hence irrational?

As you entered adolescence, how did you feel about your developing sexual desires and longings? What were you taught in church youth groups, camps, and Bible studies about sex and sexual feelings? Was sexuality the enemy? How did you feel about your changing body? Women, how did you feel about the development of breasts and starting your period? Was menstruation a "curse" or a blessing? Men, how did you feel about beginning to experience erections and wet dreams, sometimes at the most unwelcome and embarrassing times? Did your parents treat you differently, and how did you understand that?

During the prepuberty period and adolescence, it is not uncommon for people to have sexual experiences with persons of the same sex. Children and teens are often very curious about the bodies of others. Adolescent sexual arousal is so powerful and so easily triggered that healthy, normal teens can experience sexual arousal to thoughts, sight, or touch of a person of the same sex. This often deeply frightens the teen, who worries he might be gay. Sex play is fairly common, including with the same sex. And a significant portion of people who grow up healthy heterosexuals have full homosexual experiences, including experiencing orgasm through such experiences. Did you ever experience sexual thoughts about or sex play with the same sex? Did you have any sexual experiences with the same sex? How did you feel about those experiences then, and how do you feel about them now? Does some attraction to persons of the same sex still occur?

What decisions did you make individually and in relationships before you met your spouse? What was your experience with masturbation? Almost all males have masturbated, though experience ranges from infrequent experimentation to obsessive preoccupation. Women vary much more in their experience, with a substantial number having none. What was your feeling about what you did? Reactions range from deep guilt and remorse to comfortable acceptance. How much a part of your life was sexual fantasy? What kinds of sexual fantasies did you entertain?

How did you feel about sexual attraction, feelings of infatuation, dating, and so forth? What were the standards in your peer group, and how did you compare? What level of physical contact did you commonly experience in dating relationships in high school and later? What were the most extensive experiences you had? How did you feel about those experiences, and how did those experiences relate to your faith at that time? Were you harsh or lenient in your moral evaluation of yourself? How did you handle the experiences you regretted? We are so fortunate to have a forgiving God; did you seek forgiveness in the biblical manner and were you able to feel forgiven? Did you experience a sense of control over your choices, or did you constantly feel that you betrayed your own standards? Did you experience particularly destructive events such as pregnancy or abortion? Were you ever victimized by rape, harassment, pressure, or manipulation? How did these experiences shape your attitudes? How did you and your spouse conduct your sexual lives before you married; do you look back with contentment or with regret? Are there unresolved tensions between you over choices and actions back then?

As an adult, what is your level of comfort with your own sexuality at this point in your life? How do you feel about being a man or a woman? How do you feel about your body? How do you feel about your level of interest in sex?

Parents should take a look at how their attitudes about sexuality are played out in their marriage relationship. Are you able to talk about sex with each other? Many couples find this an extremely difficult area to discuss without embarrassment, defensiveness, and hurt feelings. If this is so for you, what does that indicate about your attitudes? What is your level of modesty with each other, and what does this indicate about your attitudes toward your bodies and your sexuality? Is your sexual relationship satisfying? Sex does not have to, and often cannot, meet the media caricature of sexual ecstasy, but many people do stop growing in their marital sexual relationship because the topic is too intimidating to discuss, learn about, and work to improve. Are you able to discuss birth control, and are you in accord on that topic? Is there a history of emotional injuries that you're not able to talk about with each other? Have there been major injuries to your trust of each other that affect you deeply, such as affairs, flirtations, involvement with pornography?

Parents who are in special circumstances need to ask themselves additional, difficult questions. Parents who have lost their partner through death or divorce need to face the challenge of not being able to offer the perspective of the other sex on the things they share with their child. They need also to look at the incredible drain of having sole responsibility for a family and ask how they might rearrange priorities to open up windows of opportunity for discussion of sex with the children. Widows and widowers have to ask how working through the grief of their loss is affecting their parenting.

Divorced or separated single parents also have to ask where they are in the painful process of working through the grief, anger, disappointment, betrayal, and disorientation that are all part of the process of recovery. Do you have lingering attitudes of bitterness toward your former spouse? Is anger a constant problem? To what extent are you at cross-purposes with your ex-spouse? What are your current attitudes toward sex and dating? In struggling with your own loneliness and need, are you living in a manner consistent with your own beliefs and God's standards?

We close this section with encouragement. Any steady look at our past can turn up "stuff" we would rather just leave buried. Be encouraged: You do not have to have your past completely worked out and everything in its place to be able to do a good job at parental sex education. The most dangerous situation is being unaware of your own blind spots, of the wounds in your life that are not yet healed. Awareness of those areas, which was the point of this section, can be enough to improve your functioning as a parent, and it can put you on the road to healing as you lift your weaknesses up to God.

ASSESSING YOUR KNOWLEDGE
ABOUT THE FACTS OF SEXUALITY

Perhaps the most difficult thing about assessing our knowledge of the factual side of sexuality is knowing what we don't know. Many who don't know the Bible well think they are biblically literate, because they don't know enough to know how little they know. And so it is here as well.

The best way to assess your level of knowledge about sexuality is to learn the facts. Rather than guess at what you know, take an hour or so to read about sexuality again to refresh your knowledge. Almost all of the nonreligious sex education books for parents at public libraries and general bookstores have sections on "the facts" that can serve as a good survey to check your knowledge against.

The Christian parent doesn't have to be an expert in the field of human sexuality to shape the character of his or her child. Instead, we need to know the basics well enough to speak confidently with our child; we need to have some sense of the limits of our knowledge ("Dad, what is the ratio of fluids from the prostate and seminal vesicles in the average man's semen?"); and we need to have enough comfortable humility to be able to say, "I don't know, but that's an important question, so I'll see if I can find out."

We need to be especially knowledgeable about the choices and options facing teens today. The teen world is not the same as when many of us were adolescents. You need to educate yourself about what is going on in your community among teenagers. Honest and open conversations with other parents, teachers, church youth leaders, guidance counselors, and so forth may provide quite an education in this area.

ASSESSING YOUR ABILITY TO COMMUNICATE A CHRISTIAN VIEW OF SEXUALITY AND SEXUAL ETHICS

"So why is sex outside of marriage wrong? Why would God forbid two mature people who love each other from expressing that love physically?"

"What is the Christian view of masturbation? Why?"

"How can we rejoice in the way God made us when we are supposed to 'mortify the flesh'?"

Can you give good answers to questions like these? Many of us have firm moral views of what is right and wrong, but little experience in expressing those beliefs and even less experience at justifying them to someone who can't understand why we believe as we do.

If sex education is the shaping of our child's sexual character, we must be able to do more than just present a positive, healthy attitude toward sexuality. We need to be able to build our children's moral understanding about sexuality by being able to intelligently talk with them about the Christian view of sexuality and ethics.

ASSESSING YOUR ABILITY TO TALK ABOUT SEX WITH YOUR CHILD WITH COMFORT AND CONFIDENCE

I (Stan) teach a course on human sexuality and sexual counseling to graduate psychology students at Wheaton College every year. I have addressed hundreds, and even thousands of people on sexual ethics, homosexuality, dating, and Christian perspectives on sexuality. I am fairly comfortable talking about sex to large groups of people I do not know.

Talking with my own children is totally different. These little people exist because of my sexual relationship with Brenna. Their bedrooms are near ours. They see us kiss, know when we go out on dates, even ask us, "Did you have a romantic time?" They know both of us at our best and at our worst. When we talk with them about sex, they might ask us embarrassing questions like, "Do you do that? When do you do that? Did you do that yesterday? Can I see you do that?" And the stakes seem so enormous; the weighty responsibility of teaching them rightly and well is always with us.

Can you talk comfortably with your kids about sex? What are the barriers to doing so? Is it lack of comfort with the information? with your own sexuality? with the sexuality of your spouse? with events from your past? With expressing a Christian view? Are you willing to endure some discomfort in order to build greater comfort? Are there any particular barriers you will need special effort or help to overcome? Are you willing to work to overcome that limitation?

3

Christian Parenting
as Character Formation

❖

"Okay, look—I'm not pushing you to go all the way, but at least
let me touch you! You say you like me, and I really care about
you. It's natural for guys and girls to express their caring with
their bodies, not just with words! People who care, share! And I'm not just
being selfish—I want you to touch me too! That way, we can enjoy each
other. Come on!"

Lindy is returning from a poorly chaperoned eighth grade field trip.
She looks around with a sense of desperation. The cold bus is dark, and the
exhausted teacher is sitting, head down, apparently asleep, in the far front
of the bus. A lot of the guys and girls are paired up and are "making out."
They are in their seats with coats piled up all over them so that it's not at
all clear what is going on between their necks and their knees.

Lindy and Derek have been a couple for three weeks, and she really
does like him. He hasn't been aggressive up until now; they have exchanged
only a few brief kisses. But a new side of him, a new urgency, has emerged
on this trip. He unexpectedly touched her bottom when they were standing
in the line at the museum ("You really are gorgeous," he whispered), and
suggested that they go off behind the Babylonian Period exhibit. Lindy
turned him down.

She has a sick feeling that she should never have paired off with Derek
for the trip home. She is scared, excited, feeling guilty, curious, and confused all at the same time. What will she do? She feels the pressure from

Derek; he seems to really care, and shouldn't love be expressed? And what might he say about her if she says, "Hands off!" What might he say if she gives in, and to whom? What will her friends say in either case? She knows the phone will ring five minutes after she gets home, with nosy Christa asking her what happened and "Was it wonderful?" And her parents! She remembers what her parents, especially her mom, said about petting. But then, her mom had been very unclear as to *why* it wasn't right. And what about God—would Jesus want her to do what Derek wants her to do? But does Jesus care about just touching? What will she do?

✛

Is what Lindy does in that seat on the bus determined by what she *knows*? By the facts that have been stuffed into her head in sex ed classes (how the sperm penetrates the egg, what percentage of kids engage in petting at age thirteen, what patterns of relationships exist between fathers and daughters)? Is it even primarily determined by what Christians think of as spiritual knowledge—specific Bible verses or the warnings that concerned parents have shared with her?

No. Lindy's behavior will be a function of her *character*. What she does will be the product of who she is as a person at that particular moment in her life.

Our fundamental premise is that *sex education is not really a matter of education* (when we think of education as providing information); *rather, sex education is a matter of deliberate character formation.* Providing information is part, but only part, of such character formation. For this reason, sex education must begin early, when the character of the child is the most malleable. Also for this reason, sex education—sexual character formation—is primarily the job of parents, not of schools.

Shaping our children's sexual character is just one dimension of our broad task as parents of shaping the overall character of our children. Sadly, it is an often-neglected part of our task as parents.

GOD'S BLUEPRINT FOR CHRISTIAN PARENTING

The Old Testament book of Deuteronomy contains a pivotal description of what Christian parenting is all about:

> These are the commands, decrees and laws the LORD your God
> directed me to teach you to observe in the land that you are cross-
> ing the Jordan to possess, so that you, your children and their
> children after them may fear the LORD your God as long as you
> live by keeping all his decrees and commands that I give you, and
> so that you may enjoy long life. Hear, O Israel, and be careful to

> obey so that it may go well with you and that you may increase
> greatly in a land flowing with milk and honey, just as the LORD,
> the God of your fathers, promised you. Hear, O Israel: the LORD
> our God, the LORD is one. Love the LORD your God with all your
> heart and with all your soul and with all your strength. These
> commandments that I give you today are to be upon your hearts.
> Impress them on your children. Talk about them when you sit at
> home and when you walk along the road, when you lie down and
> when you get up. Tie them as symbols on your hands and bind
> them on your foreheads. Write them on the doorframes of your
> houses and on your gates. (Deuteronomy 6:1-9)

This passage teaches us many things about God, about our relationships to Him, and about our purposes for living. But some of its most important lessons are about God's blueprint for parenting in the godly home.
The first sentence teaches that obedience to His commands is vital if we
ourselves are to learn to fear the Lord. While it is clear from other passages
in Scripture that we come to believe in the Lord and then obey because we
believe, this verse suggests that we also obey in order to believe. This is
a profound truth about all Christian life: obedience flows from belief and
belief flows from obedience.

Our obedience not only influences our own faith, but the faith of our
children as well. The living obedience of parents is the foundation for any
purposeful teaching that we do with our children. Our teaching should and
must flow from our living. Our lives, our obedience as parents, are a living
witness to God's work, for good or for ill.

The truths about our God are meant to consume the totality of our
lives. These verses direct us to shape our children's total environment to
conform to and reflect the truths, decrees, and commands of the Lord. We
live in an age when one of the unforgivable sins is certainty. Any belief can
be tolerated, as long as it is only passively accepted in a lukewarm fashion:
"This is true for me, but I surely can't presume that it ought to be true for
you." But God Himself mandates that we stake our whole lives on Him and
His Word; we are to love and obey with all of our being. The truths of the
Christian faith are to be so important that they shape every aspect of our
lives, especially in our families. We are to talk about God's truths. We are
to obey God's truths, bringing them to life before our children. We are also
to embody God's truths in symbolic form and truly immerse our children
in the truths of the faith.

The Old Testament saints knew how to immerse their families in the
truths of the faith. For example, they erected altars to commemorate special acts of God. We see Abraham building an altar when the Lord first
commanded him to depart from Haran on his tremendous journey of faith

(Genesis 12:7). He built another to commemorate God's marvelous promise of a land that would be given to him and his descendants forever (Genesis 13:18). Imagine Abraham's clan later passing by these altars, with Abraham using the occasion to tell his family again of the Lord's faithfulness to him.

We, on the other hand, live in a society rich in symbols of materialism and sensuality (television, movies, billboards, glossy magazines, etc.) but impoverished of symbols of faith. If our homes are as lacking in symbols that remind us of God's work in our lives as is our secularized society, then our children will be deprived of valuable reminders and support systems for their faith. We need visible symbols, like Abraham's alters, as well as symbols such as family rituals, special occasions, holiday celebrations, and so forth.

The Power of Stories

Have you ever stopped to ponder why the biblical revelation is given predominantly in the "story" mode rather than the "teaching of principle" mode? Have you ever wondered why Jesus Himself spent so much time on parables and stories when He could have been spinning out detailed systematic theology and ethics? The Apostle Paul taught largely by principle, but Christ Himself and most of the Old Testament writers rely more on stories. This probably reflects the power that stories have in our lives. We need principles such as "Thou shalt not commit adultery," but we probably need stories such as Joseph fleeing from Potiphar's wife just as much. Conservative Christians today are long on logic and principles and short on stories. Our churches are often big on exegetical, logical teaching and preaching. Stories are a vital way we can surround our children with symbols and reminders of the faith. This is our third principle:

> **PRINCIPLE 3:** Stories are as powerful or more powerful than principles or "logic" as a teaching tool in shaping our children's character.

Psychological research is also suggesting a return to the storytelling teaching method of Jesus.[1] It appears that people have two types of memory. One type is memory for words and knowledge. This kind of memory codes information that doesn't touch the heart of the person, information that is cold, neutral, and distant such as addresses or algebra formulas. A second and separate kind of memory is personal, related to experiences we have had and who we are as a person. Stories that affect people, that move us emotionally, are thought to be stored away by the second type of memory. This finding may help to explain how it is that great literature can "get into our souls" whereas cold statistics and facts never seem to have quite that effect. It also helps to explain the very powerful effects of the media, which almost always present stories that create the feeling that we have shared the experiences of the characters in the story. And herein lies the greatest danger of the media—they often present powerful stories that distort the truth.

Stories are an especially powerful way of teaching values. We can be swept up into the power of a story, and in taking it into our heart we take in the values of that story as well. Stories have heroes that our child can identify with.

Stories come in many forms: written stories, movies, plays, songs. Our foundation, of course, are the stories of the Bible. We have tried to make the Bible stories of faith come alive to our children by reading, discussing, and even enacting them. We should immerse our families in the lives of the saints of the Scriptures. Your local Christian bookstore can help you select picture or story Bibles for children that can help the stories of the Scriptures come alive. It is vital that we talk about these stories, making the characters come alive by imagining what they were thinking and feeling. It is also vital to apply the lessons from the lives of the saints to our lives today by asking our kids questions about the lessons of the stories.[2] Christian biographies of saints of days past can be a wonderful resource as well.

We feel that our children have benefited greatly from some of the other stories we have tried to immerse them in as well. Reading with our children is a family ritual. Fiction is also a great resource, both Christian fiction and nonreligious fiction that expresses the great eternal values of our faith. For example, we have read through C. S. Lewis's *Chronicles of Narnia* several times, as well as encouraging their viewing of the recent PBS dramatic film renditions of several of them. Our older kids have loved the *Archives of Anthropos* book series by John White (InterVarsity) as well as J. R. R. Tolkien's *The Hobbit*. We prepared carefully by listening to the musical soundtrack before taking them to see the stage production of *Les Miserables*, which they dearly loved. We endured the bawdy aspects of that production because of the profound and moving picture it painted of faith, virtue, and love. We try to select movies with some degree of care, searching for movies with enduring values that we hope to promote. The images of these and many more stories are imprinted upon the hearts of our children. Stories have a power to move the human spirit, to powerfully imprint values and truths, a power that mere logical lessons cannot approach. We must carefully choose the stories which are shaping our children's lives.[3]

Deuteronomy 6 teaches us to strive to shape our children to accept the faith of Abraham and Moses, of Peter and Paul—a saving faith in the one Lord God and His Son, Jesus Christ. Three elements of family life are absolutely critical: our *personal obedience to God* as parents; our communication or *teaching of His Law,* His truth, to them; and our *immersing their lives* in reminders about the faith.

THINKING ABOUT YOUR CHILD'S CHARACTER

How can we understand the process of shaping character? What are the factors that will determine the choices Lindy will make on that dark bus ride back from her field trip?

The core ideas we want to focus upon in understanding your child's character are your child's *needs, values, beliefs, skills,* and *supports.*[4]

Think of an athlete in training as a long-distance runner. What are the major factors that go into that child being a success in competition? First, her basic *needs* as an athlete must be met—she needs to get proper sleep, to eat well, to have time for practice, and so forth. Second, she must have *values* that support her efforts. She might desire to win her parent's approval, impress a boyfriend, win a college scholarship, or distinguish herself to enhance her ability to witness for Christ; any number of purposes are possible. She must have core *beliefs* that support her endeavors, including such beliefs as "running is important," "I can excel at this sport," "I can trust the guidance I get from my coach," and so forth. She needs *skills,* both of thinking and of acting. Thinking skills might include knowing how to pace herself, how to develop a strategy for a race, and how much and when to practice. Acting skills might include the raw physical ability it takes to run a race, and the ability to catch herself when she stumbles. Finally, who she is as a runner is powerfully influenced by her *supports.* A track-meet roommate who keeps her up all night before the big race, muddy conditions on the day of the race, a distracted coach, strong winds, and so forth can detract from her performance, while good coaching before the race and cheering family and friends can make all the difference as she approaches the finish line.

These concepts about character will form a foundation for our discussion in the rest of the book. They have implications in all areas of child-rearing, but we will stick to sexuality here. Figure 1 (page 46) is a summary of these "five building blocks of character."

SHAPING YOUR CHILD'S CHARACTER

Needs, values, beliefs, skills, supports. In our diagram, we suggested that our needs are our guts, our "bowels" to use a biblical metaphor. Our values form our hearts; our core beliefs constitute the mind of our character. Our skills are our bones and muscles by which we act. We stand on our supports and push back against the challenges that come at us.

Figure 1: Five Building Blocks of Character

You, the parent, are the most important influence upon your child's character. You will either be a haphazard and thoughtless teacher who gives little thought to what you are doing in your parenting, or you will be a prepared, thoughtful, responsible teacher. You get to choose, with God's help, which you will be.

How will we shape our children's character? In essence, this entire book is a catalog of ideas on how to do this. Ideas for how to shape your child's needs, values, beliefs, skills, and supports will occupy us in every chapter. But in general, we would remind you here that:

- We teach by *what we say to* our kids.
- We teach by *what we do to* our kids. Consequences, punishment, and praise all teach richly.
- We teach by the *stories that we tell* our kids and expose them to.
- We teach by *who we are* before our kids. This is the most powerful teaching method. Isn't that frightening? It is to us. Kids soak in the material of our lives like sponges. Our lives are a story we are telling our kids.

To come back to the Deuteronomy 6 passage, we, as parents, are to so create an environment in our families that our children *soak in the truth about God just by being in our family*. In our parenting, we are living out and showing forth what they will understand to be God's personality in our love and discipline of our kids.

We will also exhibit God's personality in our marriages by how we treat each other as spouses. That is the primary message in Ephesians 5, is it not? That Christian marriage is meant to be an object lesson to the world, including and especially to our children, about the character of Christ's relationship to His bride, the Church.

One final word. As we discuss shaping our children's character, let us not forget who is in charge. God is sovereign, we are not. And on the other hand, our children are blessed by God with the capacity to make meaningful choices; they are not and never will be robots that we program at will. The control we exercise as parents can never override either God's sovereign control of our existence or our child's God-given capacity to make his or her own choices. We must discern what we can and cannot control; there are no surefire techniques to *make* our children be a certain way. What we can do is to conduct ourselves in such a way that we make it most likely that they will develop in the ways we hope they will. And that is our solemn responsibility before God.

4

Understanding Your Child's Sexual Character

✛

We have suggested that your child's needs, values, beliefs, skills, and supports are the five building blocks of his or her character. Let us examine each of these in more detail so that we can understand character better, and better understand how we might shape it.

NEEDS

Every human being shares certain needs. Beyond our obvious physical needs, we believe there are two basic psychological needs. These needs are never utterly fulfilled—like the need for food, they have to be addressed again and again in life. But like the physical need for calcium to make bones grow strong at critical periods in life, the period of childhood dramatically shapes how your child will experience his or her needs throughout the rest of life. When these needs are met adequately in childhood, your child will face adolescence and adulthood with a foundation of vital strength for facing the challenges of life.

In Genesis 2, the Lord God is described as creating the first people. Adam was placed in the Garden of Eden "to work it and take care of it" (verse 15). After commanding Adam to not eat of the tree of the knowledge of good and evil, the Lord God said, "It is not good for the man to be alone. I will make a helper suitable for him" (verse 18). When Eve was brought before Adam, Adam said, "This is now bone of my bones and flesh of my flesh; she shall be called 'woman,' for she was taken out of man. For this reason a man will leave his father and mother and be united to his wife, and they shall become one flesh" (verses 23-25).

We can discern two elements of God's will for us as persons in these verses. First, we can see that we are made for relationships, both with God and with another special human being. We are relational beings! Second, we are made for significant work, for a purpose that transcends our own individual pleasure and sustenance. (See also Ecclesiastes 9:7-10.)

In Genesis 1 we see how God, a relational being, decrees the creation of relational beings, humanity, in saying, "Let *us* make man in *our* image, in *our* likeness, and let them rule over the fish of the sea and the birds of the air, over the livestock, over all the earth, and over all the creatures that move along the ground" (verse 26, emphasis added). God Himself is a relational being. As a triune being He related to Himself and talked to Himself before the creation. He made us relational beings who like Himself are designed to exist in relationships as part of our very nature.

God is also a creating being and a ruling being, and we create and rule in a reflection or image of His divine nature. God commands the first man and woman to be fruitful and multiply, something we cannot do without relating. As fruit of our relating, new life is created! We are not creators, but we are procreators. And Adam and Eve are told to rule (Genesis 1:26), which was their work in the created order. Specifically, they were to till and keep the garden.

We draw from this passage of Scripture and elsewhere the notion that there are two foundational needs that all humans share: relatedness and significance.

Relatedness

Our need for relatedness means that we need to love and be loved, to affirm and be affirmed. Being loved forms a foundation for life and gives us a stability we cannot have without that bond. "What a man desires is unfailing love" (Proverbs 19:22).

Many problems, especially sexual problems, appear to begin when this fundamental need goes unmet in childhood, leaving a child feeling unloved or rejected. Books about sexual addictions talk about people who go into adolescence and adulthood with an unresolved "hunger" for any personal connection that will begin to satisfy this raging need that parents were meant to fill.

There is no one way, no quick and easy formula, to meet this need for loving relatedness. Families differ in how they express genuine love and acceptance. There are also cultural differences. Children will differ in their individual needs; one child's needs might be met by one hug a day, while another might be in constant need of reassurance and affection. The needs of our children change over time. Truly responsive parents will respect and adjust to the changing needs of their child.

Significance

The need for significance is equally profound. We are each meant to have a vocation, a calling to meaningful work in our lives, from which we derive a sense of significance. Our vocation may or may not overlap with our employment.

God regards all work is as meaningful. The common distinction between "sacred" and "secular" vocations has no foundation in Scripture. God has meaningful work for us to do, but the meaningfulness of that work is not defined by its grandeur or its earthly success. We need to recapture the biblical sense of the Apostle Paul's instructions to slaves, who in their day did work that was utterly despised by free men: "Slaves, obey your earthly masters in everything; and do it, not only when their eye is on you and to win their favor, but with sincerity of heart and reverence for the Lord. Whatever you do, work at it with all your heart, as working for the Lord, not for men, since you know that you will receive an inheritance from the Lord as a reward. It is the Lord Christ you are serving" (Colossians 3:22-24). Clearly, the significance of our work is defined not by how it meets earthly criteria for success, but rather by whom the work is done for and by the spirit in which we do it. Any work that can be done for the Lord is significant work. We can change dirty diapers for the Lord, type memorandums for the Lord, empty garbage cans for the Lord, debug computer programs for the Lord, install appliances for the Lord, and pastor churches for the Lord. What more significant work can there be than that of the mother who stays home with young children in order to pour love and meaning into their young lives?

There are several common problems with significance. Some today deny any purpose. If there is no purpose, then we can never feel significant. When people come to believe that their lives serve no higher purpose, the internal barriers that prevent us from sinking into all sorts of idolatry break down. If we serve no higher purpose, what meaning do the prohibitions against sexual licentiousness, intoxication, pride, and the raw abuse of power have?

Many today deny the significance of small purposes. Americans esteem big successes. We respect and admire the pastor of a church of five thousand but are bored by the faithful pastor of a small flock of seventy-five. We are fascinated by the flashy representative of the Christian organization who speaks all around the country, and ignore the quiet and stable faith of the custodian who cleans his offices at night. We admire the pediatrician who earns a large income while dispensing medical treatments, and have no thought for the mothers who comfort the child with love and attention at home. Christians need to work hard to shed their success mentality and learn to recultivate their understanding of the significance of daily life and accomplishment. We need to learn to be faithful in the small things (Luke 19:11-27).

Meeting the Relatedness and Significance Needs

We need to constantly work to meet these two primary needs of our children. We need to meet their need for loving relatedness by having our relationship with them be a foundation for their lives. We should strive to fill them with an indisputable sense of being loved, of being accepted by the most important people in their lives. We can give them an indisputable sense of their value to us. We need to do so from their earliest days when they do not understand words at all, but can understand that the parent looking into their eyes exudes a sense of joy and warmth and love, that a loving embrace expresses the deepest acceptance imaginable that the parent feels for the child.

Meeting our children's need for significance is both a future-oriented and a present-oriented enterprise. In the present, we can give them a sense of significance by assigning them a meaningful place in the overall functioning of the family, and by esteeming the significant work they do. It matters to us whether they do their homework and clean their rooms. We can see their play and friendships as some of their most important work, for out of these will emerge patterns for their entire lives. We can see them as having a *calling* here and now to be about the Father's business (Luke 2:49). The most significant work for any of us to do is work that can be done by any of us—to be Kingdom representatives regardless of age and ability.

We also give our children a sense of significance for the future through our expectations for their lives. We affirm their growing gifts and abilities as shown in school, in sports, in friendships. We express confidence in the future God has in store for them, and in their ability to contribute meaningfully to God's work in His Kingdom. Interestingly, research consistently finds that children with high academic aspirations—high hopes that they can do well at their school work and that their good work will be of real value to them—tend to delay or avoid sexual experimentation and pregnancy. It appears that these children have hopes and values beyond their own immediate physical gratification.[1]

Finally, we help to meet our children's needs for loving relatedness and significance by living out how these needs can be properly understood and met. As Christian spouses, we are faithful to our partners and love them sacrificially. We delight in our relationships with our spouses, and build our spouses up in front of our children. We are filled with the love God has given us as a gift. We talk about the significance of our own work, not giving in to society's judgment and saying things like "I'm just a bookkeeper," "I just earn $18,000 a year; I'm a peon," or "You can do better than me if you try hard." Rather, as Christian parents we exult in the significance that God gives to our work. We say, "I am a warehouse manager, and I help to make sure that the clothes made in our factory get to the stores quickly so that people who need clothes have plenty of clothes to choose from. God made people to need clothes, and I help get people what they need. I do that for the Lord."

Understanding and acting to meet the needs of our children for relatedness and significance is the foundation for shaping their character. We can never meet all of their needs, and we should not try to do so. But we can provide them a foundation in meeting their needs for relatedness and significance. This foundation can be the basis on which they face the world in strength, able to make decisions that God will bless. Imagine the difference between a fifteen-year-old girl out on a date who is confident of her significance and filled with her parents' love for her, versus a disillusioned and hopeless girl who is thirsty for anyone to accept and love her. Which girl is going to make the right decision when pressured to have sex?

If they can trust our ministry to them in these most fundamental areas, they will trust us in other areas as well.

VALUES

Our children's character is founded also upon what they value, and parents are the most important influences in forming those values. The needs for relatedness and significance are objective; they are there whether we feel them or not. But we all embrace unique sets of values as we grow up. If the needs for relatedness and significance are the final destination, our values are the compass that tells us how to get there. Values tell each of us what helps us in our life quest for relatedness and significance on a moment-to-moment basis. We do not typically try to be loved and significant directly, but we generate values, purposes, or goals as ways to get what we really need.

Think of all the different things one can value, good and bad, as ways to get the acceptance and love we need: communication, beauty, vivaciousness, domination, going along with the crowd, superficiality, politeness, humor, seductiveness, honesty, sexual conquest. And any of the following and more can be thought of as ways to achieve significance: punctuality, workaholism, diligence, wealth, power, deceit, frugality, competitiveness, precision, evasion of responsibility. One person develops an unspoken plan for achieving significance by compulsive work habits that will force his supervisors to respect him; another attempts to meet the deep need for relatedness by a series of superficial and promiscuous sexual relationships. A young teenager, despairing of real purpose for her life, tries to fill this gaping void with slavish conformity to her peer group. The kinds of goals we work toward range from the grandiose to the pathetic. One person yearns to be President or to possess a million dollars by age forty. Another lives day to day trying desperately to avoid criticism that would be devastating, or to receive the approval of others who are seen as respected and esteemed.

What we *say* about our goals or values is important, but our goals or values are probably most honestly and directly expressed in the choices we make. The father who says he values time with his children but never makes the choices necessary to spend that time with them is speaking clearly about his real values through his actions. People often seem blind to their own values. We know what we *ought* to value much more intimately than what we *truly* value.

Parents teach their values to their children most powerfully by the values they as parents live by. This is one of the most frightening facts about parenthood. Our children read us like a book for what we value. Our lives tell our children what we deem important and not important. Do we overdose on work and put little effort in friendship? Have we despaired of ever being significant and thus hide behind a sneering veneer of cynicism about our own vocation and those of others? Are we slaves to the approval of others and evidence little commitment to goals which are ours alone and for which we need no one else's approval? Do we take greater joy in our material possessions than in service to the Lord? Do we always have time for television and other recreational pursuits and no time for community service? It behooves all of us to do an honest assessment of where our time is going and what this says about our values. Then we have to go the additional step and ask, "Is this what I want to teach my child to value; is this what really matters?"

We also communicate our values in our praise. Do we praise our children for grades they get, or for the skills that they are developing? For winning, or for using their gifts well? For being quiet, unobtrusive, and leaving us alone, or for doing something right even if it makes us uncomfortable? Do we praise our children for fitting in, for being popular, for going with the flow, or for showing strength, independence, and character even when, because of it, they are not as accepted by others as they might otherwise have been?

We need to think deliberately as Christians about the values we want our children to manifest. It is vital that we get down to the most fundamental levels of what we value, and make sure that we are always encouraging that in our children. A vibrant faith is their most fundamental need for the future. We try to shape our children to value such a faith by modeling that faith ourselves, by talking openly about how important that faith is, and by praising any manifestation of such a faith in our children. We often remind our children, "We really are proud that you are doing well in school (or piano, baseball, friendships, Bible school, etc.), but never forget (and help me to never forget) that the only thing that matters is whether you love God with your whole heart and are following Him in obedience. If you do that, your life will have value. Without that, nothing really matters. God is calling you right now to be a student (pianist, second baseman, etc.), and I think God is happy that you are doing well at that for Him!"

Next, we believe it is critical to shape our children to value *Christian virtue*. Beyond any particular outcome or achievement in our children's lives, they will be successful and blessed if, based upon the foundation of their lively faith in Jesus Christ, they manifest the vital Christian virtues of love, faith, and hope (1 Corinthians 13). The fruit of the Spirit in Galatians 5:22-23 include "love, joy, peace, patience, kindness, goodness, faithfulness, gentleness and self-control." While these fruit flow from the presence of the Holy Spirit in a person's life, they are also clearly built upon preexisting human traits and characteristics that we can begin to develop in our children. In an era of rampant cynicism and hurtfulness, do we cultivate the trait of gentleness in our children? In a time of personal dissipation, impulsiveness, and licentiousness, do we encourage our children to develop the trait of self-control? In an era that demands instant answers and instant success, are we able to teach our children to value patience?

Most directly relevant to this book, we must teach our children to value purity and chastity as ends in themselves. Do we lead them to commit themselves to such chastity? Do we teach them to value faithfulness to their vows to God and to their future spouses? We should. It's good in the eyes of God for an unmarried person to be a virgin. It's good to handle oneself with self-control and to have pure motives in relationships. This doesn't mean it's bad to feel sexual feelings or to struggle with those feelings. In fact, being the sexually alive person God meant us to be is God's desire. To be sexual *and* pure is God's intent. Our children's deep need for relatedness—to God, to a future spouse, and to loving friends—will be most deeply and fully met by living by God's standard of purity. Whereas the world says that immoral sex is a way to get your love need met, the best evidence suggests that living life by God's rules is the best way. Chaste people are likely to have more satisfying and stable marriages, and to have better sex lives in their marriages. God's way is the best way.

Finally, we remind you that we teach our children values by the stories we expose our children to—stories in the forms of books, movies, songs, and more.

BELIEFS

In addition to our basic needs and the values that direct us, human beings also are distinguished by our unique core beliefs. If needs are the destination and values our compass, then our beliefs form the road map for how we will live our lives. We often absorb these beliefs as children from what we see modeled in the lives of our parents. Many of us never seriously question these beliefs; they become so second nature to us that they are as transparent as the air within which we move every day. For many, awareness of their basic beliefs only comes at times of crisis, when we cry out because our way of understanding our world is not working, when everything is chaos and nothing is happening the way it "should." Our crises can be an avenue through which God reveals our core beliefs and the ways in which they are failing us.

Growing up in a Christian home or being a long-time member of a Christian community is no guarantee that our basic beliefs are healthy. The fear of the Lord, the respectful study of His Word, and careful attention to apostolic teaching are vital, but as fallen human beings we often take in the wrong understandings from God's Word.[2] Examples of the distortions that we take in follow:

- I am acceptable to God only if I am good in every way.
- Life should be easy, fair, peaceful, and happy, even through the worst crises; if it is not, then I am being punished for my weak faith.
- God wants to meet my every need perfectly, so if life is tough it must be because of my sin and defective faith.
- Good Christians do not feel angry, fearful, or down.
- Imperfections should be hidden so I do not disgrace God.

We need to carefully grapple with just how biblical and wise the beliefs we have absorbed and passed on to our children really are. How can we come to understand the basic beliefs which we as persons have brought into our parenting? We must realize that many of our most basic beliefs are not put easily into words. We can become investigators of our own belief systems. It can be helpful to ask ourselves what the rules are that we live by. We can step back from our life and ask, "What would an outside observer guess to be the rules that I live by, if he were to observe me intimately?" It can also be very helpful to examine the rules of the families within which we grew up: "Blood is thicker than water." "Don't contradict your mother." "Avoid conflict at all costs." "Earn our approval or you don't even deserve to exist." "You must fight to survive." We absorb and live by many more of these dysfunctional rules than we usually recognize, and it is easier to see the beliefs in someone else than in ourselves. Look at the beliefs in your families that you may have brought with you.

This entire book is, in part, about the *proper* beliefs about relationships and sexuality that we want to pass on to our children, so a few examples here will suffice. Many of the most important core beliefs are so fundamental that parents often take them for granted and hence ignore them. We want our children to believe, in the very core of their beings, that they are loved. We can teach this to our children in words, but a purely intellectual teaching of such a core belief would be empty indeed. Imagine the parent, the all too common parent, who can shout at a child, "Don't you know I love you!?" and yet rarely sacrifice for the child, rarely comfort the child, rarely express affection to the child. We teach our children that they are loved by speaking of and by acting on our love.

We want our children to believe that their choices matter, that they make a difference. We teach them that they are responsible for their actions *and* for the consequences produced by their actions. Everyone deplores young adults who never meet up to expectations but always have a ready excuse for why their own failings are always someone else's fault. Yet many parents sow the seeds for such irresponsibility by always stepping in to pick up the pieces for the misbehavior of their children. We teach our children that their choices matter by the way we respect our children and discipline them. We respect our children when we let them make choices and honor their choices. This can begin early on by simply giving children the choice between two outfits to wear or between finishing and not finishing supper. We let them live with the consequences. We gradually enlarge the arena of their choices as they grow, with the end in mind that they are becoming adults who will be in charge of their life.

We also teach a child the connection between actions and consequences, and the child's responsibility for both, through discipline. Discipline, at its best, allows children to experience the natural consequences for both their positive and their negative behavior. The most natural consequence of positive behavior is praise. Many negative behaviors have excellent natural consequences that can teach children the connections between their actions and those consequences. The natural consequence of a child ignoring the parents' command to not touch the hot muffler on the lawn mower is burned fingers. The natural consequence of refusing to eat good food in a reasonable period of time is the hunger the child experiences several hours later. When we wheedle and beg a stubborn child to "pleeeease eat," we are teaching that child that we will take responsibility for the consequences of his or her choices. The greatest enemy to our teaching our children this lesson on a day-by-day basis is our tendency to say—to always say—"Now is not the time to deal with this. I'm too [*Choose one:* stressed out, tired, embarrassed, pressed for time, emotionally drained] and my kid is too [*Choose one:* difficult, hyper, overstimulated, fatigued, cranky, temperamental]." Parents who can firmly but lovingly tell their young child, "If you touch that stove I will spank your hand; the stove is a no-no," and then follow through with the promised discipline when the child disobeys, are teaching the child that choices matter and that when he or she chooses a course of action, he or she also chooses the consequences that follow from it. Parents who do not set up reasonable boundaries around their children's behavior, or who continually undermine their children experiencing the consequences of their behavior, are teaching their children to disassociate their actions from any consequences that might occur from them.[3]

A deeply held belief that "my actions have consequences and I am responsible for both" is vital in the area of sexual behavior. The child who enters adolescence believing "I can do anything I want; consequences don't matter for me; Mom and Dad always make it better and pick up the pieces" is at great risk sexually. We must seize the opportunity when children are young to deeply and thoroughly instill in them an awareness of the short- and long-term consequences of their actions.

We want to teach our children that they can approach the world with cautious trust. We do not want to send them out into the world as naive potential victims; neither do we want to send them into the world unable to give of themselves freely to the spouse they may someday marry. The first opportunity children have to learn that God and certain other human beings are trustworthy is in their relationship to their parents. We teach our children that they can trust by being trustworthy parents.

Other important beliefs include a belief in our child's own identity as a child of God, that God made our child in just the way that He sovereignly intended, and that the goal of life is not to be happy but to love God and to become "good" in the way God intended.[4] If our children believe they belong to God as His sons or daughters and ambassadors, that God made them just as He intended, and that they are meant to pursue goodness, they have a road map for life they can trust.

SKILLS

Christians are used to thinking in terms of needs we must meet, purposes we must pursue, and beliefs we ought to embrace. We are not so used to thinking in terms of our skills and how they help to form our character. But many of the things that we take to be permanent, inborn traits in people are actually learned skills. For instance, one of the things we do in graduate training programs in psychology is to train people to be better listeners, because listening effectively is a critical aspect of caring and respect. A person who doesn't have the personal capacities to love and care for others will never learn to listen well. But many people have the capacity to love and yet lack the skills to listen. And many of the elements of being a good listener can be taught.

How are skills acquired? Psychological research suggests that *praise* occupies an especially critical place in the development and use of skills in the developing child. Children will tend to develop those skills which are praised. Skills are also learned through the models a child is exposed to. Children are enabled to do things by watching their parents do them; sadly, they also learn skills from exposure to media such as television and movies. Children can, to a lesser degree, learn skills from hearing descriptions in words of how to behave. Skills are perhaps most effectively learned by actually doing. And so, we need to deliberately think about the kinds of skills that will help our children to be effective, godly adults, and work hard to encourage those when they are young.

As we said in our earlier example of the athlete in training, skills have thinking and acting components; most skills are combinations of both. In our opening example of chapter 3, Lindy must be able to *think* of possible things to do on the bus and decide from among those options. She must then be able to *act out* the option she has chosen. If she can think of only two options—to let her boyfriend do anything he wants or, at the other extreme, to scream for help—her choices are impoverished. She really has many more options than those. If she has trouble choosing options, she will be paralyzed. Further, she must be able to act on her choices; if she has never before forcefully told another person, "You will *not* touch me and if you persist there will be consequences," then the very newness of such an action may make her unlikely to do it. Many skills have both thinking and acting facets. Let's briefly examine a few key skills.

Empathy is a critical skill. Empathy tends to develop naturally, but parents can encourage or undermine the child's capacity. We teach empathy through our capacity to empathize with our own children. Do we show ourselves able to understand things from their perspectives? We also encourage the development of empathy by actively teaching them to take the time and the energy to understand what is happening from the other person's perspective. We can help the young child to pay attention to what his friend is feeling when he has just taken that friend's favorite toy away from him. The capacity for empathy is critical in the area of sexual character, first, because the child who is going to develop good friendships and have rewarding romantic relationships is one who can be sensitive and empathic to others' feelings. Sadly, men are often terribly deficient in this ability, a weakness their wives suffer with. Second, empathy helps the child to better understand the consequences of sexual behavior. The consequences of adolescent sexual behavior are unlike anything else the child would have ever experienced. The child who can understand and empathize with the devastation of an unwanted pregnancy, with the guilt of a person who has gone through an abortion, or with the grief of a friend who finds out she is infertile because of an earlier sexually transmitted disease, is going to be at less risk for sexual irresponsibility.

Another critical skill is interpersonal strength or assertiveness. Christians often associate assertiveness with a kind of mouthy selfishness, an attitude of "I'm looking out for number one and the rest of you can go to blazes!" But the opposite of this kind of forceful selfishness is not weakness. Jesus Christ had the strength to do anything that He chose to do, and He used this forcefulness on occasion when it was the Father's will. He condemned hypocritical Pharisees, He cleansed the Temple, He exhorted and rebuked His disciples, and He fearlessly proclaimed His good news. There is no Christian virtue of weakness. We would argue, rather, that strength that is submitted to God's use and is under God's control is a great virtue. Our children should learn to be quiet and to be submissive, but they should not be battered into quietness and submissiveness. Rather, we should seek to develop their assertiveness, and then teach them how to submit that inner personal strength to God's use. We need to praise our children for speaking their minds, for asking questions, for demonstrating their strength. We need to mold them so that they make better and better judgments as to when to exercise this strength, especially in preserving their purity.

Self-control is also a vital skill. Like all of the fruits of the spirit, self-control has its natural and supernatural sides. The development of self-control begins with the child being effectively controlled by external factors. The parent implements rules, and backs up those rules with consequences. But children need to become less and less dependent upon external factors, rules, and guides, and more dependent upon the rules that they have taken within themselves. We can encourage this by asking them about the family's rules, by getting them to repeat as their own rules those that had previously only been externally delivered. For example, if a parent has had a terrible time at the dinner table with the child playing with his or her food and breaking the important rules for the supper table, the parent can ask the child before and during the evening meal what the most important rules are at the dinner table. Having children generate the rules themselves, rather than having them only externally delivered and enforced, can help them to convert from external control to self-control.

"Delay of gratification" is a critical skill. Children need to learn early on that greater joy often comes through sacrificing immediate gratification of a desire for the sake of obtaining something much better later. This can be taught in many ways, but a child's handling of money is an excellent way to teach delay of gratification. Encouraging children to save money to buy things, and not "bailing them out" when they make poor choices, can be an excellent way to teach this value.

There are also a host of skills that relate to forming friendships, dating successfully, and establishing personal intimacy. We can help our children learn to be good conversationalists. We need to teach them to listen both by listening to them and by talking to them explicitly about what it means to be a good listener. We can teach them how to praise others honestly, to be abundant in expressing the positive. We can teach them how to share their opinions in a way that respects others but communicates confidence in themselves. We can teach them to be kind. We can teach them how to think about dating relationships—how to creatively think of alternatives for entertainment with their peers; how to view what dating is all about; how to establish rules and structures for dating that will prevent them from getting into trouble.

Finally, we might mention the skills of decision making. Teaching our children to accurately understand the nature of the problems they confront is a first step. Generating alternative views of the problem is also helpful. Teaching them to generate all possible solutions to the problem is the next step to solving the problem. We then need to help them to be able to effectively evaluate the feasibility and possible outcomes of different responses to the problem. They then need to be able to pick a solution they can implement themselves.

SUPPORTS

When we think about character, we usually think about things "inside" the person. But what people do, and indeed who people are, is strongly influenced by their environment. Have you ever gone into a new situation, one you had never faced before, and found yourself confused and disoriented? Often in such situations, we respond in ways that surprise us. We wonder, was that really me who said that or did that? What we are experiencing in these situations is the influence that a new situation has on our character.

Scripture recognizes the importance of our environment in influencing who we are as a person. Proverbs, the book of James, and many other passages of the Bible urge us to flee temptation and keep our distance from "the world" (1 John 2:15). From these powerful passages, we can tend to think of our environment as only an enemy. But our environment can also be a source of strength. Many of the recommendations in the New Testament epistles are targeted at shaping the environments in which we move and live as Christians. The epistles of the Apostle Paul are filled with as many instructions about the formation of our Christian communities as the formation of our individual Christian characters. The implicit reason for these instructions seems to be that we as individual persons will be lifted up to be better and stronger Christians by virtue of finding ourselves in supportive Christian environments. And so we might say that our environments both support us, giving us strength and pushing us toward greater Christlikeness, and challenge us, drawing us away from God and toward the way of the world, the flesh, and the Devil. If we truly care about the formation and maintenance of their Christian sexual character, we will carefully attend not only to what goes into our children, but also what surrounds them.

We begin by carefully attending to the *family* environment. Have we created an environment of love, respect, listening, affirmation, humor, and support? A number of studies suggest that a close relationship between parent and child is one of the best predictors for the child acting in a sexually conservative manner in adolescence. A close, supportive relationship with the parent becomes a part of the environment, a support, that determines who that child is. Additionally, the supportive family helps to meet critical needs of the child, reinforces proper values and beliefs, and reinforces important skills. But family environments can be more of a challenge to chastity than a support. Where children are deprived of the affirmation and acceptance they so vitally need, they will go elsewhere to get it.

Second, a child's environment is powerfully shaped by the peers and friends of the child. The sexual behaviors of adolescents are strongly influenced by the actions of peers, or at least by what is perceived to be the actions and attitudes of peers.[5] If we care for our children, we will try to influence, with respect, their choice of friends and the ways they spend time with those friends. As parents, we can try to channel our children's peer groups into productive and rewarding recreational activities as opposed to destructive pursuits. We can encourage some friendships and discourage others. We need to be extremely cautious in doing this, lest we manipulate our children or interfere in an inappropriate way.

Churches form an important part of our child's environment. One major study showed clearly that "at-risk" behaviors such as frequent alcohol use, theft, cigarette smoking, and drug use occurred at about half the rate among young people who were active in church as compared to those who were not. With regard to sex, 22 percent of those who were active in church were sexually active, as compared to 42 percent of those who were not active in church at all.[6] If mere involvement can produce such reductions in sinful behavior, then imagine what we might do in a church actively targeting contemporary problems faced by teens and working hard to reduce those problems.

We must also teach our children how to shape their own environments. We can actively train our kids to recognize *high-risk situations*, how to avoid them or get out of them early, and to develop the skills needed to deal effectively with such situations. Lindy, in chapter 3, could have benefited from knowing that bus rides after dark can be pressure situations, from knowing how to negotiate limits on relationships early, and from having thought through how to resist sexual pressure. For children to do this, they must develop an understanding of their own limits and how to compensate for areas where they lack strength.

CONCLUSION

Needs, values, beliefs, skills, supports. These are the building blocks of character in general, and of sexual character in particular. Your children will stand the greatest chance of living a chaste life—a life conforming to God's will about sexuality—if

- their needs for relatedness and significance are met in the family, and if they themselves understand these needs for what they truly are;
- they value the right things, the things God values;
- they believe God's view of their own sexual natures;
- they have the skills to make good decisions and to act on those good decisions with strength and confidence;
- there are more positive supports for their making right decisions than there are negative challenges that pull them away from the right path.

Part Two

THE CORNERSTONE YEARS: INFANCY THROUGH KINDERGARTEN

5

The Biblical Foundation
for Sexuality Education
in the Christian Home

❖

T
here are four major "acts" in the biblical "drama" of God's dealing
with His people: creation, fall, redemption, and glorification. The cur-
tain has not been raised on the final act as yet. In this drama, we never
finish an earlier act before we move into the next; rather, the new chapter
unfolds as the previous act continues.

God began with His good work of creation. The Fall marred the creation, but the reality of God's marvelous creation continues on, modified by
but never destroyed by the Fall. Then, through Jesus Christ's birth, life,
death, and resurrection, God's work of redemption intrudes on the drama
and changes the reality of both creation and the Fall. God's redemptive work
changes everything, and yet creation is still an underlying reality, as is the
Fall. Creation-Fall-Redemption is an important scheme through which to
see all of life, but it is an essential part of seeing our sexuality through
God's eyes.

We see this scheme clearly in the Apostle Paul's first letter to Timothy,
where Paul warns this younger disciple that in the latter times to come
heretical teachers following deceitful spirits will attempt to lead the faithful
astray. Paul writes, "They [the false teachers] forbid people to marry and
order them to abstain from certain foods, which God created to be received
with thanksgiving by those who believe and who know the truth. For
everything God created is good, and nothing is to be rejected if it is
received with thanksgiving, because it is consecrated by the word of

God and prayer" (1 Timothy 4:3-5).

The early Christians were fighting a nonstop battle with Gnosticism, which taught in part that the two essences of the world were physical reality and spiritual reality. They further taught that spiritual reality was good by its nature and that physical reality (the physical world and the physical body) was intrinsically evil. Many modern conservative Christians lean in the direction of this heresy when they take biblical warnings about the world and the flesh (for example, Ephesians 2:1-3) to mean that physical creation is bad and that our physical bodies are the enemies of our spiritual natures.[1]

Paul rebukes negative views of food or sex (the main objection to marriage for the Gnostics) which, according to the apostle, "God created to be received with thanksgiving" (1 Timothy 4:3). Paul approaches the issue of sex starting from creation; declaring that "everything God created is good" (4:4). But he acknowledges that the Fall has marred that creation, and that we must, in a sense, "wipe the dirt off" of God's beautiful creation. This is one of the fruits of God's redemptive work, that the beauty of God's original creation can be partially restored when it is "received with thanksgiving" and "consecrated by the word of God and prayer" (4:4-5).

So Paul in this passage approaches sex *first* from the viewpoint of creation, *second* from the perspective of the Fall, and *third* from God's redemptive work.

This is the proper order for parents as well. *In teaching our children about sex, we should work from the fundamental reality of creation, through the effect upon creation of the Fall, and then to the healing effect of Christ's work of redemption upon our sexuality.* We are out of order if we start, as so many Christians do, with the Fall in dealing with our children about sex. Even more tragic than starting with the Fall is the greater error of dealing *only* with the Fall in our sex teachings.

Based upon their struggles, guilt, shame, ignorance, and doubt, many Christians feel grave doubts about the basic goodness of their physical bodies and of their sexuality. But while struggles, guilt, shame, ignorance, and doubt are real problems, they are not reflective of the fundamental truth about our physical existence or our sexuality. What is the fundamental truth?

RELATEDNESS AND SEXUALITY

First, as we discussed in chapter 3, we are relational beings by God's design. We are made to love. In some mysterious way, we mirror God's capacity to be one and at the same time three (the doctrine of the Trinity) in our capacity to be separate and yet united. In fact, when we combine the creational declaration that "a man will leave his father and mother and be united to his wife, and they will become one flesh" (Genesis 2:24) with the promise of Jesus that "where two or three come together in my name, there I am with them" (Matthew 18:20; see also the discussion of abiding in Christ in John 15), we find a wonderful parallel—in Christian marriage, three become one.

The glue, in some way, for this blessed union is the husband and wife's sexual union. Sexuality in general (including our distinction as male and female, and our inclination to love and feel sexual longing) and sexual intercourse in particular were made good by God for His purposes and our good. And what were God's purposes for sex that fulfill our good?

PURPOSES OF SEXUALITY

We believe Scripture mentions at least four basic purposes of sexuality.[2] *Procreation* is the first. In Genesis 1:28, God blesses His precious creations by urging them to beget children. Some theologians have drawn a parallel between God's creative work and our ability to procreate, suggesting procreation as one way in which our lives are an image or reflection of God's nature and character. This truth also forms the foundation for the positive Christian view of family as a fundamental unit of God's blessing. God made families!

Union is the second vital purpose of our sexuality. As mentioned above, Genesis 2:24 points to the uniting power of sexual intercourse (see Jesus' discussion of this reality in Mark 10:2-12). First Corinthians 6:12-20 is even more explicit, teaching that even casual sexual union such as visiting a prostitute results in the uniting of two strangers in some mysterious way. What is the meaning of the uniting of two persons in marriage? What does it mean for two individuals to become one flesh? Sadly but happily, this is and will remain a great mystery. Perhaps one of the best expressions of this mystery is in a poem by Madeleine L'Engle:

> You are still new, my love. I do not know you,
> Stranger beside me in the dark of bed,
> Dreaming dreams I cannot ever enter,
> Eyes closed in that unknown, familiar head.
> Who are you? who have thrust and entered
> My very being, penetrated so that now
> I can never again be wholly separate,
> Bound by shared living to this unknown thou.
> I do not know you, nor do you know me,
> And yet we know each other in the way
> Of our primordial forebears in the garden.
> Adam knew Eve. As we do, so did they.

They; we; forever strangers: austere, but true.
And yet I would not change it. You are still new.[3]

Physical gratification and pleasure are a third purpose of our sexuality. In 1 Corinthians 7:1-9, the Apostle Paul speaks in the most matter-of-fact way about sexual need and the obligation of spouses to meet each other's needs. He speaks of the problem of burning with passion, and how the physical pleasures of sex in marriage is a way to deal with that problem. Proverbs 5 speaks poetically of the beauty of physical love:

> May your fountain be blessed,
>   and may you rejoice in the wife of your youth.
> A loving doe, a graceful deer—
>   may her breasts satisfy you always,
>   may you ever be captivated by her love. (verses 18-19)

And of course the Song of Songs (or Song of Solomon) speaks powerfully of the delights of romantic love and physical rapture. In summary, God, through the Scriptures, does not shy away from acknowledging the basic truth that sex feels great; indeed, God made it that way.

Finally, as a fourth purpose, we believe that God means to *instruct* us about His truth through our sexuality. Romans 1:20 speaks of aspects of God's divine nature being clearly seen in what He has made; sexuality is one of those vehicles for God teaching us about Himself and ourselves. In being made men and women who inevitably feel the urge for union with another whom we love, we are taught that we are incomplete in ourselves and that we need union with "The Other" to be truly ourselves. Of course, marriage, no matter how wonderful, never completely satisfies our need for completion, but through our sexuality, we are directed out beyond ourselves for that completion. Sexuality is then a concrete lesson about universal truth.[4] We also see God's triune nature as unity in diversity reflected dimly in our own experience. Sexuality thus teaches us about God's and our own profoundly relational natures.

If our sexuality reflects fundamental truths about our very natures, then it makes sense that God would deliberately use sexuality as a primary illustration in His Word, and in fact this is the case. Marriage is a primary metaphor for God's love of His people as shown explicitly in the living parable of Hosea's pursuit of his adulterous and promiscuous wife Gomer (Hosea 1-3); in the rapturous love poem, the Song of Songs, which many regard as metaphorical (in part) for Christ's love for His Church; and in the wedding-feast metaphor which Christ used Himself in His parables (for example, Matthew 22:1-14, 25:1-13) and which is seen in a vision by the Apostle John at the end of his life (Revelation 19:6-10). Indeed, Paul says explicitly in Ephesians 5:25-33 that marriage is meant to be an earthly model of heavenly truth; that the mystery of Christ's love of His bride is meant to be reflected in the earthly relationship of the Christian wife and husband. And the flip side of the relationship of God and His people is taught through the metaphor of sexuality. The Old and New Testaments are full of passages like Ezekiel 23, where our spiritual unfaithfulness to God is compared to sexual unfaithfulness to an earthly spouse.

And so, contrary to our doubting and hesitant attitudes toward the purposes of our own sexuality and that of our children, God has distinct and wonderful purposes for our sexuality by His deliberate intent.

THE BLESSEDNESS OF PHYSICAL EXISTENCE

We must point out again that many conservative Christians are infected with the virus of Gnostic dualism in their belief that their bodies are intrinsically evil. We see this in our confusion over what Scripture means when it condemns "the flesh." We also see this in our standard division of the human person into parts, often into the three parts of body, soul, and spirit (after 1 Thessalonians 5:23), and our implicit valuing of spirit over the other parts of the person.

But this is not God's own attitude. Our bodies, our physical existences, are a marvelous gift, a good gift, from the Creator. Three major doctrines of the historic Christian faith suggest that we need to amend our negative attitudes about our bodies. First, the doctrine of *creation* teaches us that, contrary to Gnostic heresy, physical existence (our bodies) is not an accident or a result of the Fall, but was God's design from the very beginning. God looked upon Adam and Eve, sex organs and all, ready for procreation, and declared them to be "very good" (not just the garden-variety "good" He used in rating the rest of the creation up to that point). When we look at the creation story, it is important also to note that the first mention of "soul" in the Scriptures suggests that our typical understanding of soul as something that is in contradiction or opposition to physical existence is a terrible misunderstanding. Genesis 2:7 reports that "the LORD God formed the man from the dust of the ground and breathed into his nostrils the breath of life, and the man became a living being." The Hebrew word for "being" is the same word used for soul; in other words, the man became a living *soul*. Part of Adam's "soulishness" was his physical existence. We do not just have bodies; we *are* bodies.

Second, the doctrine of the *Incarnation* supports the goodness of bodily existence. We are taught by God that Christ became flesh—"Since the children have flesh and blood, he too shared in their humanity" (Hebrews 2:14; also John 1:14). If having a physical body were inherently bad, how could perfect holiness have taken on a body? In fact, Hebrews 2 goes on to teach that Jesus was "made like his brothers in every way" (verse 17), from which we can understand that Jesus was a sexual person just like us.

Third, the doctrine of our coming *resurrection* refutes any notion of the evil of bodily existence. First Corinthians 15:35-44, 53-54 (see also Philippians 3:20-21) teaches that we will be raised and given new bodies for eternity if we believe in Christ. Contrary to the frequent image of being disembodied ghosts or spirits who will roam in some ethereal soup for eternity, Scripture teaches we will live as bodies, perfected bodies, forever. This makes perfect sense when we consider that God's original creation design for Adam and Eve, and hence for all of their descendants (that's us!), was bodily existence.

Beyond these broad doctrines, a number of specific New Testament texts affirm indirectly that physically based experience is not bad or inferior in its essence. In fact, they affirm bodily existence. First Corinthians 6:15 teaches that "your bodies are members of Christ himself," and clearly Christ would be no part of depravity or evil. Our bodies form Christ's physical presence in the world today. Verses 19 and 20 teach that our bodies are the "temple of the Holy Spirit," and that we are to "Therefore honor God with [our] body." A temple is a place of blessing and honor in biblical imagery, and to be able to honor God with our bodies, our bodies must be a suitable gift to offer to God, a gift which is pleasing to God by its nature. Romans 12:1-2 reinforces this teaching. In this passage, the word *body* is used as a synonym for the whole person; a person's body *is who he or she is* and is a suitable gift or sacrifice to God.

The "Flesh"

But what about all of those verses that warn us about the "flesh"?[5] Don't these verses force us to look at our bodies as the enemy of our spiritual nature? After all, Galatians 5:19-21 describes the "deeds of the flesh" (NASB), a long list of actions that mark those who are not destined to go to Heaven. Doesn't this passage teach that the body is the source of all sin? Absolutely not.

The term *flesh* in the Scriptures can mean a variety of things, including: (1) that aspect of the person which is frail and creaturely (for example, Isaiah 40: 6-8); (2) the physical aspect of all it means to be a person (for example, 1 Timothy 3:16, which refers to Christ in the flesh); (3) the "one flesh" union produced by marriage (Genesis 2:28); (4) those purely human acts of judgment that occur without bringing God into the picture (for example, 1 Corinthians 1:26); and (5) the outlook of the whole person oriented toward self and in active rebellion against God. It is this last meaning that is most important to us here.

The "flesh" we are to reject is not our physical existence, our bodies, but rather our sinful self-centeredness. The Galatians 5 list of the "deeds of the flesh" is an unusual list. It contains sins that we could attribute to the body (sexual immorality, debauchery, drunkenness), but also sins we would attribute to the mind (selfish ambition), to the emotions (rage, envy), and to the person's spiritual nature (idolatry, witchcraft). Whatever the flesh means in this passage, it cannot mean just the body.

In summary, the *fleshly nature* or *old self* (Ephesians 4:20-24) is the whole person or any part of the person—body, mind, soul, emotions, spirit, will, heart—that is in rebellion against God. The *spiritual nature* or *new self* (Ephesians 4:20-24) is the whole person or any part of the person—body, mind, soul, emotions, spirit, will, heart—that is submitted to God for His cleansing and direction and enabling. And thus the body really is a gift from God on a par with all other parts of the person.

THE FALL

While many conservative Christians need to be reminded of a creation foundation for our view of sexuality, we do not typically need to be reminded about the effects of the Fall. And so we will be brief. Adam and Eve's shame over their nakedness was the first and most immediate effect of the Fall; though there was nothing wrong with their physical nakedness, they could not bear the vulnerability of nakedness before God or before each other. Shame remains part of our human heritage—beyond shame over what we have done, we feel shame at what we are. Immediately after Adam and Eve sinned, God told them that power and control struggles between the two of them and between women and men forever would be one of the legacies of their choices (Genesis 3). The Fall brought the distortions of selfishness and pride into our sexual lives. Disease, pain in childbirth, and death all entered the world and our sexual relationships. We became people who could worship sex like an idol. We became capable of treating people like objects to be used for our selfish gratification. The motives of rebellion against God, greed, insecurity, anger, possessiveness, and others became part of our experience. And we became capable of becoming enslaved to our lusts. Truly our depravity is total—every tinge of our sexual natures and of our whole natures as persons is tainted with the dye of sin.

REDEMPTION

Finding life in Christ through the forgiveness of our sins is the starting point for the eradication of the effects of sin on all areas of our life, including our sexuality. Remember Paul's words in 1 Timothy: "Everything God created is good"; it is to be "received with thanksgiving" and "consecrated by the word of God and prayer." We are to sanctify our sexuality first by receiving forgiveness for what we have done wrong. We are to reclaim the good gift of our sexuality with thanksgiving. And then we are to dedicate our lives, with the help of the Holy Spirit, to becoming more Christlike, to becoming more of the person God meant us to be. And that includes the sexual dimension of each of us—we are to discover and shape our sexuality in the manner God intended us to. We are to accept and delight in the gift of our sexual natures. A major part of this book is dedicated to enabling us as parents to help our children be the sexual persons God meant them to be.

APPLICATIONS OF THE BIBLICAL FOUNDATION

We may boil down the practical implications of the material above to some core objectives for shaping the sexual character of our children in these early years. In these cornerstone years, we major on themes based on a creational understanding of our sexuality:

- Establish that they are loved beyond measure by you the parent and by God, their true Father.
- Teach them that God intended the family to be the primary arena for the experience of life-devotion, love, and unity.
- Develop their trust in God's Law as reliable and good.
- Convince them that their physical bodies, their sexual natures, and their capacity for sexual pleasure are all good blessings from God.

We will develop the first three in this chapter, the last in the next chapter.

"You Are Loved"
The foundation of all sex education is enabling your child to give and receive love. At the heart of Christian theology is the notion that our God is a relational God who loves, and who imparted into His creation the capacity to love and be loved: "For God so loved the world . . ." (John 3:16); "God is love" (1 John 4:16). Deuteronomy 6 suggests that the heart of Christian parenting is to create a family environment where the truth of the Christian faith will be incarnated, made substantial and real, in such a way that our children will find it natural to believe the gospel and live it.

Which is more convincing: the distant, rigid, unemotional parent who forces his child to memorize "God is love" and other Bible verses while rarely embracing the child, or the loving parent who shares with her child the joys of God's love while holding and caressing that child and thus embodying that love in a vivid way? A counselee of Stan's who struggled with an obsessive preoccupation with sex but had a poor sexual relationship with his wife recently described his family: "Oh, it was a Christian home all right. We had Bible verses and 'God's rules' and hymns shoved down our throats at all hours. And through it all, I always knew that it wasn't me that mattered; it was the rules. I had to perform to meet up to the expectations, but no one cared about me. As long as I knew verses and was a 'good boy' I got approval. But neither my father nor my mother really cared about me; they never wanted to know what *I* thought after I spouted off a verse. If I expressed a doubt or asked a question, I was a 'bad boy' who had to get back in line. I never knew love. They wanted my performance, but not *me*."

Why does the developing child need love so much? Why does it have such a devastating effect when those needs are not met? Why is the absence of love likely to so disrupt the child's sexual life?

The physical birth of the child is a marvelous event. Infants are exquisitely beautiful and profoundly helpless. In spite of all the scientific research, the psychological and emotional world of the very young child is still something of a mystery.[6] Numerous research studies indicate that children are quite aware of the world about them, responding from their earliest days to all sorts of input from their senses, and developing preferences even at very early ages.

For all of his awareness, however, it is likely that a newborn in the first few months of life has no distinct sense of himself as separate from his mother, father, and the rest of the world. As every observant parent realizes, the child doesn't even know that he has arms, hands, and feet, or that these can be controlled. The hilarious experience of watching a child discover his own hands, or that he can ring the bell that is stitched to his booties, is a joy to every parent.

But before these discoveries are made, the child seems to not understand her own separateness from other things. She doesn't know where the boundary line is between herself and everything else. Through such discoveries as being able to control her hands and feet but not being able to directly control her mother, father, or toys in the crib, the child slowly begins to develop a sense that she is separate from the rest of her environment. This leads to what some researchers have called the "psychological birth of the child" (as opposed to physical birth).

During this gradual psychological birth, the child must separate from everything around him, including his parents, and establish a distinct sense of identity. Many psychologists believe that this process begins in the third to fifth month and continues into the second full year of life of the child. It is also believed that this period sets the most basic foundation for how the child understands himself and what kind of identity he forms later on.

Will the child separate to such a degree that she will be cut off from others forever? While in order to be healthy the child must establish a separate identity, she also needs to be able to trust and love. Many psychologists today talk about the vital importance of the very young child *bonding* with one or both parents, usually the mother, during the first year of life. While the emotional availability of parents to their children is always important, there probably is no more crucial period than the first two years of life. Bonding or attachment seems to flow naturally from the parent's provision of loving affection, warmth, and gentleness. This bonding provides the basis of security from which the child can venture forth and explore the world. A child who is securely attached to the mother will frequently venture forth to explore her world, only to return after short periods for a time of "emotional refueling" with the mother, followed by more and more confident explorations. If this process is successful, the child emerges between eighteen and thirty-six months of age with a secure sense of identity.

One important characteristic of relationships that meet a child's needs for attachment or bonding is what psychologists call reciprocity. Children know they are affected by the parent; they need to know and feel also that their parent is affected by their behavior. It is vital for parents to be sensitive to and respond to how the child reacts to them. Examples include picking the child up and soothing him when he cries, feeding her when she's hungry, smiling back at him when he smiles or laughing when he chuckles. When we do this, we are saying to the baby, "You are so important that you, a little one, change my life. I am so much bigger than you, and yet you have an effect upon me." This sense of responsiveness may form the basis of the child's later ability to trust others—God, a future spouse, and others. In early childhood, meeting children's needs in response to their concerns is a way of preparing them to be able to trust, which is the critical foundation of living Christian faith.

This sketch of the development of the healthy child bears striking resemblance to the creation and fall story, in which Adam and Eve lived in utter dependence upon God, and yet were given by God an existence and identity separate from Himself and the opportunity to choose. Christianity steers between the unacceptable alternatives of pantheism (where everyone and everything is God and all identities are blurred; we have no separate identity) and deism (where a "Prime Mover" is utterly divorced from and uninterested in the world and we are thus separate, adrift with no relationship to our Maker to give us a foundation for our identity; we are utterly alone). We live out in our families the same drama that occurred in the garden: We shower our children with love while allowing them, as they are able, to make choices that will shape their identities. We pray they will choose better than Adam and Eve. In this way they are separate in identity but rooted through love and trust to others. This is a transformation that only a loving family can work.

It is vital to note that careful reflection on the process of childhood development can often make a parent absolutely terrified about making mistakes. Thankfully, parents do not have to meet their child's needs perfectly. One approach to psychology has coined the concept of being a "good enough" parent; a parent who is able to do a basically adequate job of meeting the child's needs. We think of parenting as being like the weaving of a grand tapestry; there are no critical threads, but rather what matters is the overall shape the artwork takes. And in our original sketch of the character of the child, bonding forms the foundation for meeting your child's need for loving relatedness for the rest of life.

Is loving your child as an infant really a part of shaping your child's sexual character? Absolutely. Our sexuality is a part of our relational natures, our capacity to give and get love. Learning to love and be loved in the family is the true bedrock of all sexual development. Recent research indicates that many women who experience significant sexual problems in adulthood seemed to have a common factor in their backgrounds—their "early love objects," possibly their mothers but most often their fathers, were perceived as being unreliable or untrustworthy.[7] Stan has counseled a number of persons who basically have a profound distrust for their spouse based on never having had parents be really trustworthy when they were very young. We are preparing our kids for oneness in an eventual marriage when we give them a secure base of trust from which to launch out into the world.

The Centrality of Family

There is a battle raging in our society to define the family. Proponents of gay rights, for instance, are attempting to redefine a same-sex couple as just as legitimate of a family as a heterosexual couple. Where should the line between family and nonfamily be drawn? At stake are such issues as acceptance in the Body of Christ, health care coverage, housing rights, inheritance laws, custody and adoption of children, and taxation policies. Undergirding the practical battle is the moral question of whether there is one ideal of what a family is meant to be, or if humans are free to define family as suits their needs of the time.[8]

We draw our blueprint for action in this area from the way Scripture deals with the perplexing problem of polygamy. We have puzzled long and hard over how polygamy is never condemned in Scripture, in spite of the clear principle in Genesis 2 that marriage is the union of one man and one woman (how could three, four, or more people become one flesh in polygamy?) and in spite of the clear condemnation of adultery throughout Scripture. In Scripture, polygamy appeared early in human history with Lamech in Genesis 4:19. Many of the great figures of faith in the Old Testament were polygamists in some form or another: Abraham kept concubines (Genesis 16, 25:6), and David (2 Samuel 3:2-5) and Solomon (1 Kings 11:1) both had many wives. Scripture records these realities without condemnation, but dispassionately describes the devastating personal and spiritual consequences of these patterns of life.

Historically, polygamy appears to have died out in Hebrew culture during the time of the prophets, after the division of Israel and Judah and during the time of the great exiles of the Old Testament Jewish people. By New Testament time, we see clear condemnation of polygamy in leaders of the church (for example, 1 Timothy 3:2, an interesting parallel to the instruction that kings of Israel are not to have many wives in Deuteronomy 17:17), but even the New Testament does not go so far as to declare polygamous marriages to be "invalid" or polygamous families to not be families.

The thrust of Scripture seems to be this: God has an ideal for marriage and hence for families. That ideal is for one woman and one man to be united for life, and from that union children are to spring. This is what family is meant to be. We cannot say that other groupings of people are not families, but we can say that other groupings do not fully represent the ideal of what families were meant to be. Marriages are meant to be earthly models of the singular devotion of Christ and His Church to each other (Ephesians 5), a devotion that unites two different but equal and complementary types of beings (Christ and His people; a man and woman), and unites them permanently.

Family—the ideal type of family God meant all people to experience—is thus important to God as the primary place where He intends us to learn and experience love, devotion, and union. We need to teach this courageously, but not arrogantly, to our children. We need to teach that it is God's ideal will for them to marry and have children, if He should so bless them. We should extol the benefits and goodness of this path of life. But we should not in arrogance deny that some people experience much that is good in other family structures. Many people have no choice in entering other family forms: many single parents would have never have chosen that way of life had other options been possible, few singles are unmarried by deliberate effort, and few childless couples are childless by choice. Others are in "nontraditional" families because of choices that in retrospect they recognize to have been wrong (for example, the teenage single mother). The good that God can work in those families must not be denied. Even more, it is our obligation as believers to contribute to those persons experiencing as much of God's blessing as possible by supporting, helping, and loving them and teaching our children to do the same.

Perhaps the best way to teach these lessons is to seize upon teachable moments at weddings, confirmations, or baptisms; upon hearing of a divorce in the neighborhood; upon seeing a gay couple holding hands in public; or in interacting with children from single-parent homes. We can use these times to talk about God's ideal. We can teach our children that their heart desire, which they will increasingly recognize as they grow, is to have one special other person with whom they can share life permanently. That is a good desire. We can teach them that desire for oneness and union will not be met the way God meant it to be in cohabitation, a homosexual "marriage," or other arrangement that is outside of God's ideal will. We can also use these times to talk about how we should think about arrangements that do not meet that ideal. In doing so, we should have the humility to admit that our own "traditional" families always fall short of God's ideal as well, so that no one is in a position to boast.

God's Law as a Trustworthy Guide

In disciplining our young children, we want to teach them to trust God's Law and that there is value in obedience to that Law. We do this by trusting God ourselves, by teaching God's rules, and by explaining and defending and praising those rules. Even more broadly, we want to reenact God's redemptive dealings with us, His children, in our families. The heart of Christian faith is rooted in our responsiveness to God's love for us—realization of our sin, confession of that sin to God, and receiving forgiveness and restoration of relationship from God. Even when forgiveness is extended, the consequences of sin still follow; asking for forgiveness for having gossiped does not erase the broken relationships and hurt feelings our actions created.

This is the drama we should reenact in our discipline. We have tried in our own family to never let our children have a moment to doubt how deeply they are loved. When they do something wrong, our relationship is fractured, but not broken. We confront the wrong, and ask them to acknowledge (confess) it. We insist that our children label what they did as wrong. We briefly explain why it was wrong, hopefully explaining how God's rules make sense. The consequence then follows: a spanking, a timeout, a loss of privileges. When they say they're sorry, we then offer our forgiveness and wholeheartedly return to a normal relationship without holding a grudge or punishing them by rejection. We try to make this reconciliation a time of close affection, hugging and comforting our children to make the reconciliation feel real. We hope that by reenacting daily the biblical drama in a small way in our family, we are laying the groundwork for our children to instinctively know the truth of the gospel as revealed in the Scriptures. Life in our family, hopefully, thus becomes a living lesson in God's truth.

6

Teaching the Goodness
of Our Bodies
and of Our Sexual Natures

✣

Jen was from a family that never talked about sex. Her parents treated the whole area of sexuality as a shameful and unfortunate aspect of life. She and her husband Roger were happy by and large, and she really respected his integrity and commitment to the Lord. They hardly ever talked about their sexual relationship. Sex for her was not unpleasant, but it was not the rapturous experience she had expected. But she was ecstatic to be a new mother of a beautiful little baby boy. Little Luke, six weeks old, was the joy of her life.

But there was a dark cloud in her life. She had begun to notice that her little infant often had erections when he was nursing. She had first noticed it when he had done a BM in his diapers while nursing, and she had rushed to change him, interrupting the feeding. When she opened the diapers, her little one clearly had an erection. Since then, she had, out of concern, touched his crotch briefly during nursing, and found several times that he had one again.

What did this mean? Was this normal? She had thought that boys did not begin to get sexual until after puberty. How should she feel about it? Was she doing something wrong to cause him to react this way?

THE BEGINNINGS OF SEXUAL DEVELOPMENT

Your child has spent nine months developing in the womb before you ever get to hold the baby in your arms or see him or her with your own eyes.

Your child's genetic gender was set at the moment of conception, depending on whether a y-chromosome sperm (male) or an x-chromosome sperm (female) from the father fertilized the ovum contributed by the mother, which contained an x-chromosome. Though the genetic gender was set from conception, male and female fetuses are indistinguishable according to gender until approximately after the first trimester of fetal development.

From about the fifth to seventh week of fetal life, male and female children develop identical genital structures, which scientists call a "genital mound." It is a bump, almost a wart, that looks identical for male and female fetuses at first. The first change that begins to distinguish boys and girls is the conversion of identical little internal buds of tissue into the ovaries in a girl and the testes in a boy. After these "sex glands" are formed, the genital organs begin to form. From about the seventh or eighth week through about the midpoint of life within the womb, an amazing transformation occurs. The exact same tissues in the gential mound (nerves, muscles, skin) are transformed into the head of the penis in a boy and the head of the clitoris in a girl, the shaft of the penis in a boy and the shaft of the clitoris in a girl, the scrotum in a boy and the labia in a girl. By the final stage of pregnancy, the normal child's external sexual anatomy matches the identity of its gonads (ovaries or testes) and its chromosomes.

The brains of boys and girls are different from early development on, though the differences are just beginning to be understood. It is most likely that the same hormones that influence the differentiation of the genitals also cause the brains of boys and girls to develop with slight but important differences. At the very minimum, these brain differences prepare the female's brain to regulate her periods of menstruation and fertility later in life, while a boy's brain lacks such cyclical regulating structures. Other more complicated gender-based behavior patterns may be influenced by brain development during the time in the womb.

Children Are Sexual
Because of brain structures and their genitals, it is indisputable that our children are sexual beings, even in the womb. This is corroborated by recent ultrasound studies suggesting that male children may even experience erections of the penis inside the womb before birth! The infant is a sexual being after birth as well. It is not uncommon, for instance, for an infant boy to experience an erection within moments of birth, and very commonly while breast-feeding. Similarly, scientific studies have suggested that it is not uncommon for infant girls to experience the feminine signs of sexual arousal (firming of the clitoris and vaginal lubrication) during nursing. Boys will experience periodic erections throughout their childhood, frequently if they touch themselves for pleasure, but even if they do not. These will become much more frequent during and after puberty.

It appears that girls similarly experience regular vaginal lubrication, though they can be quite unaware of this, especially if they have never heard that this happens.

It is for this reason that Jen needn't worry about her infant son Luke's erections. Even as a baby, he is a sexual creature. Young children probably respond with sexual reactions such as erection or vaginal lubrication because they respond as whole beings to any pleasure they experience. God made each of our children to be sexual beings; He made our bodies sexual in indisputable ways by His divine will; and He called our sexuality good. Thus our vital task as parents is to pass on to our children the same blessing God gave to Adam and Eve—knowing that the goodness of God's work in them is deeper and more fundamental than the sin that afflicts us.

How should we talk to our children about these realities?

> During his bath, four-year-old Kevin gets an erection while soaping himself off.
> **CHILD:** "Daddy, why does my penis get hard like this sometimes?"
> **PARENT:** "Well, God made us men so that our penises are very sensitive. It feels good to touch them sometimes. When your penis starts to feel good, a little extra blood from other parts of your body goes into your penis, and that makes it get a bit bigger and harder."
> **CHILD:** "Is it a bad thing?"
> **PARENT:** "No, not at all. God made you that way. When you get an erection as a boy, you don't have to worry about it at all. Later, when you are ready to be a husband and a daddy, it will be very important for you to have an erection because you can't become a daddy without that."
> **CHILD:** "Why? What does it do?"
> **PARENT:** (This father thinks, *Darn, why does this kid have to be smart enough to ask that?!*) "Well, the main reason is that your body will make little cells that are like seeds, and to make a baby when you are a grownup, you will have to put one of your cells called sperm together with a cell from your wife called an egg. That tiny cell will come out of your penis and having an erection will help to put it closer to the egg from your wife. And when those two come together, they start a baby your wife will carry in her tummy for nine months before it is born. Isn't that a miracle?"

Parents can't do anything to stop their children from being sexual. If a parent such as Jen were to respond negatively to her child for being sexual (spanking him, rejecting him by withholding attention, or some other punishment), the trauma to her child would be significant. She would be punishing him for being how God made him, a sexual child. She would be teaching him to repress or reject an aspect of himself that God gave him as a gift. At these earliest ages, the child needs no verbal comment or particular response from the parent; the child, after all, doesn't even know he has a penis! But the infant can sense whether he is wholly loved by the mother, or if the mother is hesitant, withdrawn, or rejecting. Early on is the time for the parent to work on his or her own responses to the child's sexuality. When you are changing diapers, look at your child's genitals and say a prayer of thanksgiving that God made that child sexual. Be honest with yourself and with God about any negative or ambivalent feelings you have and resolve to do something about those feelings by reading, praying, and/or talking with someone who can help.

Not only are children sexual, but parents are too. We as parents may need to receive for ourselves a grace and acceptance similar to what we want to give our kids. We as parents are not always comfortable with our own sexual reactions. For example, a woman's breasts are richly endowed with pleasure sensors that are connected to the healthy woman's sexual responsiveness. Many women experience breast-feeding to be pleasurable (after getting over the initial highly uncomfortable adjustment period), and it is not at all uncommon for mothers to experience sexual arousal from the stimulation of nursing. This may be somewhat akin to the way a man may experience any stimulation of his penis as arousing even when he doesn't want to be aroused. A father holding a squirming child in his lap may begin to get an erection when he does not feel erotic feelings toward his child. In all such cases, it is vital that the mother or father be honest and realistic with herself or himself to admit that sexual arousal is occurring, be clear about what is causing those feelings and what they mean, and focus the meeting of his or her sexual needs on his or her marriage partner rather than the child. Such responses are not sinful or depraved; they are one more manifestation of how we are all sexual beings.

TEACHING GOODNESS BY TEACHING WORDS

Direct sex education of our children begins with the naming of body parts. We teach our kids that they have elbows, chins, eyes, fingers. Why do we then teach them that they have "woo-woos" and "ding-dings"? God made their sexual organs with the same degree of deliberateness and perfect divine intent as He made all other parts of their bodies. We should teach our children basic proper names for their sexual organs. Boys should be taught that they have a penis and scrotum (the skin/muscle "bag" under the penis); inside the scrotum are their two testes (or testicles; singular—testis or testicle).

Labeling female genitals is a bit harder, because the proper name for the entire external genital area, vulva, tends to be less common than any other proper name. It does not help that most of the slang terms for female genitals are quite negative and unattractive to women. A girl can be taught that the genitals she can see are the vulva, and then be taught the different parts, or she can be taught just the significant parts for this age, which are the labia and the vagina. To see her own vagina, the girl will need to sit down and either use a mirror or be able to bend down. She can be told that while urine does come out of a boy's penis, it does not come out of her vagina; her urine comes out of a small and hard-to-see hole just up from her vagina toward her navel. A girl may discover and ask about her clitoris, located just above her urinary opening; she should be told, "That is your clitoris; God made that part of you to give you good feelings, especially when you are a grown and married woman." We will discuss touching and self-pleasuring in the next chapter.

TEACHING GOODNESS BY SHARING OUR PRAISE TO GOD

In teaching our children about their own bodies we should emphasize that their bodies are a beautiful work of art that they can thank God for. Their own body should be "received with thanksgiving" (1 Timothy 4), as we discussed earlier. When our children were young, we tried to encourage them to an early sense of thankfulness by playing "What's that? Who made that?" It went like this: "That's my *chin!*" "Who made that?" "God did!" "That is a beautiful chin! I love that chin! What's that?" That's my *penis!*" "Who made that penis? Did the doctor?" "No, God did!" "That's right, and God made your penis just right; it is beautiful! And what's that? . . ."

Bath times are also a great opportunity to affirm the beautiful creation of our children's bodies. "I'm so glad that God made you a boy, Billy. God made you wonderfully." As parents, we can show our children our honest wonder as we consider the complex miracle that is the human body. We can help them to be full of thanksgiving because we are filled with deep gratitude and appreciation of who God made them to be. We can say, "What a beautiful body God has given you!" We can touch them in appreciation and wonder, but also teach them the privacy of their genitals by not touching them there except to wash or care for when injured.

GOODNESS AND TOUCH

We should mention that some women grow up never touching themselves on the genitals. These women tend to grow up unaware of themselves sexually and to have difficulty in their sexual relationship in marriage. Many a young girl has been taught that her vagina is dirty; after all, she bleeds from there. Some women have been taught to wipe themselves with tissue, wash themselves with a washrag, and never touch their labia, vagina, or clitoris directly at all. By comparison, boys have to handle their genitals in the process of urinating and in bathing, and often seem to be much more comfortable with and accepting of their own genitals.

We feel teaching young girls never to touch themselves is very destructive. The woman's genitals are not dirty. Medical studies have suggested that in terms of germs the healthy vagina is about as clean as or cleaner than the mouth. Through its secretions, the vagina cleans itself. Teaching a girl not to touch herself alienates her emotionally and experientially from her own sexuality and promotes an ignorance and sense of dirtiness that will have destructive effects in the long run. Girls should be taught that their genitals are a beautiful creation by the Master Artist and are one of God's gifts to them as a person.

EXPLAINING REPRODUCTION, PREGNANCY, AND CHILDBIRTH

We should explain basic reproduction to our children at an early age. Even before age three, most children can understand that babies grow inside the mommy's tummy until they are too big for the mommy to carry anymore, and then the mommy goes to the hospital so that the doctors there can help the baby come out of the mommy's tummy through her vagina. The following dialogue might be typical for a young child of four:

PARENT: "That's right. Sue went into the hospital today to have her baby; she might even be having it right now."
CHILD: "Mommy, is the baby really in her tummy?"
PARENT: "Well, yes and no. The baby is not in her stomach where the food goes. But right below her stomach, every woman has a uterus or womb. You have a womb too, Caitlin. It is right down inside here (touches Caitlin between her navel and her genitals), and do you know how big it is? Make a fist with your hand; good—it's about that big and it's inside of you. Every baby—Sue's baby and you when you were a baby—starts out very tiny, as tiny as a speck like this (points to a tiny crumb on the kitchen counter) inside the mommy's womb and then grows over nine months into a baby who stretches the womb and the whole of the mommy's tummy to be as big as Sue's tummy was!"
CHILD: "Doesn't it hurt to grow that big?"
PARENT: "Well, sometimes it doesn't feel great, but it happens very slowly, and that helps, and mommies love their babies a lot and that helps, *and* God made women like me and like you in the most amazing way to where our bodies can stretch out and hold a

baby. It is even more amazing to me that the baby can come out through our vaginas."

CHILD: "My vagina is too small for that!"

PARENT: "Well, it certainly is now! But God has made you so that when you are bigger, and pregnant, you will be able to have a baby come out there because those muscles can stretch really big to let a baby through. It hurts quite a bit, but you love the baby so much you are glad to do it, and you are so happy to have the baby that the pain is well worth it. When I held you, I didn't think much about any hurt that I had."

CHILD: "But how did the baby get in there? Do I have a baby in me now?"

PARENT: "No, you don't. Babies are made when God helps a special little piece of the daddy's body called a sperm mix together with a special little piece of the mommy's body called an egg. These special little pieces are only for making babies. And do you know what? You have those special pieces, those eggs, inside your body right now, though they aren't ready for making a baby yet. When you're old enough to have a baby, God made your body so that it will get those eggs ready. And if you do have a baby, God wants you to have that baby after you are married so that your baby will be lucky like you to have a mommy and a daddy who both love her very much."

CHILD: "I hope Sue doesn't hurt too much from having the baby."

PARENT: "Me too. Maybe when Sue gets back from the hospital she will show you how the baby drinks milk from her breasts. Another wonderful thing that God made women like you and me able to do is to feed our babies right from our own bodies. Your breasts are little right now, but later they will get bigger, and when you have a baby, they are ready to make milk for your baby. Sue is planning to feed her baby by letting him nurse from her breasts. That's what I did with you and with your brother."

POSITIVE ANTICIPATION OF SEXUAL GROWTH

We should also help our children to view positively the development of what doctors call "secondary sex characteristics," the various changes other than genital structure, that distinguish men from women after puberty. Young women experience growth of the breasts and of pubic hair (as well as leg and armpit hair), and develop an adult female body form, including wider hips. Young men experience growth of the penis, scrotum, and of pubic, facial, and body hair; a general growth spurt; and deepening of the voice. These can all be anticipated positively for the child:

CHILD: "Dad, why do you have hair on your chest and everywhere while I only have hair on my head?"
PARENT: "Well, if you look closely, you have hair on your arms,
legs, and all over your body. When the time is right, though, your
hair will start to grow in many places, and it will get darker and
thicker. This will happen some on your arms and legs, but especially on your face, where you will someday be able to grow a
beard, and especially right over your penis. In fact, growing hair
right over your penis is one of the first signs that you are beginning
to change from being a boy to being a man."
CHILD: "But what if I'm not ready to become a man?"
PARENT: (Laughs) "Well, God knows when you're ready; He made
your body so that it just starts to change whether you think you're
ready or not. And don't worry; I want to help you during the time
you are becoming a man. I'll gladly tell you anything you want to
know or talk with you about what it feels like. It can be a little scary."

Many a parent has grown up in a family where sexual development is
treated negatively. Whether it is a talk about "the curse" (menstruation), or
derogatory talk about men as sexual animals or women as sexual objects,
these sorts of ideas can be very confusing and disheartening to children. We
must strive as Christians to have the attitudes toward our wondrous bodies
that God Himself seems to have.

TEACHING AT A "TEACHABLE MOMENT"

It is vital that parents initiate the instruction of the child. The best sex education parents can give their children may not occur from premeditated "lessons," however, but rather during special moments when children are naturally interested in finding out about sex, optimally, when they themselves
initiate the conversation by asking a question. Thus our next principle:

PRINCIPLE 4: The best teaching of a child occurs at "teachable
moments" when discussion and instruction mesh naturally with the
events and needs of daily life. One of the best goals for parents to
strive for is to become "askable" parents whom kids can come to
with questions.[1]

To oversimplify, there are three key components to a well-rounded ability to instruct one's kids about sex. The first is the parent-initiated instruction session; you have something you want your child to understand, and
so you tell the child. These do not have to be dour discussions in front of
a chalkboard, but can be lively and interesting. The key is that they are

initiated by the parent because it is "time" for the child to know about some subject.

The second component is the use of the "teachable moment." To seize a teachable moment, the parent spontaneously moves from an event and creates a teaching from the event. Whether the event is a beer commercial during a ball game, bath time, toilet training, a neighbor who is obviously pregnant, baby-sitting lessons that lead an older child to watch while you are changing a diaper, seeing a woman breast-feeding her baby, unusual genitals on a zoo animal ("Mommy, what is *that*?! Is it sick?"), a neighborhood dog mounting and thrusting its pelvis on a child's leg, an innocent report of a dirty joke going around that the child does not understand, or whatever, the parent seizes the moment to teach the child.

> A father rounds the corner in his home to find his four-year-old girl sitting in the middle of her room naked and bent over looking at her vaginal opening. She has her fingers pulling apart her labia. As she hears him, she suddenly sits upright and looks guilty. This is a situation that would be very easy to pass over, to ignore, to let his wife deal with. But how could this be a teaching opportunity?
> **PARENT:** "Hi! What were you looking at?"
> **CHILD:** "Nothing . . . (a look of guilt and embarrassment)."
> **PARENT:** "Were you looking at your vagina? That is a fine thing to look at, you know."
> **CHILD:** "No . . . yeah."
> **PARENT:** "It really is a wonderful part of you to look at and to understand. Do you know why? Because God made that part of you just like He made the rest of you. Who made that vagina?"
> **CHILD:** "God did!"
> **PARENT:** "And do you know what your vagina is for? It is so amazing that God made you so that some day, if you marry and God blesses you with children, a baby will live and grow in your tummy for nine months and then come out through your vagina so that you can hold it, and nurse it, and love it like we love you."
> **CHILD:** "Does Tammy (a neighbor who had just given birth) have a vagina and is that where her baby came out?"
> **PARENT:** "Yes, that's right. And do you know if boys have a vagina?"
> **CHILD:** "No, they don't. They have a penis."
> **PARENT:** "That is exactly right. Boys are blessed by God to have a penis, but girls are blessed by God with a vagina. Boys will never know what it means to have a baby grow inside and then to let it out through a vagina. Do you ever want to have a baby?"
> **CHILD:** "Yes, I do!"

When the parent has proved himself or herself as being capable of talking about sex with some degree of comfort, then children will begin asking questions. Responding to and encouraging questions is the third vital part of a well-rounded capacity to do sex education in the home. It is vital to encourage questions, to praise kids lavishly for asking questions. This should be easy to do, because there are few greater gifts than having a child who will bring his or her questions to you. But you typically must earn this gift by establishing a track record.

> Your child happens to find a used sanitary napkin in the trash with a little blood leaked through. The mother takes the opportunity simply to explain menstruation.
> **CHILD:** "Mom, what is that? Is someone bleeding? Did someone cut themselves?"
> **PARENT:** "No, honey. That blood came out of my vagina. But I'm not sick or cut. Do you know why that happened? It is because I'm having what women call my 'period' right now."
> **CHILD:** "Your period? What's that?"
> **PARENT:** "You know how God made all women so that they can carry a baby in their tummy, in their womb? Well, the baby needs some way to get food and air for the nine months it is in there, and the baby gets both from the mommy's blood. But I don't have a baby in my tummy right now. God made women so that when they're old enough to get a baby in their tummy, every month they get a little extra blood in their womb so that just in case a little baby starts to grow in there it will have food and air. But if there is no baby, the extra blood just comes out so that new fresh blood can be ready the next month if a baby comes then. So I bleed just a little every month, and that's what a period is."
> **CHILD:** "Does it hurt? It always hurts when you bleed!"
> **PARENT:** "Well, it doesn't hurt like a cut hurts. But it doesn't always feel great either. It hurts a bit for a couple of days, but it's not too bad. I'm just so glad that God made my body in such a special way that I can carry a baby inside of me and take care of it. That's a real miracle! And my period every month reminds me of what a miracle my body is! Yours too!"

BUT WHAT IF I DON'T KNOW THE ANSWER?

Parents are often daunted by the prospect of being asked questions they can't answer. To deal with this concern, we suggest first that a parent be prepared to say, "Well, I don't know the answer to that, but how about if I try to find out and tell you in the next few days?" It is vital then that you follow through with that commitment. Second, we suggest that tl parent be listening for the opportunity to instruct the child from God's perspective on sexuality. The questions that are most likely to stump us are the detailed questions about the functioning of the human body and the miracle of reproduction. Remember, this is the type of information *least* likely to really matter to your children in the long run. What really matters is their sexual character that you are helping to build. When a question is asked, *never miss the opportunity to build their character even if you don't know the factual answer to their question.*

> Five-year-old Billy raises a perplexing question after seeing his younger sister nurse.
> **CHILD:** "Dad, how do a mother's breasts make milk?"
> **PARENT:** "You know, I really don't understand it myself. I know every woman has little things called milk glands or ducts in her breasts that make the milk. I guess they take water, sugar, and other things the baby needs out of the mother's blood and mix them together in a new way to make the milk. What amazes me is that God made women so that the milk they make for their babies is the perfect food for them. It is one of God's ways of showing His love for the baby by taking such good care of him or her."
> **CHILD:** "What do you mean, it is the perfect food?"
> **PARENT:** "Well, did you know that during the first few days after a baby is born, the mother's breasts don't make milk at all, but make some liquid that is like medicine for the baby that makes it much harder for the baby to catch any sickness? That stuff protects the baby. After that, the mother's milk is better for the baby than anything else. Cow milk is perfect for cow babies, goat milk for goat babies, and human milk for human babies. Each kind of milk gives that kind of baby just what the baby needs. God knows so well how to take care of us perfectly; that's why it is so important that we trust what He tells us in the Bible. God loves us and wants to make our lives good."

PRESERVING MANNERS AND PRIVACY

Occasionally, the overly curious child, after a discussion of human reproduction, can ask the mother very pointedly, "Where did I come out of you? Show me!" Such a question presents a parent with a wonderful opportunity to teach the child basic sexual manners without discouraging curiosity. The best answer to this is for the mother to say, "No, my vagina is a private part of me that I share only with your father. Your vagina is a private part of you, too; Mommy and Daddy only touch you there to wash you. But I will draw a picture (or show you a picture in a book) that can show you what that part of a woman looks like." This matter-of-fact way of dealing with this request can be quite beneficial for a child.

Parents are often concerned about the issue of nudity in the home. "Family traditions" in this area range from paranoia about anyone seeing anyone, resulting in locked doors and frantic screams for kids to get clothes on, to almost social nudity that seems founded in a naive disregard for any possible negative fallout from such practices. And the biblical virtues of modesty and concern for chastity are difficult to apply since standards of modesty vary so from culture to culture. Our highly conservative, restrained, and modest friends here in Wheaton would have been branded as profligate exhibitionists had they worn their discreet one-piece swimsuits publicly just fifty years ago.

We have no certain answer to this dilemma. But we do regard the concerns on each end of the spectrum as legitimate. On the one hand, overly restrictive attitudes about nudity are dangerous. They communicate that our sexuality is suspect at best and dangerous at worst, and that people's responses to our bodies are not to be trusted even within our own families. On the other hand, overly casual attitudes about nudity fail to help the child learn appropriate boundaries for his or her own sexuality and do not encourage a proper sense of privacy. Further, inappropriate nudity can prematurely "sexualize" a child. An overemphasis upon or unconscious encouragement of the child's visual examination of other members of the family can lead to inappropriate curiosity or even fondling, excesses we should guard against. We would recommend that parents not obsessively guard against any seeing of family members naked, but that nudity not be flaunted in the family. Within those broad parameters, there is room for freedom of choice based on personal comfort levels.

7

Handling Sexual Curiosity and Sexual Play, Self-Stimulation, and Dirty Language

❖

C urt has a bad back. His physician had recommended back rubs with a vibrator when he was stooped over in pain. One evening, he could hardly move. He kicked himself mentally for having helped that neighbor load his moving van. Dana, his wife, had volunteered to rub his back with the vibrator to try to relieve the pain and allow him to be able to move tomorrow. Their two-year-old, Susie, watched with great interest, making frequent comments: "I love you, Daddy. Does it hurt bad? I'm sorry. Mommy, what is that thing you're rubbing on Daddy? Does that feel good, Daddy?"

After the back rub, Dana helped Curt get off the bed and go into the bathroom.

When they walked back into the bedroom, they stood paralyzed. Little Susie had turned on the television and was calmly watching a children's program, sitting with the vibrator between her legs, turned on, pressed against her genitals.

"Susie, does that feel good?" stammered Dana.

"Yes, Mommy, it really feels good. Daddy was right, it feels real good," Susie replied.

SEXUAL PLEASURE—A GOOD GIFT FROM GOD

Curt and Dana found out that even two-year-olds know their genitals can be a source of physical pleasure. Children learn the location of their genitals just as they learn about other parts of their bodies. It is quite clear that infants experience touching or rubbing of their genitals as pleasurable. Some children even develop patterns of deliberate self-stimulation (what we call masturbation in adolescents and adults) during the first year of their lives.

The foundation for talking with our children about curiosity and sex play is an extension of our discussion from chapter 6 on the goodness of our physical bodies and of our sexuality. If our bodies are the result of a divine act of creation by God, then our capacity for sexual pleasure is a divine gift. Our task is to help our children see that sexual pleasure as a gift, to see their potential to abuse that gift as a result of the Fall, and then to teach them to enjoy that gift in the way the Creator intended.

Why talk to children about sexual pleasure at a relatively young age? Because your best chance of influencing their beliefs will come from being the one who will form the "infrastructure" of their thinking about sexuality. We offer this as our next major principle:

PRINCIPLE 5: First messages are the most potent; it is far more powerful to form a child's view of sexuality from scratch than it is to correct the distortions the child will pick up in the world.

Why wait until your child learns some distorted view of sexual pleasure on the school playground or from a discarded *Playboy* magazine some neighbor kid found in his father's trash? Why risk your child misunderstanding your views because all she hears from you is silence? Why risk the television and other media being the main source of your child's understanding of the supposedly irresistible, undeniable, unalienable right of complete and total sexual gratification? We propose instead that we, the parents, lay the foundation. We should have the first say, when our influence is greatest and our children's trust of us is highest.

Our sexual organs are made for pleasure by God's design. The capacity for pleasure does not lie dormant throughout life, switching on mysteriously on the wedding night. While the capacity for experiencing ejaculation in the boy and menstruation and pregnancy in the girl have to wait for puberty, the capacities to experience touching of their genitals as pleasurable exists throughout life. Just as the glorious beauty of a flower is difficult to explain other than as a gift that flows from God's generous nature to us, so also with sexual pleasure. Evolutionary thinkers propose that male orgasm serves a purpose in the propagation of the species—it induces male animals to have sex so that they help keep the species alive.[1] But the same thinkers have real problems making sense of female orgasm; it serves no purpose other than the pleasure of the woman. Indeed, in lower animals the female of the species doesn't seem to have orgasm at all, but rather is driven to sexual receptivity by purely hormonal drives.[2] The clitoris of the woman is exquisitely sensitive and pleasurable, and it serves no known purpose other than to give the woman pleasure from her sexual relationship. As such, evolutionists have trouble understanding how such an organ could have evolved by chance.

By all indications, the pleasure afforded by our sexuality is a gift, pure and simple, from God! And this is how we should describe it to our children. But we should go further; we should describe it as a gift for which the gift-Giver has a purpose in mind.

> Cindy and Bill placed little three-year-old Steve in the tub with the warm water running vigorously out of the tap. They were chatting quietly in the kitchen when within seconds they began to hear squeals of laughter and delight from the bathroom. Bill walked in to check on what was going on, and found Steve holding his penis under the running water and squealing with delight. Oblivious to his dad for a moment, Steve stepped back from the water, looked down at his penis with wonder, and then stepped back to the tap so that the water ran over his penis again, resulting in more squeals. Bill stepped back out of the bathroom for an instant to regain his composure, and then went back in, turned off the water, and used this "teachable moment."
>
> **PARENT:** "You were running the water over your penis."
> **CHILD:** (Steve nods, unsure of how his dad is going to react.)
> **PARENT:** "I heard you laughing. Were you laughing because it felt so good?"
> **CHILD:** "Yeah, it felt funny!"
> **PARENT:** "It really does feel funny and good. Did you know that God made your penis that way, so that it could make you feel really good?"
> **CHILD:** "He did?"
> **PARENT:** "Yes, it's true. And do you know why God did that? Because when you grow up and marry, God wanted you to be able to share some wonderful fun with your wife and *only* your wife. God wanted to give you a way to love her and her a way to love you that is so special it will help to hold the two of you together like you are glued together! And so he made your penis so that it feels special and He made her vagina area so that it feels special, and someday the two of you can feel very special together! So every time you think about your penis feeling good, you can think of how God made it that way as a special gift to you to make you happy."

We believe it is good for the child to discover that the genitals are made for pleasure. This gives the parent the opportunity to put that gift in its right perspective. God made and gave the gift, but the gift is meant to be used in a certain way.

It may actually be perilous to interfere with the child discovering that his or her body is a source of pleasure. According to two prominent sex educators, "We can say today that one of the main sources of failure to achieve sexual satisfaction in adult life is interference by parents early in life with the child's discovery of his or her own body as a source of pleasure."[3] While we would not take this as far as many secular sex educators do, it does seem likely that messages from parents that are punitive and disapproving of the child's discovery of his or her body as a source of pleasure truly can program doubts and negative reactions into the child's earliest understandings of himself or herself. It is one thing to teach manners; it is another to punish a positive experiencing of sexual pleasure.

HANDLING SEXUAL CURIOSITY AND PLAY

How should we respond when we find our dear little one playing doctor in the basement, or peeing together with four other little boys in a secluded spot in the backyard, or negotiating "show me yours and I'll show you mine" in her bedroom with the child from next door?

The single most important principle is to not exaggerate the importance of the incident, but instead to use it as a teaching opportunity about the privacy of your child's body and what a blessed gift and miracle that body is. If a parent handles such incidents in a calm, positive, and reasonable fashion, it can be a very constructive experience. If parents overreact, they run the danger of instilling in their child a deep sense of guilt or that sexual interests and feelings are bad, and of encouraging a misplaced curiosity about this forbidden and dark aspect of life.

Our response to instances like those described above should incorporate the following elements:

1. We should reaffirm the goodness of the child's body as God's special creation and gift to him.
2. We should use the opportunity to teach the child that because of the special nature of God's gift of sex, her body, especially her sexual organs, are meant to be private. God means them for a special purpose, and not for play toys with other kids! (See the discussion on privacy in chapter 8.)
3. We should affirm the goodness of our child's curiosity. We might say, "I understand exactly why you are interested in other people's bodies and they in yours. We all know inside that those parts are special, and we want to know about special things. It's like wanting to unwrap a Christmas present before

Christmas! It's just natural to feel that way. And it's also natural to want to know more about private things; it makes us feel grown up to know about private things."

4. We should set clear boundaries and expectations. To continue the hypothetical monologue above, "But even though it is a fine thing to be curious, I don't want you to show your penis (vagina, privates) to other kids. And I don't want you to ask to see theirs. If you keep those parts of you private and special, it will help you to always feel that God made you in an especially wonderful way."

Such a parental response should lay the groundwork for children to handle themselves properly. Should sex play reoccur, parents should repeat the above admonitions but add a concrete punishment such as a timeout or loss of a privilege for disobeying the parents' directions. Parents should be careful in such times to *punish for disobedience of the parent.* Don't slip over into punishing the child for sexual curiosity, or worse yet for some sort of "perversion."

Some sex play will be with children of the same sex. This is quite natural, and parents should not be inordinately concerned about this. Children naturally have as much curiosity about their own gender as the other. Children wonder if other kids look like they do. Same-gender sex play should only be a concern if it becomes a recurrent pattern. We will discuss how to handle this in the next chapter.

One final word on this matter. It is our sense that when parents do overreact to kids in this area, it is because they assume that the kids have the same sexual motives as adults—lust, adult sexual desire, and so forth. Except for sexually abused or traumatized children, this is not likely to be the case. Some adult child molesters are reported to utterly misinterpret children, claiming that they (the molesters) thought the child's interest in his or her own genitals and in seeing or touching others meant the child wanted actual sex with the molester. This is a total misunderstanding. But our point here is that we parents must not make that kind of mistake. We must not attribute adult sexual motives to our kids' sexual curiosity and sex play, nor to their self-touching.

SELF-STIMULATION

As you may perceive already, we do not feel that occasional self-touching by children is a problem morally or psychologically. Morally, all of the typical concerns about adult masturbation simply seem to not apply to young kids. Children do not lust, as we understand it for adults, and they are not "programming their minds" with destructive fantasies (we will deal with moral concerns about masturbation in chapter 16). Children need to understand that their sexual organs are a marvelous creation and gift, that they are capable of giving pleasure by God's design, and that it is good for them to be aware of their own sexuality and comfortable with themselves.

Sometimes the child's self-touching can occur at an inappropriate time or place. This gives the parent the opportunity to teach the child manners and discretion. A gentle but firm instruction in manners—"Honey, please don't rub your penis through your pants when you are around other people. Your penis is a very private part of you and other people can feel very uncomfortable if you do that"—is probably all that is needed for most children in this area.

But some children can move toward too much self-stimulation or inappropriate self-stimulation. For instance, one couple we know had an eighteen-month-old daughter who they had always thought of as very active and a "wiggle-worm." In one of Stan's classes on sexuality, the father began to realize that she was wiggling with a purpose. The parents were in the habit of carrying her on their hip, one arm supporting her bottom, with her legs on either side of the parent's body, so that her vulva was resting on their hips in such a way that a little wiggling produced pleasurable stimulation of the clitoris for her. When they held her in this way, she immediately began to wiggle. They began to notice that she was also now reaching her hand down into her diaper to stimulate herself. And of course, they asked with some embarrassment, "What do we do?" Other older children can display similar inappropriate behavior in touching themselves publicly or by announcing their touching to others.

Self-stimulation for children is unlikely to be a problem. But it can become a problem in certain circumstances: under conditions of prolonged boredom and absence of adequate intellectual or activity stimulation, under conditions of emotional neglect or deprivation, and perhaps as an attention-getting manipulation. The early claims that masturbation made one go insane were based, apparently, on the observation that many of the inmates of the early, highly barbaric insane asylums tended to masturbate a lot. Today the belief is that, rather than masturbation causing insanity, the boredom and brutal inhumanity of these warehouses for the mentally ill led many to masturbate. The experience of sexual release was for them the last hold they had on their own humanity. Similarly, it is quite common to see the residents of institutions for the mentally retarded masturbating, if there is little meaningful activity in their institution. And so perhaps children in families where resources are low and boredom common might move in the direction of masturbating to relieve boredom.

One of the truly compulsive masturbators whom Stan has counseled masturbated on average four to six times per day well into his adulthood. He had begun this pattern in adolescence. Here the real problem was not his sexuality per se; rather, the masturbation was used like a drug to cover up or compensate for the deep emotional anguish he felt because of the horrible abuse and neglect he had suffered as a child. A child who masturbates to compensate for neglect is a concern, but this problem does not occur that frequently, and is definitely not likely to occur in the family of a parent concerned enough to be reading books on parenting in the area of sexuality!

Finally, a child can engage in self-stimulation because of the reaction it engenders in his parents. It may be a great way of getting attention or getting a highly emotional reaction from the parents. This is one more reason for parents to not overreact in this area. If the child's basic emotional needs for relatedness and significance are being met, and if his or her world is sufficiently interesting and engaging, then any interest in self-stimulation is most likely to simply be a passing one that needs no intervention from the parent other than making sure family standards of politeness and consideration for others are maintained. This is exactly what we told the parents of the eighteen-month-old who was self-stimulating. They simply changed the customary way they held the little girl; made sure she had other engaging things to do, including getting her into several play groups with other children; gently instructed her in manners; and after several months her self-stimulation simply diminished. She is now a healthy and well-adjusted twelve-year-old.

HANDLING "DIRTY" LANGUAGE

We need to distinguish between technical or proper terms, acceptable slang, and unacceptable or "dirty" language. Not everyone grows up learning technical terms like *penis* or *vulva*. And what we regard as dirty language depends upon what we have been exposed to. Some people grow up more comfortable using the terms *dick* or *peter* instead of penis, *boner* or *hard-on* instead of erection, *boobs* instead of breasts, and so forth. But a lot of slang is clearly crude or even predatory in its implications.

There is no divine blessing on certain words rather than others, but clearly we want our children to learn language that does not carry baggage that might deceive or mislead them. And not all of the polite slang is helpful to our Christian cause; we are particularly averse to using the slang term *making love* as a synonym for having sexual intercourse, because by our moral standards a couple is not really making love unless the intercourse occurs in marriage. So in response to a TV program or movie that describes two single people "making love," we are likely to remark to our kids, "They did *not* make love; maybe they made lust when they had sex, maybe they expressed affection, but they did not make love because real love unites people and is rooted in lifelong commitment." Our point here is that not all slang is unacceptable; parents must make their own decisions.

Children may bring home slang out of genuine confusion, wanting to know what a term means. They may also bring it home to test your ability as a parent to discuss hot issues, to be understanding and levelheaded. In either case, the best strategy is to treat the whole issue in a very matter-of-fact manner. Above all, the parent should never punish or scold the child for asking about the meaning of slang or for using inappropriate slang *the first time*.

> At the dinner table:
> **CHILD:** (finishing a story) "So then Jimmy said, 'And forget ever playing with my toys, *ever!*' What a prick he is!"
> **PARENT:** (recovering from shock) "Why did you call him a prick? What do you mean?"
> **CHILD:** "Well, that's what Jason calls everyone. It's a putdown. I don't know what it means."
> **PARENT:** "Well, *prick* is sort of an ugly word for a man's penis. I would rather that you not call people by words like that, because God made your penis and all men's penises to be a wonderful gift; He didn't make them something nasty. So please don't call him a prick, or a penis for that matter. I would rather you not call Jimmy anything like 'jerk' or 'stupid' either. If he behaves poorly, tell the truth: he was rude or selfish or even acted like a bozo."

> Again, at the dinner table:
> **CHILD:** "Mom, what is 'f---'? Cathy said 'f--- you' to me."
> **PARENT:** "I'm very glad you asked me. F--- means to have sex. Remember how we talked about sexual intercourse being when a man's penis goes in a woman's vagina, how God made this as a gift for married people, and how God wants you and me to do that only with the person we are married to? But Lindsey, the word *f---* is used by most people as a dirty word; that's the way Cathy meant it. She probably meant 'I'm mad at you so I'm going to say something dirty to you.' And that is sad, because she took God's beautiful gift of sex and pretended it was something ugly. I don't think that makes God happy. So would you please not use that word?"

Parents need to settle in their own minds what they believe to be the proper terms for sexual anatomy and what is acceptable slang. We then set standards of what kinds of language we will and will not allow in our home. Improper language should be handled in a calm, matter-of-fact way when it first occurs, with no punishment for bringing such terms into the home. Rather, we should welcome the opportunity to instruct our children and thank God that they can talk to us about these issues. Only when foul language is used after the child has been informed of its unacceptability should discipline for such behavior be implemented.

8

Preventing and Overcoming
Sexual Molestation

❖

Andre and Carol were horrified by what their four-year-old, Tricia, was telling them. She was in tears as she reported that Lisa, the rude and spoiled five-year-old down the street, had been playing house with her in the playhouse in Lisa's yard. Lisa had forced Tricia to pull down her pants and panties "or she said she wouldn't let me go home, Mommy!" Lisa had then rubbed Tricia's labia "really hard" and, as best the parents could gather, had tried to force her finger into Tricia's vagina but had stopped when Tricia burst out crying, saying that it hurt. Lisa had let her go only after forcing her to promise not to tell her parents. Tricia probably would not have told, either, but she hadn't been able to control her fear that night when she went to bed, and her terror and hurt welled up, leading her parents to get her to tell the secret even though she was afraid.

Janet knew something was not right. Her son Brad had never been so clingy and reluctant to go outside and play with the neighborhood kids. She had sensed a change over the last two weeks, ever since the adult daughter of the older couple next door had moved back home after leaving her husband. The woman's three kids had joined the play in the neighborhood. Ever since then, her own kids had seemed sneakier, more secretive. But this change in Brad had been sudden, just in the last two days.

She confronted Brad, saying she knew something had happened and that he had to tell her what it was. She was stunned by what he told her. Her son, her four-year-old, had been subjected to having oral sex! The seven-year-old from the new family had enticed the younger kids to act out the "movie he saw." He had wheedled and bullied and induced the younger kids to do what he directed them to. Brad and Melissa had acted out oral sex, with Melissa putting her mouth on Brad's penis while four other kids watched. Becky, the three-year-old from across the street, had acted out intercourse with the new five-year-old from the family in question, though she had kept her panties on. And all of this in Janet's garage!

These are true stories from average, "nice" neighborhoods. And sadly, much worse happens with some degree of commonality.

THE FACTS

Abuse during childhood is not so common that parents should be constantly watching for it. But some estimates are that about one in ten kids experience some significant unwanted sexual activity and that between one in one hundred and one in two hundred are subjected to intercourse.

Sexual abuse (we use the term to mean unwanted sexual contact or stimulation, not necessarily just intercourse) of children is most likely to be committed by someone familiar to the victim child. The nightmare of the anonymous stranger who commits an abuse crime with our child is a real fear, but is not the one most likely to occur, to the best of our knowledge. It is thought that most sexual abuse occurs *within families*. Surprisingly, the most frequent kind of abuse appears to be the least talked about—abuse perpetrated by an older brother on a younger sister. It is estimated that this type of abuse is five times as common as the most publicized form of abuse, father-daughter incest. Sibling incest is less discussed and much less reported, probably because intense family shame keeps it covered up, and because there is less likelihood that high levels of violence are used to force consent, which leads the girl herself and the parents to put more of the blame on her.

The likelihood of sexual abuse approximately doubles in blended families; stepbrother and stepfather abuse appear to be among the most frequent kinds of abuse. Other factors that increase the risk of abuse occurring are: a mother with extremely negative views about and reactions toward any discussions about sex, the child being isolated by having a poor relationship with the mother and few friends, and the family being poor and the parents poorly educated.[1] In homes where neither parents nor siblings are likely to abuse, some risk still exists from friends and acquaintances in the neighborhood. As the distortions of sexually explicit movies and pornography grow in influence, we are likely to see this risk increase.

It is probably the case that a strong majority of abuse does not involve intercourse, but we should not take this to mean that the events short of intercourse (oral sex, fondling) are not serious. Like an attempted rape that ends without vaginal penetration, the results can nevertheless be devastating for the victim. Do not assume the ignorant stance that "only intercourse hurts a child, anything less than that is minor." But we must be equally wary of the opposite exaggeration, which is the belief that any abuse experience always devastates your child and leaves her scarred forever. The degree of damage in the life of the child is determined by many factors, including: the nature of the sexual interaction itself, how often it happened, how the child was "persuaded" to participate, the age of the child when it happened, the degree of isolation of the child from one or both parents, how the parent or parents respond to the revelation of the abuse, the personality of the child herself, and the presence of other "counterbalancing factors" in the child's life (such as truly loving relationships with siblings or friends, successful performance in school, sustained "safe periods" of time spent with grandparents).

PREVENTION OF ABUSE

It seems to us that many "experts" today, in their rush to always make kids feel good about their sexuality and in their hesitancy to establish any moral norms whatsoever, recommend parental tolerance of even the most outrageous of childhood experiences. Listen to the following approved parental dialogue from two of our country's foremost "family sexuality experts":

> (Girl) Jimmy and I were playing doctor. He said I should kiss his sore penis to make it well. Would it be okay to do that? (Parent) Kissing is one of the ways we pleasure each other, when we know and trust each other very well. What did you finally do about Jimmy's sore penis? (Girl) I kissed Jimmy's penis after he kissed my vulva. Is that making love? (Parent) That's one kind of making love. Usually we save lovemaking for people who are very, very special to us. And it is not ever something we *have* to do—only if we really want to be that close and trusting with the other person.[2]

In the authors' discussion of this incident there is no hint of disapproval, moral concern, or even caution. This paragraph is from their chapter on explaining sexuality to five- and six-year-olds! If we are incapable of even drawing lines against playing at oral sex by five-year-olds, we are going to be in deep trouble when it comes to setting moral absolutes for teenagers. And failing to draw lines with regard to appropriate body privacy and behavior also may leave our children without proper defenses against sexual molestation.

The best way to prevent abuse of your children is to give them the beliefs, skills, and supportive environment that will best protect them.

Beliefs

Critical beliefs include "rules" that serve to protect them. Most discussions of rules for children boil down to three crucial rules (in words for children):

1. *Your body is private.* "Your body, like that of all other children, is yours alone. Your body is private, especially your genital area (your penis or vagina). God wants that part of you to be private. No one has the right to look at or touch you there except Mommy or Daddy when we bathe you or think you might be sick there, and the doctor when he or she examines you there."

2. *No secrets.* "You must never keep a secret about anyone who looks at or touches you there. Some people may try to touch you there or ask if they can, and then may tell you that you have to keep it a secret. They may even tell you that we will be mad at you and that we want you to keep it secret. That is a lie. We will protect you, but we can only protect you if you tell us the truth. We will *never* be angry at you if you tell us something like that; we will be so happy you did the right thing in telling. Remember, if anyone ever asks you to keep a secret of touching from us, it is always wrong, even if that person is a police officer, your teacher, a minister, or a nurse or doctor."

3. *Trust your feelings.* "Because your body belongs to you, we will trust you and want you to trust your own feelings if you feel bad about or don't like the way someone touches you or looks at you. You don't have to kiss or hug someone you don't like. When you don't like what other kids or grownups are doing, if it makes you feel uncomfortable, then we want you to trust your feelings and leave."

But it is not enough to give children the right rules. We also need to empower them to be able to act by those rules. Part of this empowerment comes from encouraging the development of certain critical skills or strengths in your children. The first of these is the thinking skill of being able to recognize danger situations. It is not enough to tell your children the rule about trusting their feelings, or about "good touch and bad touch." We need to encourage them to be aware of their feelings and to develop that awareness. We can pay attention to how they report their interactions with other kids at school or in the neighborhood. And when they talk of a child or adult who acts in a shady or inappropriate way, we ask them what they felt and praise them for being aware of their reactions. We praise their good judgment. We try not to encourage paranoia, but we teach them caution. Also, we will want to talk about abuse incidents that happened to other children and how our child can be wary of such situations.

Skills

The critical skill is the action skill of assertiveness. Unfortunately, girls tend to be taught by parents and society to be docile and passive, and this seems to be a particular problem in Christian homes. We must not confuse the Christian virtues of gentleness, kindness, meekness, and even submissiveness with weakness. But rather, we should link assertiveness with the biblical concept of meekness. Christians often mistakenly identify meekness with weakness. When they think of a meek individual, they think of a person so weak as to be a doormat for everyone else. Then, because Scripture identifies meekness as a positive virtue, Christians sanctify weakness as a virtue.

But this is *not* the biblical way of thinking. We have heard it said that meekness was originally a military term used to describe extremely well-trained Roman war horses. These war horses were the epitome of power and destructive potential. Trained to kill with their hooves and to bite with their teeth, they were under exquisite control by their riders. A well-trained horse was called meek. And so the best understanding of the biblical concept of meekness is power under control.

There are only two persons in Scripture who are explicitly identified as meek: Jesus Christ and Moses. Neither of these men would qualify as weak. Jesus Christ was very forceful when the situation called for such action. Moses repeatedly strode into the throne room of the most powerful potentate on earth to declare the freedom of his people. He led his people at God's command, disciplining and judging them through the hardest of times.

There is no Christian virtue of weakness. We should seek to develop the assertiveness of our children, and then teach them how to submit that inner personal strength to God's use. We need to praise our children for speaking their minds, for asking questions, for demonstrating their strength. We need to mold them so that they make better and better judgments as to when to exercise this strength. For example, it is one thing for a Christian woman to deliberately allow a needy friend, to whom she feels called to minister, to break into her family time with phone calls and visits; it is another for a different woman to be chronically unable to say no to the people who steal her precious time with her children with their insensitive demands on her time. We can all appreciate meaningful sacrifice, but none of us wants our young child to be the victim of sexual abuse or our teenage daughter to be sexually victimized by aggressive boys because he or she lacks the strength to forcefully say, "No!"

How do we build such strength? We need to teach our young children that their "no" is respected. We have a family tradition of tickle fights involving all of the family, and of "Daddy-Monster Versus the Children" wrestling matches. In both, we have encouraged our kids to forcefully say or yell "stop" when they have had enough tickling, headlocks, Vulcan death-grips, or whatever. We have taught them to abide by this rule with each other as well. "Stop!" or "No more!" is to be respected, and respected instantly.

We have taught them that anger is justified when anyone—parents, siblings, or friends—does not honor this demand instantly. We use such playtime as an opportunity to *practice* saying "No!"

Don't expect your daughter to be able to say no in other situations if she has never been allowed or encouraged to say no even in safe situations at home. We praise our kids when they do say no with friends. When your kids discuss their neighborhood play, be aware of the importance of this skill and praise it when you see it or hear of it, provided, of course, they are within appropriate limits. "Christy, I heard you really telling Joshua that you were not going to do what he said in that game. I don't know what you were arguing about, but I'm so glad you were able to say with such strength what you would and would not do. That's great!"

Supportive Environment

Creating a supportive environment for your child means encouraging your child to talk to you, to trust her feelings the way you want her to, and taking action to protect her so that she can definitely trust you, the parent. This involves, in part, being willing to stand behind your children when they don't want to hug an older cousin or choose not to sit in Uncle Sam's lap. We praise the child for being polite but assertive: "Thank you, Uncle Sam, for having us to your house, but no, I do not want to sit on your lap right now." We support them to others who don't like their choices: "No, I'm not really concerned very much that Meghan might seem rude; I want her to be very polite but also very strong. She may not always make the perfect choices, but I won't always be there to help her make choices, so I'm glad to see her willing to make some on her own now." We tell them we are proud of the strength they show.

Creating a supportive environment also means reminding them occasionally of the three critical rules we described above. It means reminding them that there are to be no secrets where their bodies are concerned. Their bodies are private, a special gift from God.

Finally, creating a supportive environment means taking the time to be aware of your child's world. We need to have a sense of which kids in the neighborhood and school are trustworthy and which are not. We need to gently encourage our child to forge friendships which are likely to be safe and positive. We need to develop a sense of which parents are wise, supportive, and in agreement with our general goals for raising children. We may need to go to some lengths of sacrifice to make our own home a center for childhood play, a center where we can carefully supervise what goes on.

All of these steps will make it less likely that our children will be victims of sexual molestation. But even the best preparations cannot perfectly guard them.

HEALING FROM ABUSE

First, you need to know when to get help. Professional counsel need not be the first resort. Caring, skilled parents can deal with a lot. But if you have little track record of talking with your kids about sexual matters, and if you suspect that very significant hurt has occurred somehow, then it may be useful to talk with someone accustomed to dealing with such problems.

Listening and Sharing

The first item on the parental agenda when a child has been abused is to listen and to talk. Beware of the tendency to feel angry that anyone has hurt your child and to then convert that anger into criticism of your child for not protecting herself better. You cannot show that you are angry at all before the child, because children almost always believe you are angry with them regardless of your statements to the contrary. Don't criticize at all. Later, much later, you can gently suggest ways she can make better choices next time.

Also beware of the tendency to conduct the equivalent of an arraignment hearing to "get the facts." Knowing the precise facts is not important compared to knowing your child's perceptions of and reactions to what happened. Responding well can also be made quite difficult by your own feelings of guilt for not having been there to protect him, and your sense of helplessness over not being able to "fix it." Forget your personal remorse and guilt for the moment; you must make your child comfortable with the difficulty of talking about what happened.

Your immediate task is to listen and really hear the pain of the child. She probably feels hurt, afraid, regretful, angry, helpless, and dirty. But she will have trouble talking about any feelings. Listen to her talk, and ask gentle questions to get her to talk more. Show that you understand the feelings she expresses. Share her hurt—"I feel so angry too; what he did to you was very wrong." Let her talk about her hurt for as long as it takes; don't rush or be impatient ("You ought to get over this"). Don't make empty promises, but do resolve to help.

The best help for healing is to share the burden of the hurt, thus relieving your child from bearing it alone. This is a direct parallel to the role of the Holy Spirit that the Apostle Paul discusses in 2 Corinthians 1:3-7. God does not promise to make our sufferings go away. Rather, He promises to be with us in our sufferings and to share our burdens. This passage explicitly says that the comfort we are given as individuals is meant to overflow in our capacity to comfort others, and this is precisely what we have the opportunity to do in being a companion to our child in her pain. Pray for and with your child for Christ's presence in your child's pain and for His divine touch in healing.

Lastly, we should express confidence that there will be an end to the pain; it will gradually recede to a dull ache and then slowly recede into the distance. The child will need to talk a lot about it at first, then gradually less, with periodic "flare-ups" when other events frighten or upset the child. These are to be expected.

In this way, recovering from an abuse experience is very much like grieving. We should not rush people through grief or minimize their hurt by insensitive exhortations to "look on the bright side," but we should share the pain of the loss. We should be there to support and to talk. The parallel with grief is a good one; abused children have lost something forever. They have lost a certain aspect of their innocence and of their sense of security and certainty in the world. They have lost forever the degree of trust they previously had. These are significant wounds, and they should be properly mourned.

Creating Safety

There can be no healing from the abuse if the child is not helped to feel safe and to be safe. It is our job as parents to provide that safety. In the two stories that introduced this section, the parents had to create that safety— they banished the offending children from their homes and yards. These parents told their children that they were not allowed to play with the offending children, not as punishment but as protection, so that they could simply say "Mom said I can't" when they were asked to play with the offending children. In one instance, protecting the child led to confronting the parent and reporting the incident to state child-welfare professionals. In the other, no confrontation of the other parents was attempted. All of the factors must be weighed, but the safety of the child, emotional and physical, must be the highest priority.

Protecting our child can force terrible choices on us. One of Stan's clients was sexually molested by her new stepfather, a pastor and former missionary, from the first few weeks after the marriage when Carol was thirteen until she left the home at age eighteen. The molestation mostly took the form of groping and fondling. Her mother, a devout woman, was financially dependent on her new husband, was struggling with the three uncontrollable children he had brought into her care from his former marriage, and was still grieving over the death of her first husband. When Carol finally worked up the courage to tell her mother after almost a year of such molestation, her mother exploded, called her a liar, and accused her of trying to break up her new marriage. She never made the mistake of going to her mother again. She endured four more years of abuse. She abruptly married the first eligible boy to come along and has paid for that choice ever since. The terrible price her mother would have had to pay had she listened to and believed her daughter would have been steep indeed. But wouldn't the life of the daughter have been worth it?

Creating safety is much easier when the molestation has occurred outside of the home. When it has been perpetrated by a brother, stepbrother, father, or stepfather, it is much more difficult. It is a sad reality that women can be so financially dependent and emotionally, verbally, or physically intimidated by their husbands that it is easier to disbelieve the daughter's story than to confront and deal with reality. We cannot claim to have a simple solution to this dilemma, but feel strongly that our children must be protected. Confrontation of abuse within families may threaten the very stability of the family and of our whole lives. But to not confront it is certainly to leave one of God's precious children defenseless. Would God want us to cling to marriage or financial security at that cost?

Reporting Abuse
One of the terrible choices we may have to face is whether to report the abuse to state authorities, and/or to make the abuse "public knowledge" in the family. Such reporting is sure to create a fire storm in the neighborhood or family. The tendency of many of us is to avoid conflict, especially by rationalizing an incident as a one-time occurrence. Sadly, such judgments are often wrong. One family we know found out after the death of a beloved patriarch that the old man had molested at least nine granddaughters, nieces, and grandnieces from the time he was fifty until he died. Most of the girls had tried to talk to their parents when it happened; every one of the parents held back from fully confronting the issue for fear of disrupting family relationships. Every one of those girls, now adults, were scarred by the incidents.

There is no generally accepted rule about when to report and when not to report. Our best advice is, first, that sexual abuse by adults is unlikely to be an isolated incident. Any act that seems unquestionably improper should probably be confronted and reported. Second, in dealing with acts between children, it seems important to distinguish between sexual curiosity and exploration versus knowledgeable exploitation or more advanced attempts to mimic adult sexuality. The example above where children were acting out oral sex and intercourse undoubtedly involved children having knowledge and experience beyond their years. Such an incident should be reported so that the authorities can find out where these children found out about these acts and what sexual abuse they had experienced.

It breaks our hearts as parents to have to intrude upon the joy and innocence of our children's lives by warning them about sexual molestation. But one of our children has been a victim of sexual molestation, thankfully not extreme. This experience heightened our own awareness of how this can occur, and how hard it is to recover from such an experience. It is worth it to protect our children. It is worth the pain and exertion to deal with it well when it does occur.

9

Gender Identification and Sexual Orientation

✛

C onnie was worried. Her son Jay did not seem to be fitting in with the others boys in the neighborhood. Jay had always been different. He had always seemed a sensitive and caring boy. He was much more inclined toward art and creative play, and seemed uninterested and even offended by the rough and aggressive play of the other boys. He liked the other boys, and would play with them one at a time at home, but he used any excuse not to take part in their wild play as a group around the neighborhood. Now Jay was refusing to take part in Tee-Ball or any other sports, while the other boys thronged to these activities. What did this mean for his future? Was he going to grow up effeminate, or to be homosexual? What should she do, and how should she think about this?

As a thirty-six-year-old concert cellist, Harrison had the following reflections on his life: "I grew up in a broken home with a withdrawn, sullen, and uncommunicative father and an overpowering and often hysterical mother. They divorced when I was ten. I always knew I was different from the other boys—I was left-handed, quiet, loved my music and art, hated sports and felt completely incompetent at them, and generally did not fit in. Other kids began calling me queer and worse very early on. The more I got into my music, the further I went in my musical education, the more homosexuals I was around. The combination of a broken home that made me very nervous about dating relationships, of feeling different and unaccepted by other boys, and of being around so many gays resulted in deep confusion for me about my sexual identity. People in the art community told me I was gay. My heart, and the Lord, told me I wasn't; that I was just different and that I was just fine being different. But my confusion and doubt ran deep, and it wasn't until I married at age thirty-four that I finally felt sure of my sexual identity. Getting married in the face of those lingering doubts was nerve-racking, but I felt it was what God wanted me to do. I feel incredibly blessed by that decision now."

GENDER IDENTIFICATION

The term *gender identity* refers to a person's inner assurance that he or she is a boy or a girl, a man or a woman. The process by which a child's gender identity is formed is not well understood by psychologists. Children begin to form their gender identity quite early. Parents typically make quite a big deal out of whether the child is a boy or a girl, and tend to base expectations for the child on the child's gender (for better or for worse). Children learn the stereotypes for their gender both from parents and from their social environment. Sometimes these stereotypes are trivial and comic ("Only women can grow long hair!"), but often they can be challenging and insightful ("Men don't cry, do they?" "Women can't become President, can they?").

Perhaps because young children are working hard to establish a sense of their own identity, they do not typically have to be taught purposefully about their gender identity, but rather absorb a sense of it in the normal course of family life. They watch us intently, filing away what they observe. Often our kids become a mirror of our attitudes and assumptions, a reality that may be either reassuring or unnerving as our prejudices are laid before us.

The final solidification of the child's identity as a boy or a girl typically takes place before the age of five, though there is substantial disagreement over whether the most important period is early (focusing on the second year of life) or late (between three and five).

Between ages three and five, children go through a period of intense curiosity about and investment in identification with their gender. This often comes out in "clannish" or competitive statements, such as "Girls are better than boys!" or "Dad, can just us men in the family go camping?" It can also be expressed in idealistic ways: "I hope I'm beautiful and loving like you, Mom, when I grow up."

It appears that the single factor most likely to encourage a secure and stable gender identity for our children in those early years is that they identify with the parent of the same sex; that the boy identify or see himself as *like* his father and similarly for the girl with her mother. This identification of the child with the same-sex parent, in turn, appears to be encouraged most *by a loving and accepting presence of that parent in the life of the child* on an ongoing basis. In other words, we do not typically do anything special to encourage this identification; we simply need to be available and have a positive relationship with our child. The same-sex parent needs to be a major force in meeting the relatedness need of the child to be loved, appreciated, and accepted. And this does not need to be totally or even largely verbal. The father who enjoys having his son along as he works on the car or drives to the store is giving out important messages of acceptance to him.

Factors That Complicate Gender Identification

There are many patterns that can cause gender identification to be much more difficult, or even cause the child to go awry.[1] In an era when marriages are breaking up at an unprecedented rate, the simple absence of one parent, usually the father, can make this identification difficult. Even when the same-sex parent is present, if he or she is aloof, cold, and distant, or is an undesirable figure (such as an alcoholic or chronically psychologically disturbed person), the child can begin to experience real doubt about becoming like the parent.

Additionally, the attitudes of the other parent can make a tremendous difference. For instance, a mother who is struggling with significant negative feelings about men in general and about her husband in particular can make snide comments about the father and men in general, and can communicate a general emotional discomfort with "things masculine." These patterns can give very confusing messages to the little boy going through the process of identification. Overprotection or other forms of pampering can make it difficult for the child to have a clear sense of self. A mother who is unwilling to "let her son go" can result in the child feeling afraid to let go of her emotionally and take the step of accepting his difference from her.

Confusion about what it means to be a man or woman can also complicate the gender identification process. We live in a time when standard gender distinctions (girls cook, boys run for President, and so forth) are falling by the wayside; there are hardly any commonly assumed gender-based ideals any more. There is general confusion about the meaning of gender. Nevertheless, most parents recognize seemingly natural preferences in their children for different types of activities, emotional reactions, and so forth. The commonly noted tendency for boys to be more aggressive and girls to be more nurturing is a case in point. The vast majority of parents that we know see such differences in their children, as when girls cuddle and are affectionate to a doll, while boys use it as an object over which to run their matchbox cars. The erosion of constricting and biased gender caricatures has many beneficial results, but it may make the process of secure gender identification more difficult, as the modern "men's movement" demonstrates.

Consequences of Incomplete Gender Identification

The worst consequence of a failure to attain a secure gender identity is trans-sexualism, commonly understood as the phenomenon of a man feeling he is trapped in a woman's body or a woman feeling she is trapped in a man's body. Thankfully, this extreme condition is quite unusual. It is also possible that some sexual perversions such as transvestism (cross-dressing for sexual stimulation) and exhibitionism (the "flasher" who assaults women by showing his genitals) may be related to diminished male gender identification. Three more common "conditions" are possibly related to an impoverished gender identification: sexual promiscuity, sexual addiction, and homosexuality.

Sexual promiscuity and its more extreme variation, which we have come to call sexual addiction, may both have their roots in an insecure gender identification. Boys are often explicitly challenged in their teen years to "prove you're a man" by engaging in sexual intercourse. This may be an apt summary of part of what many young men and women are trying to accomplish by pursuing sexual conquest or addictive sexual release. The woman who is promiscuous may be trying to repair her damaged sense of womanhood by seeking affirmation from men. The man who compulsively masturbates to pornography may in part be trying to use his fantasy life and experience of sexual climax to achieve a stable sense of manhood. There are rarely single explanations for these types of problems, but this may be part of the puzzle.

HOMOSEXUALITY

The evidence about the causation of homosexuality is fragmentary and inconclusive.[2] The tremendous diversity among those who label themselves *homosexual* also complicates any understanding of what homosexuality is, and is caused by. Under this umbrella term "homosexual" are lumped men who have been effeminate since infancy and were sexually attracted to other men from their earliest recollection; also lumped under this umbrella are women, mothers who lived as heterosexuals through much of adulthood and then turned to lesbianism to escape abusive marriages and male oppression.

The causes of homosexual inclination are unclear. There may be genetic and/or biological factors such as brain structure differences that predispose some to move in the direction of homosexuality. The evidence here is very mixed. The fact that some children show stark differences in behavior from their peers very early suggests that some significant innate influence may be at work. But even if such a factor is present, that does not conclusively solve the puzzle of the cause of homosexuality. It seems clear that there is no one cause of homosexuality. The phenomenon is just too complex, too diffuse, for any one factor to explain it all.

A great deal of evidence suggests that disruption of secure establish-ment of male gender identity is a problem for male homosexuals.[3] Some contemporary theorists believe that the core sense that one is male or female is intact in the homosexual, but the related confidence in being a *man* or a *woman* is more fragile. Research consistently finds that gays report higher rates of having been viewed as a sissy or effeminate as children. A major study by a pro-gay psychiatrist studied children who were diagnosed in young childhood to have strong tendencies toward effeminacy, and found that many more than expected grew up to become homosexuals. A second study by a sociologist reported the same pattern. It is unclear whether this finding represents cause or effect with regard to identity. Perhaps some children are inherently less masculine or feminine than their peers, and this leads them to have a fragile gender identity; in other words, perhaps behavior patterns shape identity. On the other hand, perhaps children fail to develop a firm gender identity and thus begin to develop traits of the other sex as a response to their confusion; perhaps identity shapes behavior patterns. Perhaps it is both: A child who starts life less "gender-typical" may develop a more fragile identity and thus come to act even more in ways that are not typical of his gender, which leads to more identity disturbance and so forth.

Many other factors may be involved in a young person being "nudged" in the direction of homosexual orientation. Disrupted relationships with the same-sex parent are common for homosexuals. Homosexual men are very likely to report feeling alienated from their fathers from early in life on. Heterosexual men tend to report this as well, but not to the degree that homo-sexual men do. Early experiences with sexual molestation are not uncommon. Among the homosexual men we have known, over half had had full sexual relations of some sort with an older boy or man before they were twelve. Many homosexual women have been victims of heterosexual abuse, leading them to be deeply suspicious of and anxious about male sexuality.

Before we leave this subject, we feel it important to briefly address three final topics: choice, morality, and change. First, we think some Chris-tians are naively likely to assume that a gay has a high degree of choice in becoming a person of adult homosexual orientation. Our main problem here seems to be simplistic black-white thinking: Either gays chose to be the way they are or they didn't. In light of modern research, choice has become a very complex thing. As indicated above, it is very likely that many factors give certain people a nudge toward homosexual identity. That nudge may be very powerful for some, and quite gentle for others. The presence of a weak or strong push does not eliminate human choice, however. It seems quite likely that the *choices* the child makes in childhood and adolescence in response to those influences, those nudges, will have a powerful effect on whom he or she becomes. And the early choices may have powerful lasting effects; once homosexual preference is established, it appears very hard to change.

So the presence of influences does not make choice disappear. It is not either choice or causation. Additionally, becoming a *practicing* homosexual IS a matter of choice. Human beings choose to behave.

With regard to morality, we feel it is important to note two things. First, God condemns homosexual behavior in the Bible; every time such behavior is mentioned it is condemned in the strongest terms (see Leviticus 18:22; 20:13; Deuteronomy 23:18; Romans 1:26-27; 1 Corinthians 6:9; 1 Timothy 1:10). The modern arguments for changing the church's stance on homosexual morality all do fundamental damage to our understanding of the authority of God's revealed Word. Second, the same moral foundation that supports the traditional Christian understanding of heterosexual morality supports our understanding of homosexual behavior as immoral. As we argue in the next chapter, the true heart of Christian sexual morality is the notion that sexual intercourse is meant to bind a man and a woman together as one for life, and any other use of God's gift of sexual intercourse is an abuse of the gift. All of the arguments about homosexual relationships being loving and so forth may be true, but they do not touch the inner core of Christian morality: God gave us a gift, and we betray Him if we abuse that gift.

Finally, what about change? It is commonly argued today that homosexuals can't change. Well-meaning Christians often naively argue back that change is easy—just a little repentance, prayer, and effort will have the person heterosexual in no time. Neither of these views appear to us to do justice to reality. Some homosexuals are healed, some do change. Every scientific study that has examined the effectiveness of a treatment for homosexuality has reported that some homosexuals change, though the power of those treatments is not great. Spiritual healing appears to be a reality for some, but many report that such healing was illusory or partial at best for them. We believe change is possible for some, but we never quite know for whom. But Christians must not be led into thinking that God always requires change to heterosexuality in order that the person might please God. God is pleased by a life of purity, whether that purity occurs in the context of loving heterosexual marriage or in loving celibate singlehood. The path of chaste singleness is one that all Christ-followers have open to them.

GUIDELINES FOR ENCOURAGING PROPER GENDER IDENTIFICATION

All loving parents want to prevent their children from struggling with transsexualism, promiscuity, and sexual addiction. The very idea that one would want to "prevent homosexuality" sparks rage in the gay community, and yet most gays will say openly that they would not choose to be as they are had they been given a choice. Many Christians have no problem saying

...y would like to prevent homosexuality, since they view the homosexual lifestyle as immoral. Let us then explore a few tentatively offered guidelines for how we might help to steer our children toward a solid, comfortable gender identification and heterosexuality.

First, and most obviously, parents must take every opportunity to affirm their child's gender. From their first days, children should grow up regularly hearing, "I'm so glad that God made you a girl!" or "I can hardly believe what a great job God did in making you a boy!" We should use every opportunity to make connections between the child's gender and his or her development. This may be in ways that fit common gender stereotypes, such as when we compare the little boy's fascination with sports to that of his dad's, or the little girl's kindness and gentleness with a baby to the tenderness of her mom. This can just as easily occur in ways that do not fit the standard stereotypes, as when we remark with pride about our son's musical gifts and remind him that he may follow in the footsteps of great Christian male musicians such as Bach, or when we praise our daughter's athletic skill and remark on the fantastic athletic skill that God has given to both men and women. Generally, we should take every chance to remark on our child's gender and affirm it as a gift from God that he or she should delight in. In this way, we encourage our kids to fully accept the gift God has given.

Next, we must consider the child's identification with the same-sex parent to be absolutely critical. Fathers need to be available to their young sons and mothers to their young daughters during those critical first five years of life. Since parenting of young children usually coincides with the hardest period of establishing careers, the challenge of balancing work and family commitments will need to be a matter of considerable reflection and prayer. The same-sex parent needs to be available, to spend time with the child. While there is some distinction between quality and quantity of time, parents cannot always create quality time when they only have a small quantity to give. Children have to be ready too for quality time.

Above all, *the honest and steady expression of affection by both parents is critical to gender identification.* Love your child with abandon, without concern for "spoiling" the child (as the old folk wisdom warned). Spoiling does not occur with the generous expression of love, but only when those expressions are not coupled with reasonable discipline.[4] Remember from chapter 2 that parenting that provides both generous love and acceptance *and* guidance and discipline produces the best outcomes in children's lives. In addition to meeting the child's relational need for loving acceptance, you are guarding your child against looking to have that need met elsewhere, possibly in a very inappropriate way.

Tim, a man we know, was a needy boy whose father was simply never home and was uninterested in his son. His mother, angry and hurt by her husband, was deeply involved in church and her own friendships. Tim was drawn into a "special friendship" with a grandfatherly neighbor at about age five. By the time Tim was seven, the relationship had become quite sexual, with the boy and the elderly man regularly exchanging oral sex. The pattern lasted over four years, and Tim still struggles with homosexual urges today. Guard your child from having to go anywhere else to find love and acceptance.

We must beware of the aforementioned obstacles to gender identification and take steps to prevent them from interfering with the identification process. Negative attitudes of parents toward the other sex need to be honestly confronted and dealt with; they should not be allowed to contaminate the child. Arguments and hard feelings between spouses should be worked out between them and not be brought into the parenting relationship, where they get expressed in ways that hurt the child.

Single parents raising their young children at home will often have special concerns in this area. First, we would urge divorced parents to honestly confront their own emotions about their former spouse and how these feelings might have generalized to "all men (or women)," and attempt to come to terms with how they are being expressed to their children. Don't make the mistake of thinking you can hide powerful feelings from children. If strong unresolved feelings are present, deliberate steps should be taken to resolve or manage them. Second, you must find within yourself the energy to give emotionally to your child when you yourself are undoubtedly feeling in tremendous need of having someone minister to you. In single-parent homes, there are always dangers that children will be moved into the role of parenting the parent, of being maneuvered into meeting the emotional needs of the parent rather than the reverse. This can happen so subtly and comfortably that it is always a danger. Children exposed to this dynamic can be discouraged from developing their own identity apart from the parent and can experience significant problems in separating from the parent. Third, the single parent should attempt to encourage the child's relationship with same-sex adults who are loving and trustworthy. Sometimes this can be the ex-spouse, a grandparent, a neighbor, or a significant Sunday school teacher. Such relationships do not always have to be emotionally intense or involve huge amounts of time to be important.

We have reason to see behavior that is highly inappropriate for the gender of the child as a danger signal. We must not overreact here. Parents should not rush to force their three-year-old boys to lift weights and chew tobacco while smothering their daughters with lacy dresses and baby dolls. There are significant differences between children that need be of no concern. The boy who has no interest in sports or the girl who loves sports should not immediately be branded a concern. Parents should work hard to accept the unique interests and gifts of their children. Problems can begin, for some boys, when a father is uncomfortable with the interests or temperament of the son and subtly expresses that discomfort to the son. The subtle rejection can leave the child wanting the acceptance of the father but profoundly suspicious and hesitant about the father's reactions. This response from the son makes it even harder for the father to break through and really accept and enjoy the son. One homosexual man we know was the second son in his family. His slightly older brother was the epitome of the son the father wanted: rugged, tough, funny, smart, and athletic. The younger son was all of these things as well, but not to the degree of his brother. He felt rejected by his father, and came to rely on his mother alone for love. Because the parents' marriage was rocky, she became overly close with the boy, expressing appreciation that he was not like other men. By the time he entered puberty, he was sure that he was not like other boys. The lesson here? Accept the unique interests of each child, even when he or she doesn't fit all of our stereotypes. It is especially urgent that that acceptance come from the same-sex parent.

If a child's departures from normal gender behavior become extreme, however, parents do need to be concerned. Deliberate and regular cross-dressing, more than infrequent wearing of makeup by boys, and any recurrent wishing by the child to be of the other sex appear to be of special concern. Parents can seek to redouble their efforts at the responses we discussed above. They can also work to encourage more appropriate gender behavior by having the child spend more positive time with the same-sex parent and rewarding the child for participating in "gender-appropriate" activities. If those patterns seem to keep occurring, the parents should probably consider contacting a mental health professional for consultation.

Parents must often deal with sex play between same-sex kids, boys with boys and girls with girls. Unless such behavior occurs along with the types of extreme gender confusion patterns described in the paragraph above, you probably should not be concerned and should handle it just as we suggested you handle all sexual play. It is not cause for alarm. Above all, such behavior should not be labeled "homosexual." Kids today are aware at very early ages of what it means to be "gay." Unfortunately, it is common today to believe (1) that any homosexual behavior means one is a homosexual person, and (2) that once you are a homosexual person you are that way for life. While sexual orientation does not appear to be easily changed in men, it is vital to point out that sexual orientation is probably not set finally until late adolescence or even early adulthood. Thus any labeling of a child as homosexual is horribly premature and may become a self-fulfilling prophecy, a label the child takes into his heart and lives by for the rest of his life. Remember, Kinsey's original research suggested that over a third of all men experienced significant homosexual sex play while growing up, but only a fraction of that percentage actually "became homosexual."

Part Three

THE PREPARATORY YEARS: THE PRE-PUBERTY PERIOD

10

"What Is Sex? Why Is It Wrong?"

❖

Kimberly [a twenty-one-year-old mother
of eight- and two-year-old children]
learned about sex from her boyfriend.
"When you're in middle school and you run
into a boy who's 19 and cute,
he can teach you about sex in a few minutes.
You don't want him to be the one who
teaches your kids about sex,
but if you don't, he will."

B. KANTROWITZ AND P. WINGERT
Newsweek, FEBRUARY 15, 1993

"**W**hy in the world would a parent explain sexual intercourse to young children before they even get near puberty? Isn't that pushing it? Aren't you forcing them to grow up too fast? Aren't you going to traumatize them? Do they really need to know? Wouldn't that encourage experimentation and premature preoccupation with sex?"

We're glad you asked those questions! We will try to answer them.

The timing of telling your child about intercourse is a strategic decision, not a moral decision. There is no divine rule in this area. But let us think about the context of the ancient biblical culture, the context in which Jesus, Abraham, Isaac, and Jacob all grew up and the context in which God's will for human sexuality was revealed. First, they lived in a culture dependent on what we politely call "animal husbandry" today—the breeding, raising, and using or consuming of animals. As anyone who has spent time on a ranch or farm knows (and that is fewer and fewer of us today), such societies are steeped in awareness of sexuality. Fertility cycles, births, breeding strategies, animals displaying their genitals rather than discreetly hiding them, mating, and the like are daily staples of existence.

Second, it was a culture short on privacy. Much of the Old Testament culture was a nomadic one where the families lived in tents! In the towns and cities of those periods, people lived in small one- or two-room homes that did not have glass, stereo sound systems, or any of the other conveniences that offer us almost complete privacy. Third, this was a culture in which, as best we understand it, young people married quite early by our standards; a boy became a man at age thirteen and would be expected to marry soon thereafter.

Finally, this was an earthy culture in which God spoke to His people in earthy terms. For example, through the prophet Ezekiel (chapter 23) God talked in a brutal and explicit way about His people's spiritual unfaithfulness. He compared them to two sisters who act like whores, even to the point of fantasizing that their immoral lovers have penises the size of those of donkeys and semen ejaculations comparable to that of horses (verse 20)! And God's Law, in all its explicitness (rules and stories about incest, adultery, prostitution, and the like), was read aloud every Sabbath for all to hear. So let us not assume that Victorian ignorance, silence, and embarrassment is godly behavior in talking about sex.

Whether children will be traumatized by being told about sexual intercourse depends entirely upon how they are told. Lurid, sensationalized, or overly graphic descriptions are not healthy for children, especially young children. It is this type of revelation that may lead a child to be preoccupied with sex. And this is increasingly a risk for our children in today's media-driven culture. Our son's third-grade teacher, here in staid, conservative Wheaton, Illinois (what some call the Jerusalem of the Midwest!), reported to us that it is the rule rather than the exception that nine- and ten-year-old students regularly watch R-rated movies on cable television at home. The kids who don't see such movies themselves are regaled with vivid descriptions from these movies on the playground. Our son confirmed this, relating to us how the kids listened with great interest as several kids talked about seeing the science-fiction movie *Total Recall*, in which they saw a "mutant woman with three breasts" ("They actually called them 'tits,' Mom. Is that a bad word?"), and described the sex scenes in the movie to the uninitiated children.

One of the best reasons for parents to be the first to tell their children about sexual union in marriage is to prevent them from getting an initial impression that is distorted or destructive. This is another application of principle 5 from chapter 7—"First messages are the most potent; it is far more powerful to form a child's view of sexuality from scratch than it is to correct the distortions the child will pick up in the world." Trying to build a godly view of sexuality and sexual intercourse after exposure to the distortions of the world would be like trying to teach our children good nutrition after allowing them to be raised for years on junk food. *It is for this reason that we urge that children be told about sexual intercourse between ages five and seven, between their kindergarten and second-grade years.*

TELL THEM EARLY; TELL THEM EXPLICITLY

Our next general principle is:

> **PRINCIPLE 6:** Accurate and explicit messages are far better than
> cryptic, vague ones.

We all know the old story of the child who was told that in sexual
intercourse, the father plants his sperm near the egg inside the mother.
The child looked thoughtful and went away apparently satisfied. Some time
later, the father heard his child ask the mother where they kept their shovel.
"What shovel?" she replied. "The one Daddy uses to plant a seed inside
you," the child replied. Language that seems explicit to us can be quite
obscure to a child.

We should err on the side of providing too much information and
being too explicit. By explicit, we simply mean being *detailed, clear, and
direct*. We don't mean being indiscreet or lewd. Typically, little damage
is done by giving too much information if the information given is true,
sensitively described, and offered in a positive spirit. Our observation is that
children absorb the information they are interested in and can understand,
and they seem to simply ignore or file away whatever they cannot grasp or
are uninterested in. We must strike a balance here; if we bore our children by
drowning them with detail they don't want, we discourage them from coming to us for information. But asking about sexuality is hard for children,
and if we make them feel like they are pulling teeth to get information from
us, that we usually give them half or less of what they want when they talk
to us, then they will get the information they want elsewhere, somewhere
where it is easier to get.

Our general rule is that we try to give our children direct, simple, and
explicit responses to their questions, and to give them about 20 percent more
information than what they seemed to ask for. Then we try to interact with
them and keep talking about the subject as long as they seem interested and
quit as soon as they seem disinterested.

ARGUMENTS AGAINST EXPLAINING INTERCOURSE
TO YOUNG CHILDREN

There are no well-grounded biblical or psychological reasons not to tell
children the basic facts of full sexual relations. We have heard some draw
attention to classical Freudian psychoanalytic theory as justification for
not explaining sex to kids. Freudians argue that young children are in the
"latency stage" of their psychological and emotional development from age
five until puberty, and that during this period they are naturally uninterested

in sexuality. If this is true, then to tell them about sex could create damaging problems with sexuality.

However, there is no evidence to support this claim. Elementary school kids are not disinterested in sexuality, they just tend to talk more to their peers and less to adults about the topic; they're suddenly exposed to a grand vista of peer relationships through which they can learn new and fascinating information. Further, if there really is a latency period, then kids will simply be disinterested when you talk to them, which is fine if it happens.

Far from indicating a signal for the parents not to discuss sex with the child at all, this increased discussion about sex among peers signals the even greater need for parents to be constantly striving to be the primary source from which their child learns about sex. If there are problems created by telling children about sexuality early on, the problems arise because children are being told the wrong things and in the wrong ways—often by their peers. There can be no denying that a lot of children and adolescents today are growing up with very problematic attitudes about sex. The problem is not that they were given godly instruction early on by their parents; rather, the problem is that they have learned from everywhere else, and have learned all the wrong beliefs. If our children are going to learn about sex early in our sex-saturated society, it must be our responsibility for them to learn the right views, and for God's perspectives to form the foundation for all they come to believe.

WHY IT'S SO HARD TO TELL THEM ABOUT INTERCOURSE

First, we are unused to talking about sex at all, and when we do talk about it, it is usually in the abstract. Second, there is a natural privacy around our sexual lives that is difficult to deal with. When we begin to talk with our kids about sex, there is a sense of invasion of privacy; the little people in the bedroom next door now know what we have been doing! We are also often conflicted about our own sexuality, mixed up and unsure about our own attitudes and feelings, and sometimes feeling unresolved guilt or shame about our past choices or actions. Finally, we fear our own ignorance and are afraid our children might push us beyond what we know.

But none of these reasons must stop us. We must put aside our defenses and discomfort, work through our hesitancies, and risk not having the perfect answer or being shown to not know everything. Our children are worth it.

HOW TO TELL THEM

Our messages as parents should be the first messages. Our teachings should be explicit and direct. And that leads us to our next general principle of sex education in the Christian home:

PRINCIPLE 7: Positive messages are more potent than negative messages.

As Romans 2:1-16 teaches, God's Law is written on the hearts of all persons. We trust, on this basis, that in their hearts our children will be able to recognize the truth when it is presented to them. And the truth of the Christian view of sex is a good, positive truth: Sex is a marvelous gift of God. Christians believe that good is more powerful than evil. Because the Christian message about sexuality is fundamentally positive, good, and true, we can trust in the persuasive power of the positive message about the Christian view of sex.

In fact, all other messages about sexuality other than those of the Christian faith diminish rather than enhance our understanding of sexuality. Even the playboy philosophy, which exaggerates and vaunts the physical pleasures of sex, making them the center of life, is ultimately a mere graven image of what sexuality really is about. By making sex the center of life, the true meaning of sex is distorted and thus made less than what it is.

Carolyn Nystrom wrote a marvelous book for five- and six-year-olds about human sexuality, *Before I Was Born*. We have used it to introduce each of our children to the topic of sexual intercourse. After describing the nature of marriage, she offered the following explanation of intercourse:

> Friends bring gifts to a wedding. God has a special gift for new husbands and wives too. It is called sex. And sex is a gift that they can enjoy all the rest of their lives.
>
> When a husband and wife are alone, there is no need to cover their bodies. Because of the marriage their bodies belong to each other. They enjoy touching each other and holding each other close. When a husband and wife lie close together, he can fit his penis into her vagina. His semen flows inside her and their bodies feel good all over.
>
> This is the way that babies are made. A husband can't make a baby by himself, and neither can a wife. But God has made their bodies so that they fit perfectly together. And together they can make a baby. Husbands and wives want to be alone during sex because then they are thinking only of each other.
>
> God's rules say that only people who are married to each other may have sex. It is God's way of making families strong.[1]

We have had the following type of conversation after reading the above to our five- and six-year-old children.

CHILD: "So that's sex, is it? When people talk about having sex, they mean the man's penis being inside the woman's vagina? That is *so gross*!"

PARENT: "You know, I felt just the way you do when I first heard about sex. I think maybe God makes us so that when we're too young to have sex, it just sounds gross to us. But it really isn't gross. Someday, when you really love someone and you are physically ready to have sex, then it won't sound gross anymore; instead, it will sound wonderful. I remember when your mom and I were dating, I wanted to have sex with her. But even when it sounds lovely, it isn't the right thing to do until you are married. God wants you to have sex only with your husband (or wife). Since your mom and I weren't married, we didn't."

CHILD: "Why does God have that rule?"

PARENT: "Well, like this writer said, God made sex as a special gift for husbands and wives to share only with each other. You know how you feel about your most special toys—you really don't like to share them? Well, sex is a little like that; it isn't meant to be shared with anyone but your husband (or wife). To share it with other people would ruin it. It's like two radios that two people can use to talk just to each other. If you break the radios into more pieces so that three or six people can all share the pieces, the radios are broken and they don't work. They were not meant to be shared like that."

CHILD: "Oh."

PARENT: "You know what? I like talking with you about this, and I'm glad that you want to know. Would you please tell me when you have more questions so that I can talk more about it with you? Sex is very beautiful, but a lot of people believe the wrong things about it, so you will hear other kids telling you really dumb and wrong stuff. And television will show you many people who have very wrong ideas about sex. So I want to talk with you about it so that you will know God's truth about sex."

We have typically found that knowing the most basic physical information, that intercourse is when the man's penis goes into the woman's vagina, satisfies the basic curiosity of the child. But over and above the physical facts, what children really need to get from their parents are the *spiritual truths* that sex is a good gift from God and that it is meant for marriage only, and they need to learn the *relational truth* that you as the parent are open to talking about sex with them and that you welcome their questions.

Sometimes kids may ask other more detailed questions about intercourse, questions about positions, movement, exactly how it feels, and other embarrassingly detailed questions. We might feel an instinctive privacy reaction to such questions, or simply have a firm limit of what we are willing to go into with our child. We must balance such natural reactions with an awareness of what might lead kids to ask such questions. Are they being told things about intercourse on the school playground? Are they being exposed to questionable movies at a friend's house? We would urge that you respond in a matter-of-fact way, where possible, while protecting your own privacy. It is important to be comfortable with some limits on what information you give, as some things don't have to be known until marriage.

Informing Other Kids
We also encourage our children not to bring up the topic of sex with other children, because parents may have different time schedules for telling their kids about sex. But we encourage our children to speak up when they hear another child expressing misinformation, or at the very least to come back to us and ask us the truthfulness of what they have heard. We especially warn them that they will hear some kids talking as if sex is always a dirty and ugly thing, and alternatively they will hear other kids talking as if sex is the greatest and most important thing in the world and that anyone who doesn't start having sex at a young age has something wrong with him or her.

When you talk about sex, it is best to focus on human beings. "Birds and bees" and other "animal" examples can be helpful, but parents should be aware that using nonhuman examples can be a subtle way of depersonalizing and thus evading the implications of their discussion of sexuality. Also, such discussions tend to make sex a purely biological process divorced from its distinctly human meanings as an expression of committed love and the vehicle by which husband and wife are united. It is within the context of its human meaning that Christian sexual morality really makes sense. Finally, animal examples make sex seem primitive or animalistic, which it is not. Children need to be able to connect sexuality with their own bodies and feelings, and an overemphasis on nonhuman examples can defeat this. Even young children know what it is to love deeply, to share pleasure, and to be committed to another for life.

THE HEART OF CHRISTIAN SEXUAL MORALITY

If we are to influence the moral choices of our children, we as parents will need to be able to make a reasonable presentation of what that morality is and why it is valid. Perhaps "Because I say so!" or even "Because God says so!" will suffice for some kids, but not for most. In fact, such responses will probably undermine our case; they make it look like Christian morality, in the final analysis, does not really make sense and we have to try to enforce it by bullying our children.

But the traditional Christian sexual morality does make exquisite sense. It is, like all of God's wisdom, a thing of beauty and grace. God's Law is a path that guides us toward wholeness; it is a lamp that shows us the way through the darkest night. How sad it is then that so few of us can really give a reasonable defense of what we believe about sexual morality.

We will explore why sexual intercourse within marriage is approved of and blessed by God, while intercourse outside of marriage is not. Our goal in both of these sections is to equip you to be able to talk confidently with your child about what God's will is for handling his or her sexual choices. It is vital to communicate the essence of this message to children when they are young, early in elementary school, and then to repeat and repeat the message in new forms, adding to their understanding as they are able, as they move toward and through puberty. Some, but not all, of our discussion here will be beyond what the elementary school child can understand. But it is vital that you, the parent, have the big picture in the back of your mind as you teach your young child about the morality of sex. Thus, we will mostly be talking to you, rather than to your child. The morality of all of the *other* types of sexual behaviors that adolescents engage in, such as petting, will be examined in a later chapter. Understanding God's will in the area of sexual intercourse is the foundation for building a complete system of sexual morality.

The Morality of Sexual Intercourse

An enormous number of reasons have been given for young people to refrain from sex outside of marriage. We break these down into three general groups or types of reasons. Each type serves a vital role today. Sadly, the tendency for most of us is to emphasize the first, mention the second, and totally miss the third. We regard each aspect of the support for Christian morality as equally vital. The three types of reasons for chastity are the *caution about consequences of sex*, the *value of obedience to God*, and *respect for the uniting nature of intercourse itself.*

Consequences. Based on a spirit of caution, parents reason that because of the risk of serious consequences of premarital sex for an unmarried person, the teenager should not have sex. We rightly recognize that the risks of pregnancy and disease are too great. The majority of arguments in Christian and nonreligious books exhorting teenagers to wait to have sex are about consequences. These types of arguments can be extremely powerful because they are concrete and easy to describe. "Do you want to get pregnant and ruin your life?" "Do you want to get AIDS and waste away and die?" Some of the physical and emotional consequences of premarital sexual activity truly are devastating, and children need to be informed about these consequences. This is where most of our emphasis seems placed today. Because these consequences are important, we will expand upon them in a later chapter. But putting our main emphasis here is a mistake.

The problem with arguing by the consequences alone is that it suggests that the act of sexual intercourse in and of itself does not have moral implications. The moral problem with the act comes only in the distasteful consequences that can flow from it. Do you see how confusing this message can be for a teen? It essentially says to her, "Sexual intercourse in itself does not matter. Sex is neutral. What matters is that you not get a disease or get pregnant." When we place the brunt of our concern on the possible *results* of disease or pregnancy, we set ourselves and the child up for the forceful opposing argument: "But you can prevent unwanted diseases or pregnancies by using birth control, so you don't have to abstain from sex." In other words, the bad consequences become obstacles to be avoided; they are not really a solid argument for the immorality of the behavior. The consequences can be bad, but sex in itself does not matter. At its worst, this emphasis suggests that if physicians ever do wipe out sexually transmitted diseases and produce the perfect contraceptive method, then Christian morality will be obsolete because the consequences are under control.

Thus, these arguments, while powerful, lose much of their punch when the child is urged by peers or school-based sex education to consider ways of avoiding the consequences. Sexually transmitted diseases can be avoided by proper use of condoms. The risk of abortion can be lessened by use of birth control. Being an undesirable influence on others can be avoided by doing what you want to do in secret. Guilt can be avoided by rationalizing your behavior. Difficulties in breaking up a romance can be rationalized as the price of being an adult. Emotional distress can be avoided by simply growing up and being mature. Communication breakdowns can be dealt with by viewing sex as a new and different way of communicating. And so forth.

Defending Christian morality by majoring on negative consequences of sex is a mistake. It puts the emphasis in the wrong place. The possible consequences of premarital sex are vital, but they are vital because they *support* the core of Christian morality about sexual expression; they do not in and of themselves *form* the core of Christian morality.

Obedience. The second major class of argument focuses on the value of obedience to God's command. This approach is *vital* in any sincere expression of Christian faith. Unfortunately, this reasoning can be very hard to express to a child or adolescent. It can easily degenerate into the type of interchange which we stereotype as "do it because I told you to do it!" And yet the deeper truth is that obedience is probably our clearest way to express our love for God.

"If you love me, you will obey what I command. . . . If anyone loves me, he will obey my teaching," said Jesus (John 14:15,23). Anyone, including our teenagers, can understand that claims of love that are not backed up by actions in accordance with what the loved person desires are not real. The claim to love someone, accompanied by actions that ignore the other person's wishes and needs, is a lie.

Scripture speaks clearly about one specific way in which obedience pleases God: Obeying God's rules about sexuality is a concrete way in which we can honor God with our bodies (1 Corinthians 6:20). Christians are so often predisposed to thinking of their spirituality as disconnected with their bodies that it is a delight to know there are concrete ways in which we can express our spirituality physically; ways in which we can "incarnate" our devotion to God. Using our bodies in the ways in which God intended is a concrete way to honor God.

Why then is it insufficient to present this as our main emphasis in our moral teaching, to say in essence, "If you really love God you will stay chaste because that is what He wants"? This is insufficient because we all share a distaste for relationship demands that make no sense, for having to prove ourselves by behaving in a way that seems artificial. "If you love me, you will eat that grasshopper." "If you love me, you will stand on your head and scream." "If you love me, you will never say the word *blooper* in my presence." *Why* would God want us to refrain from sex until we are married? Is there any defensible reason for this request? If He really loves us, why does He insist on this rule? Is God's will about intercourse just a meaningless test of our loyalty to Him? No, it is not.

In His Word, God promises rewards for obedience, both in the present and in the hereafter (see Leviticus 26, Deuteronomy 28, or Galatians 6:7-10). These rewards are offered *after* obedience and have no explicit tie to the obedient behavior itself. In other words, there is no promise here that the act of obedience itself will be rewarding, but rather only that we will be rewarded for obeying. In this way, God shows us clearly that *obedience in itself* is valued by Him. He wants us to obey so much that He will reward us for doing so regardless of the command. But if we stop there, we still have no idea of how what God is asking of us makes sense.

"For whoever finds me [Wisdom] finds life and receives favor from the LORD" (Proverbs 8:35). Not only does following God's wisdom in obedience result in reward or "favor from the Lord," but it is also the right way, the way of life. God's Law expresses a blueprint of what is in our best interest, of how we were meant to live (see also Psalm 19 and Proverbs 1–4). We can have confidence that following God's rules about sexuality is the best way for us to act. But *why* is it best for us? Sometimes God does not reveal why; He certainly didn't to Adam and Eve in the garden. We can answer this question only by understanding the nature of intercourse itself.

Unity. The heart and foundation of Christian sexual morality is founded on *the nature of sexual intercourse, on what God made sexual intercourse to be.* The world wants us to believe that the physical act of sexual intercourse is a neutral, meaningless act that is to be judged only by the consequences it produces (bad sex is sex that hurts people) or the intent that was in the heart (bad sex is sex that is based in selfishness). But by God's design, the physical act of sexual intercourse, and indeed all sexual activity, has an intrinsic, built-in meaning given to it by God.

The scriptural view is expressed most succinctly in Genesis 2:24, which says, "For this reason a man will leave his father and mother and be united to his wife, and they will become one flesh." The Apostle Paul expanded upon this truth in 1 Corinthians 6:15-17: "Do you not know that your bodies are members of Christ himself? Shall I then take the members of Christ and unite them with a prostitute? Never! Do you not know that he who unites himself with a prostitute is one with her in body? For it is said, 'The two will become one flesh.' But he who unites himself with the Lord is one with him in spirit." The truth here is that sexual intercourse has a meaning, and it is a meaning of union, of the uniting of two people.

No one has expressed this better than Lewis Smedes in his book *Sex for Christians*, where he says:

> It does not matter what the two people [who are having sex] have in mind. . . . The *reality* of the act, unfelt and unnoticed by them, is this: It unites them—body and soul—to each other. It unites them in that strange, impossible to pinpoint sense of "one flesh." There is no such thing as casual sex, no matter how casual people are about it. The Christian assaults reality in his night out at the brothel. He uses a woman and puts her back in a closet where she can be forgotten; but the reality is that he has put away a person with whom he has done something that was meant to inseparably join them. This is what is at stake for Paul in the question of sexual intercourse between unmarried people.
>
> And now we can see clearly why Paul thought sexual intercourse by unmarried people was wrong. *It is wrong because it violates the inner reality of the act; it is wrong because unmarried people thereby engage in a life-uniting act without a life-uniting intent. Whenever two people copulate without a commitment to life-union, they commit fornication.*[2]

This is a vibrant and important reality for Christians to capture, and it is a positive truth that is woefully absent from most books about sexual morality. We need to teach our children the positive truth and positive reality of what sexual intercourse is—a life-uniting act. Sexual intercourse glues two people together in such a way that their lives are forever different because of their union. It is for this reason that God means intercourse for marriage. Sexual intercourse is meant to be a uniting event, a uniting force.

Union in marriage is both a one-time event and a process. Based on the Christian teaching of sexual union, it is true to say that a man and woman become one when they "consummate" their marriage by engaging in the fullest possible sexual expression of their love. A man and woman become one on the day of their wedding when they pledge their lives to each other and then seal that pledge by the exchange of their bodies. But it is equally true that becoming one is a process that is never complete, one that we continue working on throughout our married lives. And sexual intercourse plays a role in that gradual process. Sex draws us together and unites us on an ongoing basis. The physical ecstasy unites us. The nakedness and vulnerability unites us. The gradual learning of mutual pleasuring and self-giving unites us. The bearing and raising of children unites us. But undergirding these relational developments that sex facilitates is the deeper truth that in some mysterious, spiritual way that we can never fully understand, sexual intercourse makes us "one flesh." Something mystical and unexplainable happens when two people give their bodies to each other. We are bound together through sexual union.

We must be careful here; we must not create distortions that can haunt our children. An adolescent can take us to mean that two people are married just because they have intercourse. That is not true. Sexual intercourse does not create instant unity, as any nonvirgin can attest. A fifteen-year-old girl must not believe she can permanently seal her relationship with her current flame by giving in to his demands for sex. The nonvirgin must not be led to believe that her life is permanently ruined because she can never again become one in marriage. A man who has had sex with fifteen different women in his life is not "one" with fifteen persons permanently, forever fragmented beyond hope of repair. These are all distortions because they deny God's capacity to heal and restore the soul broken by sin.

The positive truth of the uniting reality of sexual intercourse helps us to see the beauty and blessedness of sexual intercourse in marriage. It also helps us understand just how terrible it is when any of us abuse God's marvelous design. It is as if we take the marvelous wedding gift of a priceless painting, and then use that painting as a TV tray on which we serve and spill popcorn and soft drinks. We used the gift, and desecrated it in the process. We can also better see the damage we do to ourselves when we abuse the gift. God meant sex to unite us in marriage. We are convinced that casual sex—any sex outside of marriage—progressively makes it harder and harder for us to really bond with the person God meant to be our life partner. If sex glues us together, but we spend our youth gluing ourselves to others and then prying ourselves apart from them, we are building up our own capacities to *not* really unite with anyone. We are training ourselves to be unable to really bond in marriage. And thus the rise in divorce that parallels the rise in sexual permissiveness makes perfect sense. So does the body of research that shows that as premarital sexual experience increases, so do the tendencies toward adultery after marriage and toward lower satisfaction in marriage.[3]

The Three-Stranded Cord of Christian Sexual Morality

The writer of Ecclesiastes says, "A cord of three strands is not quickly broken" (4:12). The three general sets of reasons behind the traditional moral standard form a three-stranded cord of great strength. If sexual intercourse is what Christians claim the Bible teaches, a life-uniting event, *then obedience makes sense*. God's command is not just an arbitrary standard; it is a rule that leads us to wholeness and blessing. For we who are married, this rule guides us into experiencing the best that God has for us—unity with the person who is our mate for life. For we who are single, God's rule guards and protects us from linking our lives with those with whom we do not have life union. The sexual ethic preserves us from acts that would be self-destructive.

If sexual intercourse is what Christians claim, a life-uniting event, *then the consequences of illicit sexual intercourse make sense*. The emotional devastation of bonds that are broken by unfaithfulness seems inevitable. The fact that we are relatively unprotected physically from sexually transmitted diseases makes sense when we consider that such disease would generally disappear in a single generation if all persons obeyed the Christian sexual morality. Bad consequences occur because we break God's creational design.

The three strands intertwine and mutually support each other in an exquisitely beautiful way. Sexual intercourse is a beautiful gift with built-in meaning. Its built-in meaning of union speaks to the deepest longings of our hearts for intimacy with another who loves and accepts us, one who is "bone of my bone, flesh of my flesh." And our union with another human being in turn mirrors and reminds us of our desire for union with God.

> **CHILD:** "But what does that mean, that having sex unites you? I don't understand!"
> **PARENT:** "I don't either, Justin. Your mom and I have been married for fourteen years, and I'm still learning what it means. But let's think about it together. When you become a man, do you think you would like to have a wife whom you love with your whole heart and who loves you that way for your whole life?"
> **CHILD:** "Yeah. I want to have someone to love like you and Mom do."
> **PARENT:** "Well, I think that is what everyone really wants.

People who stay single can still have a wonderful life, beca
as Christians God will be with them and they can have spe
friends in the church. The Bible says that we were not mea
be alone. We are each made to love our children, our families, and
our friends (our enemies too!), but we are each made to have one
person in life who is especially close, so close that it is like the
other person is part of us. Who do you think that special person is
meant to be?"

CHILD: "Your wife?"

PARENT: "Yes, and your husband if you are a girl. But to keep
two people that close, God seems to have decided to make a special 'glue' to keep the husband and wife together. What do you
think that glue is?"

CHILD: "Sex?"

PARENT: "That's right. It isn't the only glue, mind you. Having
kids, sharing a home, and things like that also are like a glue that
holds you together, but sex is so special because God made it to be
that kind of glue. And you know what happens when you use glue
in ways that it shouldn't be used!"

CHILD: "Yeah, you get really mad and punish me!"

PARENT: "Well, that's true, but I was thinking first that it ruins
things, sometimes for good. Imagine that you couldn't get that
clump of hair on top of your head to lie down, so you used your
model glue to glue it down. We would have to shave the top of
your head to get it off! Your hair would be ruined when you were
hoping to make it better! Glue used the wrong way doesn't help;
it hurts. Sex is like that—when a married couple has sex, they are
using it the right way and it glues them together so that they can
love each other the best way possible for life. And you are right
about my being mad and punishing you. I would be mad because
I gave you the glue as a gift to use the right way. If you use it the
wrong way, it is like you are saying to me that you don't care for
me enough to use the gift the way I meant you to. Does that make
sense?"

CHILD: "I guess. It's like if I used the baseball glove you gave
me to scoop mud down at the pond."

PARENT: "That's right. And it is that way with God. He gave sex
to us as a gift. If we don't use the gift the way He wanted, it's like
we are telling God we don't like His gift, like we don't love Him
enough to use it just the way He wanted us to."

11

Inoculating Your Kids Against Destructive Moral Messages

✤

I n *How to Talk with Your Child About Sexuality*, the official Planned Parenthood Federation of America book for parents, the following example of an ideal moral or "values" dialogue between parent and child is presented:

> A father one of us knows reported that one Saturday, when he was driving his twelve-year-old daughter to a flute lesson, she asked, "Daddy, how old do you have to be to do it?" He took a deep breath and replied, "Well, it seems to me that having inter-course—that is what you mean, isn't it?—is a real special thing that you don't do just because you're old enough or because it feels good. The most important thing is to be very sure of your *own* feelings and not do it *because* of anyone else or *for* anyone else. Your mother and I don't believe kids your age are ready to handle it, but if you decide differently, it's important to avoid a pregnancy you wouldn't be able to manage by using birth control."[1]

Even when dealing with a twelve-year-old child, Planned Parenthood does not recommend that parents give any solid messages about sexual morality. Instead, we are to suggest that children's *feelings* should tell them when they are ready to have sex, and that the really crucial issue is the use of birth control.

In fact, Planned Parenthood explicitly says that it is useless for parents to communicate their moral views to their children. As we reported in chapter 1, they have stated that parents are "wasting their breath" in trying to teach what they believe to be right and wrong for the child.[2]

With friends like this, who needs enemies? If Planned Parenthood and the many public school and governmentally funded sex education programs are the best allies parents have against the movement of the media and popular culture to further encourage our children into immorality, then we really are in trouble.

Our concern in this chapter is how we as parents can best prepare our kids to handle the messages they will be bombarded with from outside of our families. If we are going to raise our children to live pure lives, we will not only have to teach them what is right and true, but we will also have to somehow protect them against the immoral and anti-Christian messages they will get from elsewhere.

THE PRINCIPLE OF INOCULATION

So what are our options in protecting our kids? One is to try to shield them from all nonChristian influences. The problem with this approach is that it is impossible. It is doomed to failure, and so attempting to totally shield them is a waste of time and energy. And in the area of our children's sexuality, we cannot waste precious time or energy. A second approach, simply telling them that other people will tell them bad things which they should not listen to, doesn't really seem to help. When our kids hear the other messages and find them to be sugarcoated, seemingly plausible, and much more popular than traditional Christian views, they may be unprepared to stand by what we as parents have taught them.

What we *can* do is inoculate our kids against the wrong messages and negative influences they will inevitably face. We feel this is so important that we have made it one of our core principles:

PRINCIPLE 8: We should "inoculate" our children against destructive moral messages.

What does a physical inoculation or immunization do? The body has natural defenses that can be quite effective in protecting us from disease if mobilized in time. To protect us against such dangerous diseases as polio, smallpox, or the flu, doctors isolate the virus or bacterium that causes the disease, grow a culture of the germs, kill the germs, and then inject the inert germs into the body. The body's immune system responds to the foreign germs by manufacturing antibodies and other agents to find and destroy that type of germ. Since the inert germs posed no threat to begin with, our bodies thus develop a defense against the dreaded disease without ever having been at risk of developing it in the first place.

What we want to do, then, is *psychologically immunize* our children against the germs of the nonChristian moral messages they will soon encounter in the world. This inoculation work should begin early in life, as inoculation works best when you can get to the child before he or she has actually begun soaking in destructive messages from television, school chums, or sex education classes. *Inoculation involves parents deliberately exposing their kids to the counterarguments and pressures they will be exposed to later in life, but in the safe environment of the family, and showing them how those nonChristian influences are unconvincing, false, and destructive.* For instance, rather than shielding our children from the argument that having sex is essential to really growing up, or that their hopes of ever having loving relationships with boyfriends or girlfriends depend on having sex with them, instead *we become the first to tell them this argument. Then, we help them reason against these destructive messages, thus inoculating them against this argument.*

SUPPORT FOR INOCULATION FROM SCIENTIFIC PSYCHOLOGY

As parents, we want to protect our kids. We Christian parents are often prone to think that protecting them means attempting to shelter them from opinions and attitudes that we view as contrary or subversive to the faith. But scientific research helps to confirm that this is exactly the wrong approach to take.[3] When adults or children are protected from views that oppose those they have been taught, their attitudes on those subjects remain fragile and easily changed. In other words, when we teach them what is right but don't prepare them for the powerful counterarguments they will encounter, we leave them practically defenseless. But when they are *challenged with accurate, strong but not overwhelming counterarguments to the position they are being taught, and show them that those counterarguments can be disputed*, their beliefs will actually be strengthened.

How does such psychological inoculation seem to work? In the words of social psychologist David Myers, past research has shown that "when people who were already committed to a position were attacked strongly enough to cause them to react, but not so strongly as to overwhelm them, they became even more committed" to their original position.[4] This seems to happen for several reasons.

First, being exposed to counterarguments leads the child not to be surprised or threatened when others later oppose his or her views. Some kids raised in Christian homes are led somehow by parents and church to think that Christian morality is self-evident and believed by every reasonable person, so that the mere serious presentation of other views is unnerving.

We must lead our kids to expect opposition; they will be persecuted for what they believe.

Second, when exposed to counterarguments and challenged to come up with reasons to stick with the view parents have taught, children are led to publicly (in the presence of the parent) make a commitment to the view they have been taught. Research shows that few things are as powerful as making a public commitment for keeping a person faithful to the view he or she has embraced. We will do more with the power of public commitment in chapter 18.

Third, psychological inoculation helps the children move from passive acceptance to active advocacy of the view parents are teaching. When we help our kids become active practitioners of what we have taught them, rather than passive listeners, they are more likely to make those views their own in the depths of their hearts.

Fourth, this enables kids to make an effective counterargument; it forces them to be ready to defend the reasons they have for Christian sexual morality. They will need the skill of defending their beliefs all too soon.

To teach how we can inoculate our children, we must first discuss the nonChristian morality systems that can challenge Christian belief. Then we will discuss the actual process of inoculation.

THE DESTRUCTIVE MORAL SYSTEMS

There are many different values and beliefs that stand in opposition to Christian sexual ethics. We will summarize them according to the following types: "Playboy Sensuality," the "Ethic of Intimacy," and the "Pseudo-Christian Love Ethic."

Playboy Sensuality

Explicit hedonism, though not as popular as it was in the 1960s and 1970s, may be making a comeback among young people today who have lost hope in the meaning of their lives and the certainty of their futures. If the future looks bleak and if there is no God and hence no meaning, what is there to life but the gratification of the lusts of the flesh? And more, simple appeals to lust and pleasure may be the most forceful arguments that teenagers in the back seats of cars or empty houses can make on the spot. Arguments like "This will feel better than anything you have experienced in your life," "You deserve to feel good," "This is what your body was made for," and so forth, are common. Powerful pressure may be placed on a girl by exaggerated descriptions of male sexual drive—that the boy *has* to have sex, that she is torturing him by saying no, that the drives have to be gratified or the person is hurt, and on and on. Finally, our kids will hear crude appeals to fitting in at all costs. "If you don't have sex, there must be something

...ong with you." The core moral message here seems to be that being popular and accepted and fitting in are more important than virginity and sexual restraint.

Thanks to the stark contrasts between Christian morality and playboy sensuality, it is relatively easy to think of arguments to counter this view, though the counterarguments depend on your child accepting that Christianity is true.

The Ethic of Intimacy

Most "sophisticated" people today reject playboy sensualism. In many circles, promiscuity is out of fashion. But do not fall prey to thinking that the rejection of the playboy ethic is a vote in favor of true Christian ethics. Planned Parenthood does not promote promiscuity, but neither do they promote chastity in a way that Christians can accept.

Tim Stafford, popular Christian writer and longtime author of *Campus Life Magazine*'s popular column "Love, Sex and the Whole Person," has argued that the view that much of our secularized culture takes of sexual expression can be described as the "Ethic of Intimacy."[5] This Ethic of Intimacy is a seductive view that chips away at true Christian morality. He describes it as being composed of seven basic ideas:

1. Sex is always viewed as positive. The old view that sex is part of our lower, animal nature is gone, replaced by notions that sex is usually good, and at worst merely neutral. Only sex by coercion, such as rape or incest, can be frowned on.

2. Individuals are always independent. The old idea that sex unites people is gone. People come together as long as it benefits them to do so, and then they go their separate ways to find new ways of caring for themselves. Our first obligations are to ourselves and our own welfare. There is no cause higher than my self-interest.

3. Compatibility is the key to good sex and good relationships. Compatibility just happens. Since one can never know when and with whom compatibility will happen, it is always best to "try on the shoes before you buy them." The most widely selling college textbook on human sexuality, supposedly a scientific and morally neutral text, states as a matter of fact that "it does help to know if you and your spouse-to-be are sexually compatible."[6] It is also widely believed that people who are compatible at one time may not stay that way; after all, people change.

4. Sex, and ethics in general, is a strictly private matter. If there is right and wrong, there is only right and wrong for each person. What is right for me may or may not be right for you. My life is none of anyone else's business.

5. Sex does not change the person. Sex has no necessary consequences of any kind, to good or to ill. Having sex does not change you, no matter how

many partners you have. There is nothing particularly informative about knowing that someone is a virgin, because that person is not different in any significant way from the nonvirgin.

6. There must be no double standard between men and women. What is good for the goose is good for the gander, and vice versa. Differences between the genders must be eradicated. If men are consumed with lust or promiscuous, women must try to close that gender gap.

7. The magic element that makes sex okay is maturity. You must be able to "handle" sex, you must be "ready for it." Generally, this appears to mean that you should be able to take steps to prevent disease and pregnancy. Apart from that, the meaning of maturity is completely unclear.

We see many of the elements of this Ethic of Intimacy in the works of Planned Parenthood and many school sex education curricula. Right after telling parents that they are wasting their breath inculcating a morality in their children, the Planned Parenthood book for parents turns right around and prescribes its own morality that should be taught to children. The question of when people should have sex is a moral question. They say:

> To be ready for sex, persons must:
> be sure they are not exploiting another person or being exploited
> themselves.
> be able to discuss comfortably with their partners the cautions
> against unintended pregnancy and STDs and to share respon-
> sibility for taking steps to prevent them.
> be able to accept the consequences of their own actions. Could
> they deal with a pregnancy or with contracting a disease?
> be willing to make the emotional commitment and take on the
> obligations of a healthy adult sexual relationship.
> understand that enjoying this aspect of sexuality involves the
> ability to make thoughtful decisions.
> Without this the sex act is likely to produce far more stress and
> anxiety than pleasure.[7]

Planned Parenthood goes on to discuss various reasons for why teens would want to wait to have sex, all of which are stated in a very negative and demeaning way. Sex is for the mature, so a major reason for young teens not to have sex is that "many young boys and girls are not emotionally experienced enough to deal with the strong emotions a sexual relationship can create."[8] Teens might want to wait because "early sex would make them feel guilty or anxious. Some may be afraid of becoming too emotionally dependent on a partner." Others may be "late bloomers" who "may never develop a very strong sex drive."[9] Which of these reasons for waiting to have sex will the teenager identify with? Which teens want to be late bloomers, guilty and anxious, afraid, and immature? All of these, given as reasons not to have sex, are conditions any teen would be desperate to grow out of! And so such reasons really do nothing to persuade the teen to wait to have sex.

Throughout this material from Planned Parenthood, the reader can easily see the very ethic of intimacy that Stafford has described. Inoculating your child to such views is critical for the future well-being of your child.

The Pseudo-Christian Love Ethic

As if it were not enough to face destructive messages in the world, we parents are often unwittingly sabotaged by destructive moral messages from within the church as well. Readers who are members of mainline church denominations must be especially cautious of views of sexuality that are circulating in seminaries, popular "Christian" books, and in published sexuality curricula being used in the church. These views are often most clearly stated in the painful and highly visible discussions about homosexuality in the churches.

What makes these views especially troubling is that they are the most subtle distortions of truth imaginable, requiring true discernment to detect and respond to. We have read these sorts of materials and arguments for years, and believe the following are some of the core elements of the pseudo-Christian love ethic:

1. Sexuality is God's good gift to humanity. Sexuality is so good that to mix talk about sex with talk about sin is to diminish this good gift.

2. Since we are fundamentally sexual beings, the experience of full sexual expression is necessary for full development as a person. A celibate, sexually abstinent person is really an underdeveloped person, a half-person.

3. Since our sexuality is a good gift, we are all entitled to experience the gift of our own full sexual expression to the fullest extent. God would not give people a gift like a sexual appetite, or for that matter a homosexual orientation, and expect them not to experience to the fullest what God has given them a yearning for.

4. Celibacy is a gift (1 Corinthians 7:7, Matthew 19:11ff). Since it is a gift, those without the gift are not expected by God to abstain from sex. If you aren't married and don't have the gift of celibacy, God must want you to satisfy your sexual longings.

5. The declaration that "all of the Law is summarized in the command to love" is taken to mean that loving feelings make sexual expression morally acceptable. It is argued that Christianity promotes an ethic of love that makes all mere rules (like "no sex outside of marriage") obsolete. We are to follow love, not law. Anything that we do out of genuine love feelings cannot be wrong.

6. Since God is relational and our sexuality is relational in God's image,

therefore it is primarily when we are acting out our sexuality that we are closest to God and are in touch with the "God-force" within us. We are being relational, creational, and uniting (just like God) when we are having loving sex. This last point is as yet only being promoted by several very liberal faculty members of seminaries in their books and is not likely to be heard in the pews, but it is an idea being discussed seriously in seminary circles.[10]

Our children may be especially vulnerable to destructive moral messages that come sugarcoated with "God-talk" and slightly twisted references to the Scriptures. It is vital that we inoculate our children against these messages as well.

AN ESPECIALLY DANGEROUS MORAL MESSAGE: SILENCE

Suppose sex education in your child's public school is presented without any obvious moral slant. Suppose the teachers present the facts of biology, reproduction, and birth control, and then stand back and let the kids talk about sex without interposing any moral messages at all. Suppose they listen to comments from kids and answer factual questions, but put forth no moral view of their own. Are the moral beliefs of kids unaffected by such presentations?

It appears that the moral views of kids can be profoundly affected by such a program. Silence can often communicate just as richly as spoken or written words. When a panic-stricken parent asks a teen if he is using drugs, when a wife desperately asks her estranged husband if he still loves her, a response of silence says volumes about the reality of the situation. And so it appears also with "value-less" sex education.

There is good reason to believe that adolescents expect their parents and teachers to disapprove of premarital sexual intercourse. If parents, teachers, pastors, and other "authority figures" respond in *neutral* ways, when the kids expect disapproval, they are likely to interpret the silence as approval.[11] This type of reaction has been clearly shown with younger children who behave violently or aggressively. When adults who observe such behavior do not punish or criticize it, the child interprets that neutral, value-free reaction as approval. The child thus engages in more negative behavior in the future.

The implications of this view for "value-neutral sex education" are obvious. For the teacher to present moral alternatives such as abstinence and promiscuity (with the use of birth control, of course) as equally acceptable options and then to stand back in moral neutrality, is to teach the adolescent that all choices are equally acceptable to the authority figure, the teacher. With such a value-neutral program, we are taking a tremendous risk that the message children hear (regardless of what we meant to communicate) is that "you can stay abstinent, you can be promiscuous, you can adopt the playboy philosophy, you can be a nun, you can be anything—these are all equally valid choices of which I, the teacher or parent, approve equally."

HOW DO WE SAFELY INOCULATE OUR CHILDREN?

We must expose our kids to these countervailing views so that they will not be startled to find people who disagree with their Christian positions on sexual ethics. We must help them expect opposition, even persecution. We should help them think actively about what they believe, and put words to their beliefs. We should help them express their views so they are committing themselves to follow the traditional Christian way. And finally, we should help them come up with responses to these views that make sense.

Our core method in this area has been to watch carefully the messages given by television, billboards, popular music, and movies, as well as things that our kids report that other kids say on the playgrounds. We try to catch these messages early, before our kids are even aware of the significance of what they are hearing or seeing. We try to use these messages as teaching moments with our children to inoculate them against these destructive messages.

> **CHILD:** "Dad, Clint (another ten-year-old) has a picture of a naked lady in his room, hanging over his bed. I saw it yesterday. She has her arms over her chest and her legs crossed so it doesn't show her private parts, but she's completely naked. Clint says he stares at it every night while he goes to sleep."
> **PARENT:** (In shock) "Do Clint's parents know he has that picture?"
> **CHILD:** "Oh sure; he said his mom bought it for him."
> **PARENT:** "Well, what do you think about that?
> **CHILD:** "It seems kind of weird to me; after all, he's only ten. I wouldn't put up a picture like that."
> **PARENT:** (*You can say that again!*) "I'm glad you wouldn't. What do you think a kid learns from having a picture like that in his room? Or, I guess what I'm really asking is, what do you think the people who made and sold that picture want the boys that buy it to think about women and about sex?"
> **CHILD:** "I don't know. Maybe that it's okay for women to show their naked bodies and that it's okay for boys to stare at them?"
> **PARENT:** "I think that's right. I think they believe it's okay for men and boys to stare at a woman's body, and also to think about sex. They probably also believe that the most important thing about a woman is how she looks. And you know what else? That naked woman probably wants other women to think they have to

look just like her to be beautiful. That probably makes her feel
important and it will help her to get richer because those women
will buy her exercise video and her diet books and all of the other
junk she tries to sell. But how do you think God feels about that
picture? Would God want you or me to have that picture on our
walls? (No way!) Why?"

CHILD: "Well, because God made our bodies private, and
because being beautiful on the outside is not the most important thing."

PARENT: "I think you made God very happy by the wise thing
you just said. God made sex as a beautiful gift that helps make a
husband and wife stick together for life. Sex is meant for marriage,
not for posters on kids' walls. In the next ten years, son, many
people will tell you that you are stupid for believing what we have
talked about today. They will try to tell you that it's okay to think
about sex with anyone and to have sex with anyone as long as you
don't hurt someone by giving her a disease or getting her pregnant. They will try to tell you and your sisters and your future wife
that they are a good person only if they are beautiful in the way
that woman is beautiful. All of that is a lie. All people are beautiful
in their own way because God made them. The most important
kind of beauty is whether the person is good. Is he or she beautiful inside? And part of being beautiful inside is loving God and
obeying His rules about sex."

✛

PARENT: "Bill, did you hear what that TV news reporter just
said? She said that the church would have to stop interfering with
the private moral decisions of people today or it would become
more and more irrelevant. Do you know what that means?"

CHILD: "No."

PARENT: "What she was saying is what many people say today:
That nobody, not even the church, has the right to tell people today
how they should live their lives. People have to make up their own
right and wrong in their own mind, and no one else can tell them if
they decide rightly. So if I decide I can't have sex with anyone but
your mom, that may be right for me, but another person can decide
it's okay to have sex with a lot of people, and that may be right for
him or her. Do you think there could be different rules for different
people?"

CHILD: "That wouldn't be fair. Doesn't God give rules to
all of us?"

PARENT: "I think so. Do you think so? (Yes) Why do you think a person might say that everyone's rules are different?"

CHILD: "Because that person doesn't like the rules?"

PARENT: "I bet that's it. If a person doesn't like God's rules, maybe it helps to say that they really aren't God's rules at all. You'll hear that in school soon—that no rules apply to everyone, because if they did, everyone would agree on the rules. But that has to be wrong. The Bible says that God made His rules for people, but right from the beginning people began to break the rules. Does that mean the rules aren't really good? No."

CHILD: "You mean a lot of people don't think that God's rules from the Bible are good rules?"

PARENT: "Yes. Many people don't. They say that different rules for different people are okay. But Christians believe that God made us all, and that He made rules for us all. It isn't our job to make others obey the rules, or even to yell about the rules. But we're supposed to live by the rules, and urge others to also."

We cannot, in this chapter, summarize a response to all of the anti-Christian moral values discussed earlier. The heart of our response, however, needs to be to clarify and make perfectly clear just what the opposing view is saying. We need to strip it of its sugarcoating, and hold it up for the child to see in the clear light of the Christian view of sexuality. There is no absolutely irrefutable argument against any of the destructive moral systems. We must, in trust, proclaim as effectively as we can the Christian view that stands against the other views. An example: Sexuality is a great and positive gift, as they say, but it is an area where we are fallen as well, and so God has given us rules so that we may know for sure how to use the gift.

Sometimes we must not wait for an impromptu moment to teach, but must initiate a conversation because we are concerned about what our kids are headed into.

PARENT: "Sarah, now that you are twelve, I want to warn you about some of the things that others will soon say to you about sex, if they haven't already. You will hear boys saying that you have to give them sex to fit in, or that you have to have sex because it's the greatest thing in the world and you are sick and crazy or a chicken if you don't. That's bad, but I think you're smart enough not to fall for that baloney. I don't think you will want to fit in with people who want to make you have sex to belong. We've talked about sex, and so I think you know that while sex is wonderful, it is wonderful in marriage, where it not only feels good but it also helps to keep you in love with your husband for all your lives. Those things don't worry me as much. One of the things that worries me the most is those who say that having sex is part of growing up, of being mature, of being an adult."

CHILD: "Yeah, there are kids who say that already. They say, like, 'How are you going to know if you really love someone if you don't have sex?' And they say if you really love someone you will have sex with them."

PARENT: "And what do you think about that?"

CHILD: "I'm confused. You have told me that sex is a way of expressing love. And I'm afraid of not knowing how to have sex when I do get married."

PARENT: "Those are good thoughts. You see, that's why I was worried, because what you're being told is partly true, and partly false. Sex and real love are meant to go together. That is why, when you start dating, you will feel excited about the idea of sex with a boy whom you really care for. There's nothing wrong with that. But real love is lifelong love. And that's what marriage is—a commitment to love each other for a lifetime. Some say, 'Try sex and see if you're in love.' God says, get to know each other without sex, test your relationship by being patient and waiting, and then see if you really love each other by seeing if you are both willing to promise to love each other for a lifetime. Then you have sex when you are married to cement your relationship together. Do you hope to have one man to love forever?"

CHILD: "Yes! I would hate to wind up divorced and remarried three times like Aunt Kathy."

PARENT: "I'm glad you feel that way. Did you know that people who do *not* have sex before marriage are more likely to have a happier and longer-lasting marriage than those who do, and that they are more likely to enjoy sex with their husbands too? That takes care of your worry about learning to have sex—marriage is the perfect place to learn. Who would you rather learn with, a husband who is committed to you for life and loved you enough to wait for months or years to have sex with you, or a boy who tries to make you have sex on the third date and likes you only because he hopes to get sex from you?"

12

Laying the Groundwork for Adolescence

❖

The late elementary school years, before puberty begins, are the vital time for positively introducing children to the wonderful and amazing changes that lie ahead of them. So much rides on the crucial decisions they will soon be making. We must carefully continue our work of building the foundation of character they will take into their adolescent years.

This is an easy time for parents to let down and not do their work of sex education and character formation. Our kids may be so involved with their friends and with school that they ask fewer questions. We often dread the transition our children will make from childhood to adulthood, and so we are reluctant to talk about it. We fear the enormity of the challenges they will face. We feel a sense of loss as they cease being the little kids who depended upon us so completely. And we can remember so clearly the confusion and pain of our own transition through puberty, and block out our own memories in part by ignoring the fact that our own kids are headed down the same road. And yet, the elementary school years are perhaps the most vital time to impact your child's character.

THE BEST PREDICTORS OF SEXUAL BEHAVIOR

Interestingly, four factors have been shown in scientific research to be powerful predictors of teenage sexual experimentation. The first three of these factors seem to us to be grounded in the need for relatedness—the closeness of the relationship of the child with his or her parent; the closeness of the child to his or her peer group and the amount of sexual experimentation that goes on in the peer group; and the teen's religious beliefs and practice. The final factor seems to us related to the need for significance, and that is how intent on and confident the child is of success and achievement in school. All of the aforementioned factors exert their powerful influence on sexual behavior in adolescence, but *parents will be too late if they wait for adolescence to begin working on these factors*. To affect the closeness children feel with parents, their sense of significance, and their choices of peers, we must begin working early.

The Power of a Close Parental Relationship

In elementary school, children begin to move outward from the family unit, building friendships and steadily coming under more and more influence from those outside of the family. They spend more time with friends in the friends' homes, thus falling under the influence of the values of other families. Relationships with their friends, their peers, become more and more influential. Kids begin to hear different messages from influential adults, especially their teachers in school.

Once the child is in adolescence, the closer the child says her or his relationship is with parents, the less likely the child is to be having sex. A close, positive relationship between a mother and daughter has consistently been shown to predict the daughter having relatively less sexual experience.[1] It seems that a close relationship between parent and child instills in the child the desire to want to live out the values and moral beliefs of the parent. In other words, the greatest power of a parent to influence the children's morality lies not so much in how loudly or cloquently that parent expresses his or her moral views. Rather, *the power of a parent's moral message lies in the power of the love relationship between the parent and the child*. If we want to have an impact on our children's morality, we must be close enough to them that they will want to follow in our moral footsteps. We want to make this our next major sex education principle:

> **PRINCIPLE 9:** The closer and more positive the relationship between parent and child, the greater the parent's influence upon the behavior of the child.

In elementary school, perhaps especially in late elementary school, the parent has an opportunity to foster a continuing close relationship with the child or to let the child slip away. It is easy to let the child slip away as he or she gets more independent, more involved with friends, and more difficult to communicate with. To continue to build a close relationship, we have to put effort and creative energy into the relationship. We need to think of good opportunities to spend time with the child. These are not times to necessarily lecture or instruct our child, but simply to enjoy being with him or her. One of the great dangers of the busyness of our lives, of our investment in careers, church, and everywhere but the family is that we will simply not be there for our children, available to be close and to enjoy them.

We need to build a relationship grounded on encouragement and praise. We need to put away "anger, rage, malice, slander, and filthy language" and instead base our relationships with our teens on "compassion, kindness, humility, gentleness and patience" (Colossians 3:8,12). Ever mindful of their fragile sense of self at this age, we must take every opportunity to build them up, communicate our confidence in them and our excited expectation for what life has in store for them. We must avoid unnecessary battles, which become ever more likely as we move through puberty into adolescence, allowing our love to cover a multitude of sins (1 Peter 4:8), and forgiving as Christ forgave us (Ephesians 4:32).

We must continue, here in the elementary school years, to work on being an askable parent. Among other things, we can do the following:

- Praise our children asking questions, any questions, but especially questions about sexuality and relationships. We should acknowledge how threatening it can be to talk about such things.
- Praise manifestations of understanding of what we have been teaching. We can ask, for example, what God would think about the way women are portrayed in a television commercial or the way sex is treated in a sitcom, and praise their insightfulness as they use what we have taught them.
- Restrain our impatience; give them time to develop their questions. We should attempt to provide a good answer to *any* question the kid asks, regardless of how confusing the question is. Often our discomfort leads us to hurry the kid up or demand clarification that the kid cannot provide; this comes across to the child as rejection or other negative reactions.

How does a close relationship between parent and teen come to exert a restraining influence on a teenager's sexual choices? To understand this, we must realize that there appear to be two aspects of morality, the rule-obedience aspect and the loyalty-relationship aspect. Men tend to emphasize the rule aspect; morality consists of obedience to rules. Women tend to emphasize the loyalty dimension of morality; true morality lies in being loyal to those one is close to. Both aspects of morality are found in the Scriptures. Our moral character results both from following just and right moral laws, and from loyalty based on love. We follow God's Law both because the Law is good and right (Psalm 119) and because we love the Law-Giver (John 14:15,23).

In the turbulent adolescent years, a close personal relationship with a parent, especially between a young woman and her mom, can serve as an "anchor." It is a foundation for fundamental personal loyalty. When the girl is making sexual decisions on a date, she will see the morality her parents taught her not just as abstract rules, but as issues of personal loyalty. She will have to decide, not between a persistent boy and an abstract principle, but between her relationship with the boy and her relationship with her mother. And hopefully she will have come to see her parents as representatives of God's very character in her life.

Remember also that your child, like you, needs to be loved and affirmed. When the teen's relationship with one or both parents provides rich love and acceptance and praise, that child doesn't have as great a need to go into a dating relationship, a sexual relationship, to get the love he or she needs. If we keep them full at home, we send them to the grocery store satisfied rather than starving.

Let us mention here what we feel could be a great misapplication and abuse of this principle. A close relationship is founded on respect, appreciation, and genuine care for the other. It is not founded on fear, mistrust, dependence, or insecurity. Some relationships that appear to be healthy and close are in reality stifling and sick. The greatest danger of trying to forge a close relationship is that we will become clinging and manipulative rather than close. Beware of statements that use guilt or obligation to force children to act like they are close to us, statements like "After all the effort I gave (diapers changed, nights stayed up), you should do. . . ." We have to trust that we have given our children skills and values to make good choices, but they are not really their choices until they have to make them for themselves. And then we as parents have to choose to have a good relationship with this independent, developing adult, which is much harder than having a relationship with a little robot we have under our control.

It is in this context of discussing having a real relationship with your developing child that we can best answer the daunting question, "What do I say if my child asks me what I did, what rules I lived by, before I was married?" Some parents will have the joy of honestly saying they followed God's plan for them. Others will not. One popular Christian book actually urges parents who have engaged in immoral behavior in the past to do their best to evade the question, and if they cannot wiggle out of it, to create the impression (without actually lying) that they preserved their purity.

True, close relationships are grounded in honesty. Honesty is essential. We urge that parents who did not engage in premarital sexual intercourse tell this to their child, and use it as a positive example for the child. Parents who did engage in premarital intercourse must first sort through their own understanding of what they did, how they dealt with it before God, and how they look at themselves now in that light. Knowledge of the sexual actions of their parents may be too much for younger children, so parents might want to tell a younger child (perhaps twelve or younger) that they will talk about their own past when the child is closer to adolescence. This should not be done in a tantalizing or teasing way, but straightforwardly.

When your child is beginning dating may be a good time to talk with the child if he or she has previously asked about your choices. If the child has asked before, you probably shouldn't wait for him or her to ask again, but instead take it upon yourself to initiate the discussion. We ask too much of our children when we put them off and expect them to persistently pester us with the same question.

No parents, especially those who have pasts involving extensive promiscuity, should feel compelled to disclose details of their past or describe it in such a way as to compromise their own privacy or the imaginations of their kids. A simple statement such as "I made very foolish choices in a relationship when I was in college" or "No, I was not a virgin when we married. I was not a Christian then and really lived by the rules of the world rather than of God" should be enough. Kids' requests for more details should be turned down.

Your response should also include the following elements. First, you should discuss how you feel now about your choices then. Statements like "Well, everyone has to sow a few wild oats" will obviously not help your cause, whereas "I look back now and see that I felt as if no one loved me, that I had to give sex to be liked, and that I took horrible risks with my life" will be helpful. Second, you should discuss the consequences of your choices, both the clearly negative consequences (emotional pain, feeling cheated, realizing that you used people, disease, pregnancy, abortion) and the consequences that seemed positive at the time—"You know, I really felt as if sex made my relationship with that man into true love, and I enjoyed sex, but when it ended I realized that having sex made it harder to see that this was not a marriage relationship of real love, but just an infatuation that could not last. I also realized that the good feelings physically did not make up for all the pain and regret I felt later." Third, you should challenge your children to do better than you. Challenge them not to let your failure become their failure. Finally, discussing such an experience is a perfect time for a powerful lesson in God's forgiveness and redemption for your child. It gives you a chance to testify to how God makes all things right through His grace.

We know such a process strikes fear into the hearts of many a parent. But we should have the courage of the gospel in sharing with our children God can make all things right. We should have the courage displayed in the Scriptures themselves, which show the saints of God throughout the ages, warts, sins and all, as they grow in grace. We are in good company in taking on such a daunting task!

The Power of the Peer Group

The sexual activity of a teenager's peer group is another factor that predicts a teenager's sexual activity. One recent study found that the adolescent's perception of how much sexual activity was going on in his or her peer group was the single most powerful predictor of whether that child was sexually active himself or herself.[2] This seems to go back again to the power of the need for relatedness. We all want to fit in and be accepted. If a child is not close to her parents, and if she is seeking the approval of a sexually active peer group, she is very likely to begin having sex. Based on this, it is vital that we as parents take a very vigilant role toward our child's involvement in a group of peers.

These researchers argue that how the child selects a peer group is influenced by the strength of the relationship between the parent and the adolescent. In other words, we can have the most powerful influence on our child's selection of friends by simply working hard to stay close with our child ourselves. The child who has a strong relationship with the parents, who is closely attached to the parents, is going to tend to seek out a group of friends whose values, morals, and activities would tend to meet with the approval of the parents. If we are close, we are less likely to need to directly intervene in our child's selection of friends. We will be more likely to be able to sit back and enjoy the friendship selections that our child makes with the confidence that our child is firmly committed to our values. And this kind of peer group helps to keep our children from experimenting with sex. Kids who feel distant and disconnected from their parents are more likely to choose a peer group that is at odds with the morality and wishes of the parents.

If we sense a distance in our relationship with our children, and are worried about the peers that they are choosing as friends, our task is much more difficult. Under these circumstances, we need to be very careful not to instigate terrible power struggles with our children that further alienate them from us. This calls for the wisdom of Solomon.

If we are really worried about their selection of friends, we may have to take direct and decisive action to break them away from those friends. This can be extremely difficult, and parents need to really count the cost of taking this gamble. We have to first realize that there are large areas of their lives that we cannot begin to control. They can spend time with undesirable friends at school, at school activities, and so forth, and we may have little to say about this. Secondly, while we can, to a certain extent, prevent them from associating with certain undesirables, we cannot create friendships with desirable kids for them. Our own children have to be actively involved in that process.

Sometimes you will be more likely to meet with success if you don't try to separate your kids from an undesirable peer group, but rather encourage them to also be active in other, different peer groups. In other words, you may not get them to stop hanging around with one group, but if you can also get them in a church youth group or other more desirable group, at least you will have begun to blunt or diffuse the influence of the negative peer group. We don't create friendships for them by encouraging them to be involved in groups, but we at least encourage them to be in the "right place at the right time" where they are more likely to form the right kinds of friendships. Also, explicitly talking with other parents who are involved in the same dilemma can be extremely helpful.

The Importance of Personal Faith

Research clearly suggests that adolescents who have a firm personal religious faith are less likely to be sexually active than their peers.[3] We have commented briefly on how to shape our children's faith in chapter 3. We believe that a firm faith in Christ does at least four powerful things for our children. First, it places them in a relationship with the living God, who through the work of the Holy Spirit can plant His Law in their hearts and give them His own strength to face their trials and temptations. Second, a relationship with God is perhaps the most critical relationship every person needs to meet his or her need for relatedness and significance. Third, a living faith reinforces the moral beliefs that we have advocated teaching throughout this book. Last, a living faith helps to place our children in a community of faith, a fellowship of fellow believers who are together trying to live according to God's will. This peer support is essential.

For all of these reasons, we should work diligently during the elementary school years to build up the living faith of our kids, that they might be strengthened for the challenges of adolescence.

The Value of Academic Achievement

The degree to which the child values academic achievement predicts early sexual involvement.[4] Children who have academic goals, especially those who are confident of going on to college and who believe that school is an exciting place to work hard and achieve, are much more likely to delay their sexual experimentation than academically discouraged or hopeless kids. It seems that children who have lost hope of success in their preparation for meaningful work are more likely to pursue physical pleasures. If their future is dark anyway, why not?

We are convinced that the real issue in this research is not whether the child values and gets high grades. This would sound like kids that make A's will remain virgins and kids who get C's are destined to fall into promiscuity. No. It seems to us that the real issue here is whether children have a hope for a meaningful life, a meaningful life where they have something constructive to offer to the world that gives them a reason not to fall into the empty pursuit of pleasure wherever they can find it. We can forgo the satisfaction of our selfish desires when we have a higher purpose that calls us beyond ourselves. In the absence of any higher purpose, we naturally move toward the simple gratification of our own wants and desires.

We should encourage our children's performance in school and their having goals to work to their best ability. But at a deeper level we need to give our kids hope for the significance of their lives regardless of how well they do in school. We do this by having an attitude that respects the dignity of all work, an attitude that suggests that they can serve a purpose in God's Kingdom regardless of whether they are a theoretical physicist or a ditchdigger.

If we build up our relationships with them, gently guide the formation of their peer groups, and give them a deep sense of hope and significance for the future, we will be laying vital foundations for their living sexually pure lives.

SKILLS TO DEVELOP

Now let us discuss some of the kinds of skills that will serve our elementary school aged children as they move into adolescence. Perhaps you are accustomed to thinking about some of what we will call "skills" as traits—characteristics of persons that are either there or not, and which cannot be changed. But we think that these are, at least in large part, skills that can be learned through example and experience. We as parents have to have the skill ourselves, and then exercise our creativity to think how to encourage our child to develop it.

Empathy, the ability to feel another person's feelings, is a critical skill. Empathy tends to develop somewhat naturally in young children, but it seems that parents can encourage children to develop a deep understanding of others, or they can blunt their children's development of this capacity. We teach empathy, first, through our capacity to empathize with our own children. Do we show ourselves able to understand things from their perspectives? Do we understand accurately when they are angry? When they are upset? When they are grieving? When they are fearful? When they are confident? When they are joyful?

We also encourage the development of empathy by actively teaching them to take the time and the energy to understand what is happening from the other person's perspective.[5] We can help the young child to pay attention to what his friend is feeling when he has just taken that friend's favorite toy away from him. Helping an older sister understand the crushed feelings of a baby brother whom she has rejected is important. We often jump in and discipline for wrong behavior without taking the time to instruct the child to perceive what happened from the other child's perspective. When we take the time to do this, we are developing the capacity for empathy.

Skills often have thinking components and action components. The above are the thinking or perceiving aspects of empathy. One action aspect of empathy is the capacity to find out what the other is feeling even when we cannot intuitively sense it. The capacity to listen well, to ask sensitive questions, and to enter creatively into the other person's frame of reference are critical skills of action to develop.

The capacity for empathy is critical in the area of sexual character for at least two reasons. First, the child who is going to develop good friendships and have rewarding romantic relationships is one who can be sensitive and empathic to others' feelings. Being able to have rewarding intimate relationships with others is a critical strength that can help to prevent problems in the sexual decision making of the child in adolescence. Sadly, men are often terribly deficient in this ability, a weakness their wives suffer with.

Second, thoroughly developing the capacity for empathy helps children to better understand the consequences of their sexual behavior. The consequences of adolescent sexual behavior are unlike anything else they would have ever experienced. If they cannot understand and empathize with the devastation of an unwanted pregnancy, the guilt of going through an abortion, the grief of becoming infertile because of an earlier sexually transmitted disease, and the pain of being used, they are going to be at greater risk for sexual irresponsibility.

Another critical skill to develop is *assertiveness*. We should seek to develop their assertiveness, and then teach them how to submit that inner personal strength to God's use. We need to praise our children for speaking their minds, for asking questions, for demonstrating their strength. We need to equip them to say no and to stand by their guns. Many rape-prevention writings say that too few women have ever practiced saying no, announcing early on that they do not like what is happening on a date and that they will not cooperate. They actually say it is helpful for a girl to practice screaming, yelling for help, and struggling to resist an attacker. We need to mold our kids so that they have the strength to live by their decisions, and the wisdom to make good judgments as to when to exercise this strength.

Self-control is also a vital skill. Self-control is listed as one characteristic of the fruit of the Spirit in Galatians 5:22-23. Like all of the characteristics, however, self-control has its natural side and its supernatural side. We should pray for as generous a dispensation of self-control for our children as God will give, and then work like crazy as parents to develop it as a natural skill in them. The development of self-control begins with the child being effectively controlled by external factors. The parent implements rules, and backs up those rules with consequences. In this way, children are brought under "external" (parental) control. But children need to become less and less dependent upon external factors, rules, and guides, and more dependent upon the rules that they have taken within themselves. Teaching our children the rules that should guide them, and then encouraging and praising them as they follow the rules themselves can help to develop such self-control. Parents who keep tight external controls on their developing children for too long often stifle, rather than encourage, the development of self-control. After all, why should the kids work to control themselves when Mom and Dad always have such a tight leash on them?

One special type of self-control is the capacity to *delay gratification*. This is also a critical skill to develop. Delay of gratification is shown when children can refrain from a short-term pleasure to get a greater reward in the future, when they can turn down one piece of candy now to get a sack of candy on the next day. The application of this skill to sex is obvious—we are urging our children to bypass the short-term pleasures of teenage sex (such as physical gratification and acceptance) in order to avoid the larger but more distant and probabilistic negatives (such as disease and pregnancy) and to get the wonderfully positive long-term rewards (a happier and more satisfying marriage). And clearly we begin laying the foundation for their capacity to delay gratification early on. Do we teach our children to wait? Do we model patience? Do we gratify their every whim on demand? Are we alert to examples of beginning development of this skill and encourage and praise them for it? Do we try to make the long-term rewards of self-control more real for our children by reminding them of those rewards and manifesting them in our own lives?

Finally, we mention the skills of *decision making*. Wisdom cannot be taught, but kids can be aided to make better decisions. Teaching our children to accurately understand the nature of the problems they confront is a first step. Teach them to patiently make sure they know what they are facing. Help them to see other ways of viewing a problem—"Maybe you really will have no friends if you don't have sex, but maybe they're just testing you to see if you can be a friend and still not engage in sex." Teaching them to generate all possible solutions to the problem is the next step to solving the problem. We then need to help them to be able to effectively evaluate the feasibility and possible outcomes of different responses to the problem. They then need to be able to pick a solution that they can implement themselves.

13

**Preparing for
the Physical Changes of Puberty**

✤

At about age ten, in the fourth grade, some children will begin the marvelous transformation process we call puberty. Public school sex education often begins in earnest during these years. We as parents should take the lead during these years, before puberty begins, to positively introduce our children to the wonderful and amazing changes their bodies will soon be going through. We need to help them anticipate with excitement the changes ahead, including pubertal growth and the onset of menstruation. We also need to set the stage for their understanding of sexual attraction and excitement.

Our main focus in this chapter is reviewing how you can teach your children about the changes ahead. But first, we want to discuss the value of repetition in sex education.

THE VITAL ROLE OF REPETITION

Allow us to offer our next key principle of Christian sex education in the family:

PRINCIPLE 10: Repetition is critical; the most important messages about sexuality rarely "get through" on the first try.

Young children love repetition. They seem to never tire of reading the same favorite book or playing the same favorite game over and over. Family rituals become like a bedrock of stability and security for them. And children learn through repetition. We all do. There is a comfort and joy in repetition. In many of our churches we repeat the Lord's Prayer and the Apostles' Creed, and if we allow ourselves, we continue to learn from and be comforted by such rituals, whose meaning is never lost but only deepened with practice.

The lessons of Christian sex education also need to be repeated over and over. After all, the world will be repeating its lessons on sexuality over and over to our children. In TV program and commercial after program and commercial, movie after movie, joke after joke, on and on the sexual messages of the world will come at our children. Our lessons cannot be offered to our children once for all, after which we sit back self-satisfied and lazy. Our lives are lived in the midst of a grand spiritual battle; we are called upon to arm ourselves with the full armor of God (Ephesians 6:10-20). In warfare, you never stop practicing the basics of your battle plan; you use repetition to stay sharp, to keep your major objectives in view. So even when our children have "gotten" the lesson, we still must reinforce it with constant attention and repetition. And the later elementary school years are a wonderful time for repetition, before puberty, middle school, and social changes begin to inject their complications.

EXPLAINING PUBERTY TO YOUR CHILD

There are biological realities that make the situation our children face today very different from what was common at any other point in human history. Up to about one hundred years ago, the average age at which young people went through puberty was around seventeen or eighteen. Young people did not become fertile, capable of bearing or fathering children, until about the same time at which they were considering marriage and moving into their vocations.

But the timing of puberty has been radically decreasing. The average age for onset of menstruation for girls is now under age twelve. Some girls, in fact, are beginning their menstrual periods as early as age nine, though others can begin their periods as late as age sixteen or seventeen. Boys are beginning to go through puberty between the ages of thirteen and fourteen. Live sperm can appear in a boy's semen as early as age ten. When we put these average ages at which young people are going through puberty together with statistics showing that the average man marries at age twenty-six and the average woman at age twenty-four, we can see that it is not at all uncommon for persons to be *sexually* mature for just as long in their life before they marry as they were sexually immature. The average boy spends thirteen years before puberty and then thirteen years after puberty before he marries, and the average young woman today spends twelve years before puberty, and then twelve more years as a sexually mature woman before she marries.

So young people today are experiencing puberty earlier than previous generations, and are having to handle being unmarried but sexually mature (physically) for a much longer time than has ever been true in human history. Parents should also take note that kids who are early maturers, who go through puberty early, have been shown to be more likely to get involved in premarital sex at an earlier age.[1]

These are just a few of the reasons why it is very important to teach our children what to expect as they come into puberty. These are perhaps the most critical years, because after puberty begins, discussing sexuality feels much more personal to your child. Discussions before puberty are discussions about the future, but with the acute self-consciousness the child feels going through puberty, discussions after that point about their bodies and their experiences can be more difficult. In late elementary school they can still with some ease talk about what will be happening to their bodies. During puberty, it will be easier in turn to talk about what lies ahead in dating and teen relationships.

We would like to summarize very briefly some of the things you need to know and might want to tell your children, in the kind of language you might use with your child, during their late elementary school years. As you discuss these changes with your sons and daughters, you should work hard to be positive and affirming, telling them that they will be receiving a gift in installments over the next few years, the gift of an adult body. God is the gift-giver, and God means them well with His gift. Tell them that you as a parent are excited about that gift, and want to help them know as much as possible about the gift and how to use it wisely and well.

What to Say to Girls
Girls typically grow through pubertal changes a year or two before boys. They go through unexpected growth spurts. In a society that is consumed with how much people weigh, girls are often very concerned when they put on weight unexpectedly. Their hips, thighs, and shoulders begin to round out and broaden. Their breasts grow, beginning with development around the nipple (what is called the "breast bud") and then breast growth spreads out from there. At times, a girl's breasts can feel swollen or tender. Under the influence of hormones, the quality of her sweat begins to change and she may begin to need to use deodorant. The girl has more body hair, including the development of underarm hair and possibly light fuzzy hair as a mustache. She can develop pimples and acne. She may experience a real alternation between periods of having a lot of energy and of feeling deprived of energy.

Menstruation typically begins between a year and a year and a half after the girl begins to experience breast development. She will oftentimes experience backaches, tenderness of her abdomen, and a bloated feeling in her abdomen on an irregular basis for several months before menstruation begins. She should be well educated about menstruation before it begins. Initial periods tend to be irregular, and this is not a cause for alarm.

Some families celebrate the girl's first period. They make it a time of recognition of the girl's transition from childhood to the beginnings of adulthood. Whether you have a family party, a quiet and special dinner just for daughter and mother, or just a positive talk with the daughter, it is vital to make this a time of true affirmation. Her starting menstruation is a symbol of her womanhood, of the totality of God's marvelous gift of femininity to her. We should help her appreciate this great gift.

A girl's specific sexual development starts with breast development. In the following year, she begins to get more pubic hair, which starts to grow in straight and gradually grows more kinky. Her labia, which form the outer part of her genitals, grow larger and take on a deeper, ruddier color. Many people do not realize that just as boys experience spontaneous erections, girls experience spontaneous lubrication of the vagina. Girls thus will begin to be aware of a feeling of "wetness" in their vagina and the opening between the labia.

The girl's body is also more capable of being sexually aroused after going through puberty. Her clitoris and all of the tissues of her genital area grow more sensitive during this time. Some girls will notice this and experiment with masturbation by rubbing their genitals with their hands or possibly with an object such as a pillow. All of these changes take place in spurts over months and months; remember, puberty is a period, not an event. Girls and boys appear capable of having orgasms before puberty, but their capacity for sexual pleasure (and interest in such pleasure) definitely increases at this time.

We should tell them about the experience of orgasm. (We will save our discussion about the morality of masturbation for chapter 16 and of petting for chapter 15.) In telling the child what orgasm is, we might say something like the following: "Honey, one of the changes your body will go through is that it becomes more able to experience pleasure from your sexual organs. Women and men both are able to have what are called orgasms. You've probably heard the word before. An orgasm is a time of intense good feeling that every person can have when he or she has felt sexual pleasure for some time. An orgasm feels like a sort of burst of intense pleasure that lasts a few seconds. Married people can feel orgasms when they have sexual intercourse if they learn to please each other. This is part of the joy of being together and sharing our bodies. Girls and boys may have orgasms in their sleep during a dream; the dream may or may not be about sex. Having dreams where your vagina feels wet is normal and nothing to worry about, though it can be embarrassing. Girls and boys may also have orgasms if they touch their own genitals or if they let another person touch them. The ability to feel orgasm is a gift from God; it really feels wonderful. But like all of God's gifts, we should use it the way He wants us to."

The girl's emotional development is influenced by her having gradually stronger sexual feelings and specific sexual thoughts. As with the boys, she experiences anxiety with these changes. With the onset of her menstrual cycle, she may experience significant mood shifts. Being very conscious of her bodily changes and quite unsure about how she feels about them, she may become very defensive and evasive about her body. Parents can ask about what is happening with her, and receive extremely vague replies, if any at all.

Socially, girls often vacillate between avoidance of boys and fascination with them. They try out new social skills and styles for relating with boys, playing at being shy, coy, rowdy, or flirtatious. Girls are often more successful in school at this age than are boys, and will take great comfort in their success in this area. They can become very interested in femininity, and work hard to fit whatever is promoted as the most influential ideal for being feminine.

What to Say to Boys
Boys typically begin the transformation of puberty about two years later than girls. Teenage boys between ten and thirteen go through a period of general physical development. They get taller. Their shoulders broaden, their muscles get larger, and they get stronger. A great many boys can experience slight swelling of their breasts around their nipples and some tenderness there. This is a normal reaction that some boys have to the changing hormones in their body and is not necessarily a sign of anything being wrong in their development. These general body changes are all a result of hormone changes, which also causes their perspiration to smell stronger, like an adult's. Most boys thus need to begin using deodorant during this time. Their skin and hair gets oilier. They begin to develop hairier arms and legs, and hair under their arms. They get the beginnings of a beard and mustache. They can begin to develop pimples or acne, and their voice begins to change.

A number of changes are specific to the boy's sexual development. He begins to get pubic hair, which begins growing in straight and then gradually becomes more curly or kinky. His penis and scrotum will grow larger. Boys will often notice that their scrotum is looser and that the skin of the scrotum develops more wrinkles. This too is perfectly normal.

With the onset of puberty, boys begin to have more "spontaneous" erections, erections that appear to happen for no particular reason. This is usually terrifically embarrassing for boys, and it is essential to inform them that this will be happening and is no cause for alarm. We should tell boys about orgasm in the way we discussed a few pages back. Many boys begin to experience wet dreams, where they ejaculate in their sleep, often in response to a sexual dream, and for most boys it is in a wet dream that they have their first ejaculation. Wet dreams are often a point of deep embarrassment for boys. They have no voluntary control of this response, and should never be disciplined in any way for them. It is best simply to tell your child ahead of time that this will happen, let him know that you understand that it might be an embarrassment, and give him permission to change his own sheets as often as he might like. Most boys will at least experiment with masturbation during this period of transition. Boys begin to think about sex during this time, including moving from general sexual feelings to more specific sexual fantasies.

Tremendous emotional changes are underway as well. The development of stronger sexual feelings and of sexual interest in girls can be quite intimidating and anxiety producing for boys. This is a hard transition to make, and boys can be very anxious about their sexual feelings. They worry about their normalcy. They worry about not being accepted, and are very sensitive to any embarrassment with their peers and anything else they perceive as a failure or a mistake. They typically have a strong interest in girls but attempt to hide it. They develop an intense interest in being "manly" and are likely to be overly concerned and defensive about this.

In their social relationships, boys desperately want to be accepted by their peers. The struggle to learn how to relate to girls is difficult. They need to try out new ways of relating to them, but are terribly afraid of failure. They can often overreact to their own perceived failures. The approval of their group of friends becomes very important, and no one wants to be perceived as less than a man.

We feel that the transition of boy to man should be celebrated too. But it is harder to celebrate than a girl's first period, in part because there is no one event or marker to point to as a transition point, and also because the most obvious changes in the boy are more explicitly sexual (erections, ejaculation) than the girl's period. We would probably do more harm than good by announcing that we were having a special dinner for the family because our son had his first wet dream! We do suggest, however, that the father acknowledge the growth and change he sees in his son, and that he welcome his son into manhood.

What to Say About Uncomfortable Urges

We should tell our children, boys and girls, that the sexual feelings and yearnings they will feel during and after the puberty period can be powerful, mysterious, and at times very uncomfortable. One of the most troubling but common experiences of many teens is to feel sexual arousal in unexpected ways. Boys especially can find themselves sexually aroused by girls they don't like or find to be unattractive. They may feel sexual attraction to a cousin, sister, or friend of the family. They may get "turned on" to lewd jokes describing deviant sexual acts, or to TV commercials or magazine ads. The same thing can happen to girls—they can feel aroused by someone they dislike or by thinking about rape.

Because teenage sexual arousal can be very unfocused, many normal heterosexual teens find themselves on occasion feeling a sexual response to hearing about homosexual acts or to thinking about another girl or boy's body. We should help our teenagers to take this in stride by recognizing it for what it is. They are going through a period where their identity as a sexually mature adult is being shaped. Early on in this process, they do not have as definite a "form" to their sexuality as they will later. They should be warned about these experiences, and told not to worry about them. Such occasional feelings are to be expected, and will eventually be resolved. Their job during this period is to be thankful for their awakening sexual feelings, make the right decisions that God wishes of them, enjoy their relationships, and be patient with themselves as they grow up. They do not have to act on any of the sexual feelings they experience.

Some children and teenagers engage in experimental homosexual behavior, and this needs to be discussed as well. If all of the teenagers who engaged in some sort of same-sex sexual experimentation grew up to be homosexual, perhaps a third of all adults would be homosexual. Instead, the latest research suggests homosexuals represent less than 2 percent of the population. Same-sex experimentation can take the forms of guys wrestling and grabbing each others genitals, girls practicing kissing or petting as they talk about dating, two boys watching each other masturbating, and so forth.

It is vital *not* to label such behavior as homosexual; to do so is to brand the person on the basis of an action. Never say, "Stop that homosexual play!" or "Are you trying to become gay?" Children can be branded with doubt by such statements. If we have "caught" children in such an activity, we should discipline them for their failure to protect the privacy and sanctity of their own body, but we should always do so in the context of affirming their basic "normalcy." At the same time, we should talk with them compassionately about the feelings that might have been associated with their actions: curiosity, fear of not fitting in, loneliness. We might say something like (for ten-year-olds), "Bill, because you were engaging in sexual play with Jeremy, showing each other your penises, you are restricted from playing with him for one week. Acting like that is inappropriate. It is very normal to be curious about another boy's body. But you are meant to keep your body private, so that you will be able to make it a special gift to your future wife. Your body and its sexual feelings are a special gift from God to you. I'm punishing you now because you did not make a good choice of how to use that gift." If children confess such actions to us, we should again talk with them with compassion, and also help them to structure their lives to try to make sure it doesn't happen again.

There are many helpful books written for teenagers about the changes their bodies will be going through during and after puberty. Many of these books also have helpful discussions of the changes they will be facing in their emotions and relationships. James Dobson's *Preparing for Adolescence* (Regal) is a good example of the kind of book that contains very helpful encouragement of teen chastity and generous discussion of the emotional changes that are ahead.

Teen Pregnancy
A quick word about teenage pregnancies. Even though the woman is sexually mature and capable of getting pregnant as soon as she starts having her period, her body is still not physically mature, ready to bear children, until age eighteen or later. The earlier onset of puberty today creates a situation where a woman can get pregnant before she has the strength and physical stamina to tolerate a pregnancy well. Girls who give birth prior to age sixteen are much more likely to die in childbirth; their risk has been cited as being up to 400 percent higher than adult women. Not only is early pregnancy unhealthy for the mother, but early pregnancy also creates tremendous health problems for the baby. Babies born to young girls are more likely to be premature, to have low birth weight, and to have more birth defects. Complications with birth and prematurity can lead to such conditions as mental retardation.

Don't let puberty be a surprise to your child. The elementary school years are a wonderful opportunity to prepare our kids for what lies ahead. We should use that opportunity well.

Part Four

THE TRANSITIONAL YEARS: TRANSITION THROUGH PUBERTY

14

Preparing for Dating: Dealing with Romance and Sexual Attraction

❖

"**M**om, a guy named Dirk asked me to go to the football game with him and then to go hang around afterward. He is, like, a really cool guy. Some of the other guys call him Snake, but I'm not sure why. He says that dropping out of school was a big mistake, but he's so smart that I'm sure he will get back into school after he gets a job and gets his really cool car paid off. He said getting the tattoos was, like, a big mistake, and the parts of his head that were shaved are growing out. He doesn't go to church, but he says he's really spiritual. I don't think his being five years older than me is a problem, because I'm, like, about as mature as him. And he promised not to smoke or drink while we were out. I can go, right?" Words to chill the heart of any parent.

What do you plan to do about dating? In this chapter we will outline the kinds of issues we should think and talk about with our kids, during their transition through puberty, in preparing for dating. We should then gently but firmly surround our teenagers with a supportive framework of rules about dating that will allow them time to mature and grow in strength before they face the challenges that adulthood will offer them.

DATING AND CHARACTER

What happens when your children date will be the result of the character you have helped them build over the years. Dating will be the most positive experience for them when they are well prepared. Consider the following important points of character development:

- You have built a history of helping them meet their needs for relatedness and significance in healthy and godly ways. The teenager who enters dating feeling a deep sense of love and acceptance from his parents, a love and acceptance that encourages him to love and accept himself and to feel the love and acceptance of God, is a strong young man. The teenager who, based on the confidence and encouragement of her parents, begins dating with a sense of confidence in the meaning of her own life and of her ability to serve God well with her gifts and abilities both now and in the future, is a strong young woman.
- They have some understanding of their own deepest needs, and can make mature decisions about how to get those needs met. We will discuss how to talk with your teen about the real meaning of feelings of infatuation and romantic interest later in this chapter.
- You have supplied them with the most important core beliefs about sexual morality and dating. Some of those vital beliefs include the purposes and limits of legitimate dating.
- They have come to value the right things. Here in adolescence is when we begin to truly discover whether we have taught them by example and word to value conformity, approval of others, and self-gratification, or rather chastity, strength, independence, purity, and obedience.
- They have the skills to handle themselves well. Can they say no? Can they defend themselves? Can they be decisive? Can they recognize danger situations and take steps to get out of them?
- They have a supportive relationship with you, the parent. Your support, provided in the forms of affection and encouragement, but also rules and limits, can give strength at a time when others are weakening them.

Shaping your child's expectations and views of dating is a process of shaping character, and we would do well to remember what goes into character in order to do that shaping well.

THE NEGATIVE REALITIES

Three crucial realities have emerged from the research on teen dating that parents need to be aware of as a backdrop for our discussions about the emotional and physical realities of dating. The last two need to be communicated to our kids at the right time, which will vary from child to child. Only a parent who knows his or her child well can make a truly astute judgment of when that right time is.

First, there is strong evidence that adolescents who start dating early are more likely to begin having sexual intercourse early.[1] "Early maturers" are thus more likely to get into trouble with premarital sex than are "late bloomers." And kids who are in groups that start dating early are at greater risk; early dating is not harmless. There are at least two likely reasons for this. (1) Early-dating girls typically wind up dating older, and thus probably more sexually experienced, young men who are likely to "bring them up to speed." (2) Early daters simply have more dating experience under their belts at each age so that they probably tend to get restless with their current level of sexual experience and are more willing to move on to the next level of physical intimacy. There may be good reasons to hold the line and simply not let your child, especially the early maturer, date until her emotional, spiritual, and interpersonal maturity catch up with her physical status.

Second, there is a high level of dishonesty in many adolescent dating relationships. One study surveyed one thousand boys in high school.[2] One of the questions asked was whether it was okay to "lie to a girl about being in love with her in order to get her to have sex." Fully 70 percent of the one thousand boys surveyed said yes. Such lying is coming to be of even greater concern in an age of rampant STDs and the deadly HIV virus. One woman with AIDS said, "Don't trust someone, even someone you love, to come clean. People aren't always honest about their past sex life or HIV status."[3] We need to give a clear sense to our kids of the extent of trust that is reasonable, and that when it comes to sex there are many incentives for both men and women to be dishonest.

There is probably as much dishonesty with self as there is with others. One study found that over half of the nonvirgin girls surveyed had believed that they would marry the boy they first had sexual intercourse with.[4] Interestingly, less than 10 percent of young men believed they would marry the first woman they had sexual intercourse with. More unfortunate still is the reality that, among those who engage in premarital sexual intercourse, less than 3 percent of these nonvirgins actually wound up marrying the individual whom they first have sex with. It seems likely that the young men in this study were lying to their girlfriends, but also that there was a good deal of self-deception among the girls.

Third, parents must know just how prevalent date rape is becoming. We will discuss date rape more fully in chapter 20, but will say here that a recent study reported that about 13 percent of white teenage girls and 8 percent of African-American girls reported being raped or forced to have sex against their wills. Parents must be concerned about this happening to their daughters.

THE PURPOSE OF DATING

We should begin our discussions with our kids by talking about the purposes of dating, about what dating is for. Too much of what kids pick up on their own is destructive. Dating can be the place where you prove your value as a woman by pleasing a young man, by being the woman the guys pursue, even if that pleasing and pursuit is bought with your own sexual purity. Dating can be the place where a boy shows his manhood by domination and manipulation of a woman, by "getting all he can." Dating can be seen as a life or death selection process of your life mate even in the early teen years. We need to orient kids as to what to expect and strive for.

We should set positive expectations for dating for our kids. As Christian parents, what do we believe dating is for? As we set our kids' expectations for dating, we must try to strike a balance between giving them positive expectations that will serve them well later, but *not* seem to be pressuring them to be interested in dating earlier than they want or to be prescribing to them that they now ought to be obsessed with the other sex.

We look forward to our kids marrying the right person and experiencing the joys and fulfillment that will come from that union. But we are not obsessed with their marriage in the future; we are also excited about their capacity to learn and grow and mature as young adults, and they do this partly through their romantic relationships. So what do we tell them?

Dating is an opportunity to have fun and to expand your enjoyment of different activities. Dating can be great fun. You get to do things and try activities on dates that are not part of the routine of families. Some of the ways that adolescents have fun are not healthy, however. The steady reliance of college students, for instance, on alcohol to have a good time should be of great concern to parents. But we must not let our concerns and cautions completely mar the opportunities dating gives our kids to learn to enjoy different types of people and different kinds of experiences. Church youth groups can foster healthy fun for teens both by sponsoring clean and fun activities, and by giving teens better ideas about how to have fun dates through workshops on "Great Dates" or "Creative Dating."

Dating is an opportunity to get to know a wide variety of people and learn better what you really like and respect in people. Dates can be a wonderful opportunity to know another person at some depth. You see people in a new light when you see them with their family, in new activities, with other people (such as on double or group dates), and when you spend time alone with them. Teens should be urged to trust their instincts about things they do not like about the other person. They should also be confident about taking joy in what they do like.

Dating is a great place to enjoy friendships and learn more about the other sex. Good marriages are built, in part, on friendship with your spouse and on an understanding of the other person. Our kids can begin the process of becoming good spouses by learning to be friends with the people they are dating. Again, church youth groups can help by discussing or putting on workshops about dating manners—how to be polite, how to be friends with the other sex, the elements of a good relationship, and so forth.

Dating is an opportunity to grow in your confidence and skill in handling yourself. When dating is handled rightly, our teenagers will be able to gain self-assurance as they slowly move out from the family and successfully handle the challenges they will face—peer pressure; confusion; how to stop, slow down, or deepen intimacy; and how to put a stop to a relationship that is no longer healthy or helpful.

Dating is an opportunity to feel strong loving feelings, to fall in and out of love, and thus over time to learn what true love really is. Our children must understand that they will fall in and out of love many times before they learn what real love is, though no one really understands this until they go through it. Perhaps no one has said it better than C. S. Lewis: "Love as distinct from 'being in love' is not merely a feeling. It is a deep unity, maintained by the will and deliberately strengthened by habit; reinforced by (in Christian marriages) the grace which both partners ask, and receive, from God. . . . 'Being in love' first moved them to promise fidelity; this quieter love enables them to keep the promise. It is on this love that the engine of marriage is run; being in love was the explosion that started it."[5] We should *never* interpret for our kids that what they are feeling at age sixteen is not true love. Rather, we should rejoice with them that they feel love, and encourage them that if what they are experiencing is true love, it will be deepened and made yet more beautiful by sexual purity and exercising the patient discipline of allowing the relationship to develop slowly.

Dating is an opportunity to feel and enjoy strong feelings of sexual attraction, and to learn how to handle those feelings rightly and glorify God in the process. We must again tell our kids that it is a normal and good thing for them to feel sexual excitement for someone they care for, to want to kiss, to touch and be touched, and even to want to be one sexually. But we must also tell them again that they do not have to act on those feelings, that it will not hurt them not to act on those feelings, that if it is a godly relationship then it will not hurt the relationship either, and that God wants them to follow His rules. The dating relationship is a wonderful place to follow God's desires and see how He will bless obedience and purity.

Dating is an opportunity to grow to love your future spouse. We probably should not utterly separate teen dating from its connection to marriage; after all, some people do begin dating their spouse-to-be in the teen years. But we should balance this possibility by gently letting our teen know that many long dating relationships do not make it to the altar. This is probably best handled not as a shaking-the-finger-in-the-face "Don't you forget . . ." lesson, but rather as a story that we tell our child now and then.

THE EMOTIONAL REALITIES OF DATING

We are convinced that parents often do their kids a disservice by focusing so much on the sexual dimension of dating that they ignore the greater significance of dating's emotional dynamics. We feel strongly enough about this to offer it as our next principle:

PRINCIPLE 11: Sexuality is not the most important thing in life. We must strive to put sexuality into its proper perspective.

What do people ultimately want from their human relationships? Orgasms and sexual thrills only satisfy the most superficial levels of our yearnings as persons. It is the stunted and immature human being who can fully embrace the playboy philosophy of promiscuous sexual pleasure and a life of noncommitment. Our sexuality is a vital and beautiful gift, but it is itself a signpost pointing us to a deeper reality—of our capacity to love God and to love and become one with a special person. All of the smoke about sexual feelings can hide the real fire that is creating the smoke. It is the fire of our adolescent child finding out in his or her heart what each of us must ultimately discover: That we are made to be incomplete by ourselves, and that we long for union with God and another special person to be made complete.

So let us not become one-track parents who think of dating only as the place where sex could occur. Let us think instead of dating as one of the places where our kids will experience the powerful emotional awakenings of their true self, the self that is restless until is rests in a relationship of union with God and spouse.

Specifically, we need to help our kids anticipate the emotional elation and turmoil of infatuation; the joys, frustrations, and sorrows of adolescent love. One of the most vital topics to cover with our adolescents is that of the emotional dynamics of relationships and how our emotions relate to sexual yearnings. There is a tremendous need to dispel the clouds of mystery that surround the emotions of dating relationships.

Remember the power of stories. One of the most helpful things we can do as parents is to tell *our* stories to our kids, to tell them of the ups and downs we experienced. Tell them what the power of infatuation felt like when you were sure it was lifelong love. Tell them about the obsessive way you wrote your flame's name over and over, the way your whole day revolved around when he would call you, or the way you got an electric thrill to see her smile at you. Tell them about your confusion and pain as a relationship died a lingering death. Tell them about the agony of betrayal. Tell them about the fear of asking out the one you thought you adored. Tell them of the boredom and frustration of discovering that you were not enjoying the one you were with. Tell them how your powerful feelings blinded you to his flaws and led you to exaggerate his perfections. Do all this to give your child a wider range of experiences, namely your experiences, to serve as a vantage point from which she can see her own experiences more clearly.

James Dobson has a helpful discussion of many myths of "love" in his helpful book *Preparing for Adolescence*.[6] There are many damaging and pernicious myths about love in the teen culture, and we as parents should try to protect our teenagers from them. We urge that parents talk with their kids about these and other myths about love in adolescence. The main myths he discusses that deal with the emotional realities of dating are that true "love at first sight" is a real thing, that it is easy to distinguish infatuation from real love, that fighting and real love do not go together, that true love lasts a lifetime without any effort or sacrifice, and that teenagers are more capable of real love than are adults.

Parents can acquaint their kids with some of the crucial emotional realities of dating. We should discuss the reality that most teen dating relationships are temporary—the average age of marriage for both men and women is in the mid-twenties. Our kids are probably going to go through a lot of dates, a lot of relationships, before marrying. We often aren't able to discern true love by how a relationship feels. One of the differences between infatuation and true love is that true love can see flaws in the other and still love. Any real relationship can stand the test of time, and if it can stand the test of time it can also stand the test of sexual restraint.

Often we cannot really think clearly about relationships until we go through infatuation. Dating will be a place where our child will eventually find true love, but most often dating will be a place to learn to relate and learn the difference between true love and infatuation.

THE "PHYSICAL REALITIES" OF DATING

In discussing dating we lay the groundwork for thinking about what happens physically in a dating relationship. Our first goal must be to "normalize" sexual attraction and interests. We need to stop thinking of sexual feelings as bad. Rather, we should strive to celebrate the wonderful feelings of desire that the young person has for the person he or she is attracted to. God made us to respond as whole beings; God made our children to be sexual beings who would feel sexual desire for people they care for. If we present sexual feelings as the enemy, we are likely programming our children to feel unrealistic and unproductive guilt. The core idea we want to share is that it is a wonderful, blessed, and profoundly normal thing to experience sexual attraction in any relationship where there are romantic feelings. Trouble comes in as we consider what to do with those feelings.

When we discuss dating with our kids we should encourage them to talk about their physical relationship *as* a couple. Communication is important in all areas of the dating relationship, and the couple should talk about physical relationship as well. Talking does not mean negotiating, however—our children should be urged to set standards deliberately rather than waiting to see what happens. Nothing should happen by surprise. In light of the rampant dishonesty in dating relationships, teens should be wary of manipulation. Each couple should have a sense of where they are on the spectrum of commitment and how their physical relationship affects their general relationship. Kids need also to be aware that expressing physical affection probably makes it harder, rather than easier, to understand the true character of the partner and the real status of the relationship.

A DEVELOPMENTAL APPROACH TO DATING

Kids begin "dating" at different ages in different groups. Some kids are actively "going out" in seventh grade, while others wouldn't dream of dating until tenth grade or later. Some teens are into group friendship dating, while others are into more solitary and traditional "car dating" activities. Some patterns have more potential than others to move adolescents toward more sexual experimentation— the more individual and private the pattern, the more likely it is to cause trouble.

We would urge that rather than waiting and reacting to what is thrown at them by their kids (as our opening example illustrated), parents should instead encourage a "developmental approach" to dating. *Developmental approach* is simply a fancy term for allowing your child to ease gradually into more independent dating activities.

We are very hesitant to give specific ages for specific types of dating, as such examples can quickly become rigid guidelines. But we can hardly give a good description of what we have in mind without talking about ages. There are no absolutes for setting time frames for stages of dating, but we should check with other parents in our community and church to see what they're using as their standards. Their standards should not automatically become *our* standards, but they can let us know what we are up against.

If there is any absolute, it should probably be the bottom age at which you will let your child begin dating of any kind. We have discussed how kids who mature early and start dating early are at particular risk for early sexual activity. It is vital that a parent spend enough time setting limits with the child and supporting the child that the child does not get in over her head in adolescent sexual relationships. We need to be clear with a precocious thirteen-year-old that she will not be allowed to date until the time that we have determined, regardless of how aggressive the boys pursuing her are. And if we're going to set limits, we had better have the energy and resources to back them up—it's no use settings limits on dating and then leaving the child unsupervised three evenings of the week.

And it's not enough just to set limits. We also need to help our children find other ways to get their needs met. The parent who sets limits but is not there to help and support the child is likely to be perceived by the child as cruel. We need to set the limits and provide the support.

A developmental approach to dating might take the following form: "Dating" could start first in integrated group contexts such as youth groups or school clubs. Such groups give boys and girls the opportunity to be around each other and get to know one another within the context of an activity or common interest. Rather than focusing upon themselves, they come to know each other through something outside of themselves. This can really help to decrease the pressure on the adolescents. This would be the kind of dating a parent could allow early on, telling a child, "If you want to spend time with Pam, I would like you to tell her that she is welcome to go with you to the youth group, or with us to church, or to join the theater and drama group you're in at school. That's a great way for young people to get to know each other."

The second step in dating might then be to allow group dates at structured events such as school sporting events, dances, plays, church activities, and so forth. Important rules might be that parents or older siblings must do the driving, and that the teen is not to separate from the group to spend alone time with her romantic interest. A teen might be told, "Yes, you are fourteen and so I think it might be okay for you to have a date at a group activity. But I'm not ready to allow you to go in his car even though he can drive. You may tell him the answer is yes about going to the school dance, but you can either meet him there and I will drive you, or I would be happy to drive you both."

The third step might then be group dates that occur in a more autonomous fashion such as a group of couples meeting to go to a movie and walk to get ice cream. Allowing double dating might be a next step in moving toward solitary dating.

Finally, parents may be ready to let their child go on solitary dates. We have not faced this reality yet, but at this time are not likely to let our children go on solitary "car dates" until they are sixteen. It is our sense that children can wait until they're old enough to drive before taking on the full responsibility of being out and completely on their own with another person. Solitary dating can still be handled in a developmental fashion through curfews and restrictions on activities. Remember, kids who operate under reasonable dating rules imposed by caring parents whom the kids are on good terms with are less likely than kids from permissive homes to experiment with sex. Be ready to talk about the rules, but be ready to support your child by having limits.

Parents who set up guidelines for dating for their kids are likely to get hit on the "trust" issue—"Why don't you trust me?" We should assure our kids that we do trust them, and will continue to do so until proven otherwise. But *we do not similarly trust all of their friends nor all of the situations they might get into.* It may be a good strategy to give an example from your own life when you had good intentions, but got into a situation that was beyond your ability to handle. Brenna experienced a terrifying but wonderful example of this. At age fifteen she was set up on a blind date with a college basketball player who, thanks to her naiveté at that age, manipulated her to go up to his dorm room. He clearly took the fact that she had come there as consent to have intercourse. In that situation, she could have been raped easily, but thankfully this enormous and powerful man had enough moral scruples not to victimize a younger girl. We may deeply trust our child's integrity, but our trust does not extend to situations and people our child does not control.

Remember too that we must be honest about our trust levels. If we don't trust our kids, we must tell them so. Trust is earned; it cannot be established on demand. We must give our children the opportunities to show they are trustworthy, but we don't have to play stupid or blind when they violate our trust. When trust has been violated it has to be rebuilt, and that rebuilding is a slow and painful process.

What should we do about kids who seem disinterested in dating? First, we should be patient and accepting. Many a happy, well-adjusted adult did not date much in adolescence. Some kids are too busy having fun of other kinds, or are so deeply interested in sports or academics, that they simply do not feel romance is that important. But parents should also have their eyes open for potential problems that can be partially manifested by a failure to develop any romantic interests. Probably the most common problem here is anxiety about the other sex and discomfort in relating to it. An excessive fear or guilt about the teen's sexuality can show up as an exaggerated desire to avoid all situations that could get him or her thinking about sex at all, and so the child avoids any thought of romance. Finally, some kids who are struggling with uncomfortable sexual longings such as sexual feelings for persons of the same sex will avoid dating. If you suspect a deeper concern or problem behind your child's noninvolvement in dating, we urge *you* to seek counsel from someone you trust to help you sort out your perceptions and understandings of your child. Only then may it be appropriate to suggest that the child pursue counseling of some sort.

GUIDELINES FOR DATING

Josh McDowell and Dick Day in their book *Why Wait?*[7] offer some helpful ideas for guidelines for dating. It may be possible for parents to implement some of their suggestions as a dating rule for their kids. Others may be enforceable only by the teenagers themselves. But parents may be able to suggest them or show in describing their own dating experiences how the guidelines were or would have been helpful. McDowell and Day suggest the following:

1. Teens should be accountable to definite plans and guidelines. "Hanging out" is not a good plan, especially in early dating. Specific activities at specific locations should be the rule. Having the couple engage in deliberate forethought about what they will be doing can help prevent disastrous, spontaneous "doing what comes naturally"!

2. Couples should avoid sexually explicit media as part of their activities. It is getting harder and harder today to find an adult movie that is not rated R and loaded with gratuitous sexual scenes. But there are many other activities that will not "get the juices flowing" to the same degree. Parents should urge the teenagers to choose activities wisely, and there should be limits to the kinds of activities they can pursue.

3. Teens, especially young women, should dress modestly rather than provocatively. Dress is suggestive. The women's activists who protest that men should heed a woman's "No!" at any point are right, but parents must also face the reality that young men today have been bombarded with television and movie images of reluctant and coy women whose lips say "no" but who give in under pressure. Everything a young woman does in a relationship, from mode of dress on, communicates some message about her moral standards. Young women from Christian families should not send out mixed signals.

4. Teens should choose all of their companions, especially those they date, very carefully. Our companions will shape who we are (Proverbs 13:20, 28:7, 29:3); we are more likely to become like our companions than to convert them to think and believe like us. There is no question that "interfaith" marriages face many challenges, and it is commonly recognized that compatibility in basic life values and philosophies contributes to marital stability. Many Christians interpret 2 Corinthians 6:14 to prohibit Christians from marrying nonbelievers, and many people extend this teaching to imply that Christian singles should not date unbelievers. This is a matter parents should talk carefully about with their child.

5. Teens should be prepared to talk openly about sex and their moral standards with the person they are dating. Teens should set their physical limits and standards early and firmly. No infringements of their standards

should be accepted. We will discuss enforcing those limits and protecting themselves in chapter 20.

6. Christian teens can include prayer in dating, both before and during a date. Our first "date" was actually to a talk given by Josh McDowell in 1973. His talk was entitled "Maximum Sex" (much to Stan's horror, who asked Brenna to go with him without knowing what McDowell's topic was going to be). Josh challenged Christian singles to include prayer in their dating relationships. As a result, we prayed together on our first date, and prayer has ever since been a source of strength and guidance for us as a couple. And remember from the Introduction that praying together as a couple is one of the best predictors of marital happiness. If that is so, why not get in the habit of praying with people you care about?

7. Our friends Lisa and Mark McMinn from Oregon gave us an interesting perspective on a particular problem in dating that parents should try to prepare for. It is the problem of girls often feeling *obligated* to the boy taking them out, feeling that they somehow "owe" the boy for the date. Many boys subtly encourage this feeling of obligation and have a specific repayment plan in mind for their monetary investment in the date! The place to start in dealing with this problem is awareness—we should warn our daughters (and sons) about this occurring, and make it very clear that they never owe part of their body to anyone. If the date seems to want something back, have the teen tell the date that her parents will be more than happy to refund half of the cost of the date, plus the interest that money would have earned in a money-market fund during the period they were out on the date! Even better may be to urge couples to "go Dutch" or alternate paying for dates ("This is my time to pay"). This feeling of obligation may be especially destructive, and we should prepare our kids for it.

8. Another insight the McMinns gave us was the importance of affirming to a girl that it is all right to express directly her interest in and attraction to a boy. Girls who are socialized into always being passive recipients of attention from boys are often forced to develop coy, manipulative, and seductive ways of drawing attention to themselves to get noticed. This pattern can sabotage a girl's sense of competence and strength in handling herself on dates. Also, by not communicating directly, a girl opens herself to the danger that her subtle messages will be terribly misunderstood and misinterpreted, signaling that she is sexually available, and once out on a date, her direct messages may fall on deaf ears.

9. Finally, teens should be urged to avoid high-risk situations. "Parking" alone in a car miles from anywhere is very risky, as is being alone in a house or apartment with no responsible adults around. Situations where the women are outnumbered drastically by men should be avoided or a hasty departure made. Perhaps the most risky situations are those where alcohol and drugs are involved.

Parents should take an absolute stand that their children not be allowed to consume alcohol or drugs or be around where they are being consumed. Not only are alcohol and drugs problems in themselves, but numerous studies have found that kids who take risks with alcohol and drugs are also very likely to be involved with sexual experimentation.[8] Unfortunately, the teenagers who are most likely to take risks with alcohol, drugs, or sex are the very teenagers who are least likely to recognize the dangers of the behavior they are engaging in. One implication of this for our parenting is the need to be vigilant not only about the child's sexual behavior but about any of the behaviors that fall into such risk-taking categories.

Dating is filled with opportunities—opportunities for growth and fun and closeness, but also for deception, manipulation, and victimization. By preparing our children well for what lies ahead, we make it more likely that they will experience more of the benefits and fewer of the injuries.

15

Developing Moral Discernment About Petting

✤

"Dad, is kissing okay when you're dating? What if he wants to kiss me goodnight? If all we're doing is kissing, what's the big deal?"

"Is it all right for a boy to touch the girl's breasts if they are going steady?"

"Mom, what is oral sex? Some of the girls at school say it's okay, because the guys really like it, and if you do it you're still a virgin."

"But how far *can* I go?"

We have now set the framework for our kids to think about dating. We have hopefully prepared them to understand the emotional dynamics of teen romantic relationships, and have taught them to regard their powerful sexual desires as a reflection of God's gift of a sexual nature.

But what, exactly, are they allowed to do with those sexual desires short of intercourse?

Scripture does not give us a direct answer. Dating, as we experience it today, did not exist in the ancient world. Marriages were, by and large, arranged by one's family. People were getting married, on average, very close to the time of puberty, so the need to deal with sexual desires for *years* before marriage was not typically an issue. Courtship did not involve time alone in the back seat of a chariot or in a deserted house. The independence of modern dating would have flabbergasted parents in biblical times. For all these reasons, Scripture is silent on petting.

We will use the common term *petting* in this chapter to refer to all sexual behavior between a couple short of penis-vagina intercourse. The term petting seems quaint and rather innocent, but it is not necessarily either. The term *petting* is used commonly to describe everything from passionate kissing on the neck to oral sex.

How early should we talk with our kids about the morality and realities of petting? Our kids could or will be exposed to sexual situations and temptations early on. It's not uncommon for inner-city kids to begin having sexual intercourse at eleven or twelve years of age. Even in seemingly conservative suburban settings, a substantial portion, probably between 25 percent and 33 percent, have had intercourse by age fourteen. We fail to prepare them to handle the steps that can take them into intercourse to their and our peril. During the puberty period, hopefully before they begin dating, is the time to tell our children what young people do short of intercourse in physically expressing their affection and/or sexual drives. In this chapter, we will assume that you will be talking to a thirteen-year-old.

DISCUSSING THE MORALITY OF PETTING

What is God's will about petting? Is it surely a sin for a boy to touch a girl's breasts? Does God look at that action the same way if the couple are thirteen-year-olds who barely know each other as He does if they are in their early twenties and one month away from getting married? If we say it is sinful, what is our justification for our stand? If we say it's not sinful, what is our basis? What is God's will for how a couple should express themselves physically before marriage?

What the Bible Commends and Condemns
Perhaps we can move toward greater clarity by first being certain what the Scriptures do and do not say. Certain acts are expressly condemned in the Scriptures, others are expressly commended or approved. We do not often think of the Bible commending or approving sexual actions, so let us look there first.

There are two patterns of sexual behavior that are approved of and spoken of with forcefully positive words. The first is sexual intercourse in marriage. Hebrews 13:4 says that "Marriage should be honored by all, and the marriage bed kept pure, for God will judge the adulterer and all the sexually immoral." It is clear that the writer means that the marriage bed is pure, but can be made impure when the marital relationship is violated by sexual intimacies outside of the marital relationship. Marital sex is pure; it is commended and blessed by God. The Apostle Paul, in 1 Corinthians 7:3-5, gives down-to-earth advice to spouses that they meet each other's sexual needs in marriage. Paul is clearly a realist here, one who paints marriage as a supportive relationship that can help preserve us from temptation and meet our needs. Marital sex is clearly approved of by God.

Celibacy—total abstention from overt sexual expression—is also approved in Scripture. Paul urges believers who are content with single life and not torn with temptation to remain celibate for the sake of the greater focus and energy they can devote to service of the Kingdom (1 Corinthians 6–7). Paul's words echo those of our Lord Himself, who commended the life of celibacy both by His words (Matthew 19:12) and by His perfect example of living a celibate life.

Which acts are expressly condemned in the pages of the Bible? The "condemned acts" list contains more items than does the "commended acts" list; this may reflect our human creativity in violating God's will. Let us begin with those acts for which we seemingly have absolute biblical clarity:

- *Adultery*, the sin of a married person having sex with someone other than his or her spouse, is condemned in the Ten Commandments (Exodus 20:14) and in numerous other places.
- *Incest* is condemned in such passages as Leviticus 18:6-18 and 20:11-22.
- Rape is condemned in Deuteronomy 22.
- Homosexual intercourse (or sodomy) is condemned in such passages as Leviticus 18:22, 20:13; Deuteronomy 23:18; Romans 1:26-28 (note that this is the only passage that refers to female homosexuality); and 1 Corinthians 6:9.
- *Bestiality*, acts of sexual intercourse with animals by both men and women, is condemned in Leviticus 20:15-16.
- *Cross-dressing*, where men and women deliberately mimic the other gender, is condemned in Deuteronomy 22:5.
- *Sexual intercourse between husband and wife during the woman's menstrual cycle* is condemned as unclean in Leviticus 18:19. However, this is seen by most evangelicals as a function of the Jewish ceremonial Law, which Christians are not under obligation to obey.

Now let us take on two final actions that violate God's will, but regarding which there is some confusion of meaning, namely "sexual immorality" and lust. The terms *sexual immorality* and its synonym *fornication* from earlier Bible translations (as found in such passages as Acts 15:29) are translations of the Greek word *porneia*. Translators and scholars typically believe that this term *at least* refers to all sexual intercourse outside of the bonds of marriage. There is not, however, total agreement even on this point, with some liberal biblical scholars denying that the term *fornication* has anything to do with premarital sex. The arguments of these scholars are, however, not persuasive.

The association of the term *fornication* with "sensuality" and "impurity," as in 2 Corinthians 12:21 and Galatians 5:19, however, has led many to interpret *porneia* to have meaning far beyond just illicit sexual intercourse. Many preachers and teachers would interpret petting and masturbation, for instance, to be instances of *porneia, of sexual immorality or fornication. We cannot know for certain, however, that the word really was meant to include such actions. Porneia* certainly means, at the very least, sexual intercourse outside of the bounds of marriage. It may mean more than that, but we don't know this with certainty.

Lust is equally hard to define with precision. Our Lord declared in Matthew 5:28 that "anyone who looks on a woman lustfully has already committed adultery with her in his heart." Writers have tried to determine the exact bounds of lust, without much consensus. Some seem to favor a "tight" or "limited" definition something like this: "Lust is when a person knowingly and deliberately cultivates thoughts and fantasies of illicit sexual intercourse in his or her mind *and begins to act on those thoughts* by flirting with the other person or trying to build a relationship that will eventually allow the fantasized immorality to occur." By this definition, casual feelings of attraction to another person do not qualify as lust.

But this definition seems too tight; Christ's words do not seem to imply that the person has to act for it to be lust. Indeed, His words clearly mean that lust can occur entirely in the heart.

Others seem to favor a very broad and inclusive understanding of lust, so that any noticing of others as attractive, any curiosity about the human body, any sexually charged dreams, and so forth are viewed as lust. When all sexual feelings are made lust, however, we seem to have gone too far. Such a view seems often related to a deeply negative view of our sexuality as "a work of the flesh," as intrinsically bad. Are we guilty at times of laying too heavy a burden on our young people by making them feel guilty for their natural and healthy feelings of attraction and interest? Something is wrong when all sexual interest and attraction is made to be lust. But something is equally wrong if we casually discard our Lord's warning about lust and do not strive for purity.

Different Assumptions

So what do we teach our children about petting? Petting is not one of the clearly condemned behaviors listed above. We do not know for certain that petting is *porneia*. It seems reasonable to think that the feelings that would inspire two teens to get "hot and bothered" in the back seat of a car qualify as lust, but given how unclear the definition of lust is, this isn't a very powerful argument.

Different writers seem to approach the topic of the morality of petting with very different assumptions, much as they do regarding *porneia* and lust. One group seems to reason that "If the Bible doesn't say it's right, then it must be wrong, a sin." By this reasoning, sex in marriage is blessed by God, but since no sexual actions outside of marriage are praised by our Lord, it must be a sin to engage in those actions. So by this reasoning, a passionate prolonged kiss (which is probably not what Paul had in mind as a "holy kiss" in Romans 16:16) between an engaged couple would be sinful; it is not commended by God.

Others seem to argue in quite the opposite direction, suggesting that "If the Bible doesn't say it's wrong, then it must be right and acceptable to God." By this reasoning, anything not expressly forbidden in Scripture is within the realm of Christian freedom. They might cite, "Since you died with Christ to the basic principles of this world, why, as though you still belonged to it, do you submit to its rules: 'Do not handle! Do not taste! Do not touch!'?" (Colossians 2:20-21). Stan actually had a Christian friend in high school who took this verse to justify extensive petting, including oral sex, with his girlfriends. "If the Bible does not say it is bad, then enjoy!" he said often.

A third way of dealing with petting has been called "gradualism" by some. This view claims that different levels of intimacy are legitimate for different types of relationships. The level of physical intimacy should roughly parallel the level of life commitment and growing oneness that the couple are experiencing. A proponent of this view might say that just as eating meat offered to idols was wrong for some and not for others (Romans 14), one type of petting may be wrong for one person and acceptable to another. The man touching the woman's breast would be wrong in the teenage relationship that is all infatuation and hormones, but may be right and even beautiful in the engaged couple in their thirties in the interval before their wedding.

There are problems with each of these views. The first view, "It's all wrong," seems oppressive in its almost universal declaration that all physical expression of caring is always wrong. Does God really mean for an engaged couple to not even kiss passionately before marriage? The second view, "It's all right except intercourse," legitimizes levels of physical intimacy that rival intercourse itself in the way two persons share their bodies. Can we really imagine God to be blessing two teenagers engaging in full-body touching to orgasm simply because it isn't intercourse? The third view strikes us conservative Christians as a form of moral relativism in proclaiming that what is right for some may be wrong for others. And we may be rightly troubled by how unconvincing this reasoning may be for teens, who are likely to say, "Well if petting is for those who are mature, really in love and committed, then petting is for me; after all, I'm fourteen!"

PARENTAL GUIDANCE ABOUT PETTING:
REASONING FROM SCRIPTURE

We are caught in a dilemma. Perhaps the Middle Eastern culture of Christ's day had it right—people married at about the time they entered puberty, and thus grew into their experience of their own sexuality in the context of their marriages. Some people claim it is "unnatural" for two people to develop an intense, close emotional relationship in dating without expressing themselves physically in sexual intercourse. The conservative Christian can agree wholeheartedly—it is unnatural! But we might argue that what is unnatural is not the sexual urges; it is our prolonged patterns of dating with no commitment and with lots of privacy that allows for physical urges to become almost uncontrollable.

But the fact that sexual restraint is "unnatural" in a certain way does not carry much weight. Christians are often called by God to do the unnatural. Is it natural for the angry person to become a person of self-control, for the liar to become a truth-teller, for the prideful person to become humble, or the fool to become wise? No. These are all unnatural callings, but callings which God would have us aspire to.

We must reason from the foundation that sexual intercourse, as we said in chapter 10, is a life-uniting act. Intercourse binds people together, and was meant by God to be experienced only in marriage. Full sexual intimacy is meant to go along with a life commitment and the fullest experience of emotional and spiritual intimacy that each partner can give.

Our starting point thus is that sexual intercourse is out-of-bounds for the dating couple. More, given the beauty of the gift of sexual union in marriage, we will strive to act in such a way that we guard that gift so that when we marry, we will be able to experience the fullest joys conceivable of what God meant sexual union to be.

So what do we say? First, we urge that you as parents think through the range of physical things that two people can do with each other without having intercourse. What do you believe is a level of physical expression that can be honoring to God for a teenager in a dating relationship? Have your own "inner limits" in mind as you read on.

1. We must acknowledge the goodness of the sexual desires of the teenager and of her or his desire to express those desires in a loving relationship. This may be extremely hard for us as parents; it involves us coming to see our beautiful, innocent little ones as sexual beings entering adulthood. But we are all, parents and teens, made by God to want to be physically close and intimate with someone with whom we feel love and affection. Kids should be told to expect such feelings, and to be glad that they feel them. Our fundamental attitudes as we talk of sexual feelings and desires should be positive.

2. We should confront our children with the reality that many of our sexual desires are *not* good—they are predatory, selfish, obsessed with sensual pleasure, insincere, and dishonest. We should give them a way to understand their own experience so that they can sort the good from the bad. It is part of our fallenness that we want to use each other. We want to dominate another person. We care for the parts of the other person's body but not about them. We use our infatuation with another to alleviate our own boredom or loneliness. We must also lead our kids to see the possibility that the sexual feelings of their boyfriends and girlfriends are also a very impure mixture of good and bad, of genuine affection and sinful lust. Their feelings, at the most basic level, are both a gift from God and a trial and temptation to sin.

3. We should instruct our children that no one is hurt by refraining from sexual expression. Sexual feelings do not have to be acted upon. We have to acknowledge the frustration that not giving in to sexual desire can sometimes produce, but also suggest that the frustration is a small price to pay to please God, prepare for a lifetime of love with a marital partner, and avoid the consequences of sex outside of marriage. This means, in part, that we will urge our children to err on the side of caution. Physical affection can be a blessing in a loving and mature relationship. But a mature, godly dating relationship will be more hurt by "going too far" into physical expression than it could ever be hurt by not enough physical expression.

4. As we discuss what we feel to be God's will about petting, we should not claim to have moral absolutes or revelations of divine will that we do not in fact have. We should be able to say honestly, "This is what I believe is right for you. I have put a lot of thought into this, and hope that you can find my views to be trustworthy as a guide. If you feel I have been right in other areas, I ask you to trust me here."

5. Urge that our teens exercise caution rather than an attitude of experimentation in expressing themselves sexually. We should explicitly discuss with our teens how further sexual expression typically leads to further sexual expression. It is hard to go back behind the line you had previously drawn, and after you pass over that line it's that much easier to lurch forward two more steps. "Light petting" (no one agrees what this means) may be inadvisable not because it is so wrong itself but because of what it may lead to. As we develop this theme, however, we *must not* plant in the minds of our children some sort of pessimistic sense that if once they violate the limits we discuss with them, then they are rapidly sliding down a slippery slope toward promiscuity from which there is no return. With God's help, people change patterns of life all the time. There are no actions for which they cannot be forgiven and enabled to start anew.

6. Discuss how transitory adolescent dating relationships tend to be, and how much dishonesty and game playing can be at play in teen dating

relationships. This is a good opportunity to reinforce the themes we discussed in the last chapter.

7. After prayerful reflection, we would urge you to suggest concrete limits that you want your child to hold to. We should emphasize that we have no perfect assurance that our limits are God's limit. See our dialogue presented below.

8. We should ground our petting limits discussion in the moral framework of God's purposes of His gift of our sexuality and of sexual intercourse (chapters 5 and 10). We should also draw in the basic needs we know to exist in us, in our child, and in the person she or he is dating. We will try to provide an example of this in the dialogue below.

9. Helping teens to make a personal commitment to limits that they choose for themselves is essential. In chapter 18 we develop a full rationale for this procedure.

10. Communication within the teenager's dating relationships is vital, as we stated in the last chapter. Even teenagers should be able to talk about their standards with each other and live by those standards. Our children should be encouraged to believe that a dating partner who cannot communicate about the reality of the relationship and who does not abide by the standards that both partners agree to does not deserve loyalty or affection.

We offer the following as one side of a dialogue with a thirteen-year-old on "what's right and wrong in petting":

"Christopher, I hope that as you feel more and more attracted to girls, and begin to really feel special feelings about some, that you will realize what a precious gift those feelings are. Those are the feelings that someday will probably allow you to fall in love with the woman you are to marry. God made you to have those feelings, including the feelings that men have of wanting to kiss, touch, and even have sex with a girl. But He did not make you so that you have to act on those feelings by getting physical with a girl.

"Many of the feelings we have about sex are not from God, though. When I was a young man, I remember feeling real caring for some girls, but I also remember feeling selfish, feeling that I wanted to touch and feel a girl's body because it would be fun for me, would excite me, and would make me seem cool with my friends. I sometimes would not think about the girl as a person, but only about her body. These feelings were wrong. And girls have such sinful selfish feelings too, and may also be ready to do anything to get a guy to like them as well. That's not what God wants either.

"Son, many people, many kids in high school, will have sex with people they are dating. Many of them who don't go all the way into sexual intercourse will be much too intimate, so intimate that they might as well be having sex. You know that intercourse is wrong, but what about other things like kissing and touching? What's right and what's wrong?

"'How far can I go?' is really the wrong question; it's like asking 'what can I get away with?' The real question is 'What is best for me and the girl I am dating? What does God want me to do?' I don't have the perfect answer for you. There isn't an absolute rule in the Bible. But here is what I think:

"Sex outside of marriage is wrong because the joining of our bodies makes us one, and we're supposed to be one with a person only in marriage. I should be one only with one person, my wife. You should be one only with one person, your wife, after you marry her. Oneness is something that happens immediately when you have sex, but it is also something that happens gradually in many small ways, and sharing bodies without having intercourse is one of those ways. If you get involved with a girl and enjoy just about every part of her body and she yours without having intercourse, you have begun the process of becoming one with her. You will have started down that road when it is very unlikely you will marry her. You will have also put yourself in a situation where, because of the excitement of the moment, you will find it very hard to make the decisions that Jesus would want you to make.

"I think then that you should decide not to get very physical with the girls you date in high school. You probably will not meet and date the woman you will marry until college or after. If you meet and date her in high school, you probably will wait a long time to marry. I would urge you not to go beyond kissing in your dating relationships; no touching of girls' breasts or genitals, and no letting them touch your genitals. These experiences are too intimate, too close, too powerful to play around with when you are so far from marriage. Enjoy your dating. Enjoy the respect and fun and appreciation you will find in your relationships.

"I want you to understand that if you choose not to get into sexual intercourse or into heavy petting, you will be in the minority. Guys may razz you for being a virgin, or for being a prude; girls you date may want to do more with you than you feel is right. You will also find it frustrating sometimes not to have sex and not to do petting. But this is a frustration you can live with; no one ever died or went crazy from not having sex. You will need a lot of strength to live your life by God's rules. But it's no more of a difficult task than any that God has given to His saints."

DISCUSSING THE REALITIES OF PETTING

Kids hear about petting at school and from friends, but usually in the form of slang terms that no one defines for them. They are often very confused about what exactly happens physically between people between initial introductions and full sexual intimacy. We can help them make better moral decisions if we help them know what others are talking about. We urge that you talk with your teen about what happens in petting, after laying the kind of moral framework we have just discussed.

How do we tell our children about the realities of sexual involvements in dating that fall short of intercourse? What should we tell them? Perhaps the following "monologue," framed in terms for a thirteen-year-old to understand, will help.

A word of caution: Some will find this monologue to be overly explicit. Others may feel strongly that it represents what should be said, but could not imagine saying this to their child. Friends, we *must* talk explicitly with our kids about sexuality; if we don't, they'll get their explicit instruction from their peers and on dates. We urge you to try talking about these matters, and to trust that any progress in talking about petting is a success that will bear fruit in helping your child make a commitment to chastity. But is what follows too explicit? The following monologue even brings up oral and anal sex. "Why?" you might ask. Because recent research suggests these actions are becoming more common among teens. Some research suggests that the big emphasis on not getting pregnant has led some kids to use anal sex as a preferred method of intercourse that does not run the risk of pregnancy. One study suggested that about one-fourth of all minority group teenage girls have tried anal sex, which is the most efficient way to contract the HIV infection, with only about one-third using a condom.[1] Oral sex is even more frequent, with one study suggesting that about half of teenagers had engaged in it at least once.[2] With these kinds of statistics, do we dare *not* be the first to talk to our kids about these actions? We must help them to think as a Christian about them.

"Julie, I want to tell you a bit more than I ever have before about the ways people who are dating might relate to each other sexually. I want you to understand exactly what can and does happen. I want to tell you about these things for several reasons: so you will firmly make up your mind now, ahead of time, about what you will and will not do. I also want you to know what can happen so you can see the warning signs if a boy is trying to get you to do something you shouldn't do. I want you to know reality so that you will recognize when a boy is not being honest with you.

"Some of what I'm going to talk about I think is fine in the right relationship and at the right time. Much of what I'll talk about I regard to be very wrong. I've already told you why I believe as I do about the rights and wrongs of petting. Now you need to know what can happen.

"The physical relationship usually begins with a kiss. But there are kisses and there are kisses. Kisses range from a quick smack on the lips to the kind of kissing where people's mouths are open and they stay kissing for a long time. You have heard already that when people kiss like this they often touch with their tongues in each other's mouths; you asked me about 'French' kissing years ago. This idea is really gross when you have never done it, but it is exciting and lovely with a person you really love and are attracted to. I would urge you to be cautious about who you kiss, and that you save kissing passionately for when you are older. You're thirteen now, and will have a good amount of time to learn who you really care for and can trust.

"The boy or girl who finds his or her partner attractive and exciting will want to touch him or her. Touching often begins when a boy and girl hold hands, or put their arms around each other while walking, or give each other a hug. These can be very nice ways to express affection with someone you really care for. Some boys, though, think that going out even on the first date means that you will touch like this, but you don't have to. Even these kinds of touching can be really exciting. I hope that you will never think that the feeling of excitement means you are in love; it doesn't. You may feel sexually excited with someone you just have a crush on for a few days. Boys can and do feel sexually excited even with girls they don't know or don't like at all. Feeling sexually attracted does not mean you are in love.

"You know that your genitals are the most sensitive and sexually exciting parts of your body. They are for a boy too. A girl's breasts are the next most exciting area. But your whole body becomes more sexual as you grow up and especially as you are attracted to someone or feel you are in love. After kissing and hugging, the couple may move on to touching other parts of the body. Some parts of your body are more sexual than others. For instance, for most people the thighs, the neck, and the bottom are all very sexually sensitive. That is why after kissing, some couples begin touching other parts of the body. A boy may want to kiss not only a girl's lips, but also her face, neck, ears, or arms. This can feel good, but it can make it harder to make good decisions.

"Couples sometimes then move to touching the most sexual parts of the body on top of or through the clothes. Julie, I would urge you to have this be the point where you choose not to go along; I would urge you not to let a boy touch your breasts or any of the other things I'll tell you about for the reasons I said earlier: It is too close, too intimate, and it can make it harder for you to say no to what could come later.

"Some couples may not do this kind of touching until they are ready to get married after dating for years, and some guys may try to do it on the first date. It can happen suddenly when the boy brushes his hand over the girl's breasts. Remember, you never really know for sure what the other person is going to do. You have to know your limits and make your choices, and be ready to handle things you do not agree to. If she lets him, he may touch and feel her breast for a long time; he finds this really exciting and she does too. If they both want to go farther, the boy and girl may move to touching their genital areas by touching each other between the legs; the boy may rub the girl's genitals through the girl's clothes, and the girl may rub his penis through his pants. This can be so sexually exciting to them that one or both may have an orgasm from this kind of touching. I think this is sad, as I believe that kind of sexual pleasure is something only a husband and wife should give each other.

"If they go further they will move to touching under their clothes. As I said earlier, this can happen quickly or slowly. It can happen as quickly as the boy suddenly putting his hand under her blouse to touch her breast. Couples can unfortunately go even further to touching their genitals under their clothes or with their clothes off. Here, clearly, they are getting so intimate, so close with their bodies, that they're really sharing just about all of themselves. This is far too much intimacy when you aren't married.

"I must warn you that a girl can get pregnant doing this even when she doesn't have sex. If she is excited enough to have her vagina be wet, and if he has an orgasm so that his semen spurts out, any semen with sperm that touches her wet area around the vagina can get her pregnant. The sperm will actually swim into her from the outside of the vagina even if his penis was never in her vagina during intercourse. This doesn't happen often, but it's not unknown. (See chapter 19.)

"Some couples move from there right into having sexual intercourse. At this point, they have already been so intimate, they have shared and given so much of themselves to each other, that it is only a small step into intercourse. If they don't have sexual intercourse for some reason (maybe one or both believe that is the only thing they won't do, or perhaps they are very afraid of pregnancy), sadly there are still other things that some unmarried couples do. One is oral sex. Most kids find this gross to hear about, but many kids now do this and so we have to talk about it. You've probably heard about it. When couples have already touched with their hands all over their bodies, they can move the kissing from the lips to kissing the skin, to the boy kissing the girl's breasts, to "kissing" each other's genitals. This may not actually be sexual intercourse, but you can hardly get more intimate than this. You are totally sharing your bodies.

"Another thing that couples do is what is called anal sex. This is where the couple has intercourse, because the boy's penis goes into the girl's body. But it does not go where it was intended to go, into the vagina, but instead it is put in her rectum, where her bowel movements come out. Apparently more couples are doing this today, in part because they think this is a smart way to have sex without the danger of pregnancy. Unfortunately, having sex this way is the very best way to transmit HIV, the AIDS virus. Because the rectum was not made for sex, it usually causes tearing and bleeding of the girl's rectum. Anal sex also can pass bacteria that are harmless in the rectum (because it is designed to handle them) to other areas of the body where they can cause terrible infections. I believe God did not make us to have anal intercourse.

"And that summarizes the kinds of things people can do between the time they first kiss and when they have intercourse. Sadly, some couples can experience almost all of these in one day, when they rush from a first kiss through touching to intercourse. A couple who would do that have totally trashed God's gift of their sexuality. Another couple may date for two years and only kiss before their wedding day, saving all touching and sharing of their bodies until their wedding day. Some couples date a long time before doing some touching, but go no further than light touching.

"Julie, your body is one of God's most miraculous gifts to you. He has given you the capacity to feel attraction, feel love, feel sexual excitement, get pregnant and bear children, to be a wife and mother. This is a great gift. Any good feelings you would get from enjoying intercourse or lots of sexual touching outside of marriage would not be worth your disappointing God and making it harder for you to experience all of the joys God wants for you in your marriage or your single life. I pray you will set the right standards for yourself and make the right choices. I would like you to pray and reflect on what I have said, and decide what your standards should be."

16

Solitary Sex:
Masturbation and Pornography

✛

MASTURBATION

The results of a recent poll of the readers of *Christianity Today* reflect the confusion that so many of us feel about the issue of masturbation. Among laypeople and clergy, almost exactly one-third of each group reported that they believe masturbation is wrong, one-third believe it is not wrong, and one-third believe "it depends."[1] This certainly makes our job in this chapter easier!

For some people, masturbation is an issue that generates tremendous emotional energy. But there is a sense in which real emotional heat about the masturbation issue seems misplaced. As one father recently said to us, "I just shake my head when I hear a parent agonize about masturbation. For goodness sake, kids are destroying their lives with AIDS, other diseases, pregnancy, and flat-out promiscuity. I would be delighted to know that my kid was handling his sexual needs by masturbating by himself four times a week in the privacy of his bedroom if I knew that this was keeping him off the streets and out of the back seat of the car on dates. What is the big deal?"

But our God seems to care for us so much that He is concerned about the details of our lives. And His vision for holiness in our lives extends down to the smallest of our actions and the most private and intimate of our thoughts. So we have no more warrant to dismiss this issue than we do to say, "Don't worry about a short temper and a foul mouth; after all, people are killing each other at a record pace out there. I'm just happy you aren't hurting anyone physically." But we must also keep this issue in its proper perspective.

The Realities

Masturbation is common, but perhaps not as common as the books about sexuality suggest. Stan once heard a speaker at a conference say "95 percent of men masturbate [note the present tense] and the other 5 percent are liars." His comment drew great laughter and applause. But the research here is biased by the same confusion of "regular practice" with "one-time occurrences" that biases the research about teenage sexual activity. A girl who lost her virginity in a date rape at age fifteen and has been abstinent since is often thrown into the percentage of kids who are called "sexually active" because she is a nonvirgin. The same is true about masturbation. The actual questionnaires that have inquired about masturbation usually ask, "Have you ever masturbated?" It is this type of question that generates the "95 percent of men" finding. While it may be likely that 95 percent of men have masturbated at least once, what the "average" man did in his adolescence and does now as an adult is not at all clear.

But there can be no disputing that masturbation in adolescence is common. It is beyond question that the majority of teenage boys masturbate at least occasionally. Masturbation has not been as widespread among girls, but has become more common in recent years. Many women in the older generations never heard or knew of the practice of female masturbation. But the discussion of masturbation in the media and in sex education classes, the greater awareness and knowledge of female sexuality today, and greater acceptance of women as having sexual desires have all led to more frequent practice of masturbation by girls today than in the past.

Arguments for the Acceptability of Masturbation

Masturbation seems to have few or no "negative side effects." It is common today for experts in the field of sexuality to believe that there are some positive benefits to the practice of masturbation. Some argue generally that masturbation is part of the normal process by which a child learns the pleasure his or her body can give, and hence learns to accept his or her own body. Masturbation in the teen years, it is suggested, continues that process.

There is some feeling that this may be especially true of women. Informal clinical research has suggested that women who masturbated as adolescents are more likely to be able to easily experience orgasm in their marital relationship, and that knowing and accepting the way their bodies feel sexual pleasure helps them to teach their husbands how to best please them. Additionally, some clinicians suggest that women who have never masturbated tend to have more negative views of their own sexuality and of sexual relations, more trouble accepting their own bodies, and more difficulty appropriately guiding their spouses to learn to give them pleasure.

But all of this "clinical wisdom" has to be taken with a grain of salt. The whole area of sexuality research is slanted by the liberal moral views of almost all of the leading scholars in this field. Also, many of the experts in this field seem to reduce the idea of sexual fulfillment to the question of who is having the most orgasms. Perhaps people who masturbate do have more and easier orgasms later in life, but what kinds of marriages do they have? How much true oneness do they experience with their spouses? What kind of people are they? Does the practice of masturbation influence one's values? What about the effect on one's thought life? The doubter might agree that people seem to be having more orgasms now, but ask if the exaltation of sexual satisfaction has improved our society. Perhaps we are encouraging a generation of sexual narcissists who, because of their preoccupation with pleasure for themselves, will be less capable of bonding and committing their lives to another, and will be less faithful sexually, with the resulting increase of sexual diseases, divorce, and so forth.

Some Christians argue for tolerance of masturbation on a very practical basis. "Masturbation," they say, "is a way to handle sexual urges and desires. If a kid gets 'sexual release' through masturbation, he will be less likely to press for sexual intimacies with the person he dates." The crucial issue in this argument is whether the practice of masturbation increases or decreases teen sexual acting out. Is masturbation a way of managing sexual tensions by oneself, or does it lead one to be more preoccupied with sex and hence more likely to push for more sexual experiences with others?

We are aware of only one argument that attempts to draw directly from the Scriptures to establish a basis for the acceptance of masturbation.[2] This author suggests that Leviticus 15:16-18 should set the tone for our dealing with masturbation. Verses 16 and 17 say that a man who has an emission of semen should wash and be ceremonially unclean until evening. Verse 18 goes on to say that if a man and woman have intercourse, the same cleanliness rules apply. By bringing up intercourse separately, the passage surely does imply that the emission of semen in verses 16 and 17 occurred for the man individually. The passage may be referring to a nocturnal emission or "wet dream" rather than masturbation, but the passage is not specific. This author suggests that this Leviticus passage is significant for treating a solitary sexual experience, whether wet dream or masturbation, as a purely ceremonial cleanliness issue and *not as a matter of morality*. The passage also puts no more disapproval on the solitary experience than it does on intercourse. Since Christians today commonly view the Old Testament ceremonial law as no longer valid, this author suggests that masturbation is not in itself a moral concern from a biblical perspective and is no longer a ceremonial concern either. It is neutral in itself, and can become immoral only if other elements, such as lust, are added to it.

Moral Objections to Masturbation

Stan has been teaching a course on human sexuality for over a decade, and has frequently asked students what reasons they have been given for masturbation being either moral or immoral. Interestingly, hardly anyone can report any discussions where the conclusion was that masturbation is morally acceptable. But many reasons have been given for the sinfulness of masturbation. We will briefly describe and discuss the most prominent of these arguments, in rough order from least persuasive to most persuasive, and thus come nearer to understanding the real issues that masturbation raises.

Masturbation is "onanism." The story that served as a biblical condemnation of masturbation for centuries in the church was the story of Onan in Genesis 38:1-10. According to Israelite law (Deuteronomy 25:5-10), after his brother died without leaving an heir, Onan was bound to have intercourse with his sister-in-law and impregnate her in order to continue his brother's name and family possession of their land. Onan had intercourse with her repeatedly, but "spilled his semen on the ground to keep from producing offspring for his brother" (Genesis 38:9). His reason for doing this is not clearly stated; perhaps he wanted the pleasure of the sexual relationship but none of the responsibilities of parenthood, or perhaps he greedily hoped to take his brother's land for his own and cheat his sister-in-law of her rights under Israel's law. In any case, God was displeased by what he did, and struck him dead.

The connection made between masturbation and interrupted intercourse was the "spilling of semen on the ground"; hence the labeling of masturbation as "onanism." When, in the ancient world, it was believed that the man's semen contained a whole embryonic child and that the woman was nothing but a fertile garden in which the tiny baby was planted, Onan's action of "spilling semen" was seen as tantamount to deliberately killing an unborn child. But now we know this is untrue. Onan violated a specific Hebrew law; he disobeyed God by not cooperating to get his sister-in-law pregnant. But there is no clear law against masturbation in the Old Testament. So, masturbation is not connected in any important way with the sin of Onan. There is general agreement today that this verse is irrelevant to the masturbation issue.

Pleasure, at least sexual pleasure, is bad. If pleasure in general or sexual pleasure particularly is bad, then masturbation is an indulgence of the sinful desires of the flesh, the body, for pleasure. But as we argued in chapter 6, Christians must view our capacity for sexual pleasure to be a gift from God. Is pleasure from our bodies a particular problem? If we say it is, we are going down the path of asceticism that Protestants have been so hesitant to embark upon. It is part of the Reformation heritage to reject the notion that sin resides in some special or greater way in our bodies. Rather, we are capable of sinning equally in all aspects of our persons: bodies, minds, wills, emotions, spirits, and so forth.

Masturbation leads to various dire consequences. Many stories abound in Christian circles about terrible consequences that can follow from masturbation—that it can destroy your health, drive you to insanity or deviancy, or cause you to go blind. Many Christians have heard about the idea of "compulsive" masturbation, and are afraid of this consequence in light of the Apostle Paul's admonition that we not use our freedom to become enslaved again to immorality (Galatians 5:1). First, we must acknowledge that there are no known negative consequences of masturbation; it doesn't cause any of the dreaded conditions that rumors suggest.

But what about the compulsive desire to masturbate? Stan met a friend while working on staff at a Christian camp who confessed to him in anguish and tears that he was hopelessly in bondage to masturbation. Yet he reported only masturbating once or twice a week. Could it be that the compulsion here, and with many people, was more of a *compulsion to stop* due to deep guilt feelings than it was a compulsion to continue masturbating? By analogy, it might be like a woman whose weight is normal and who feels normal desires for food, but who, in an excessive desire to look perfect physically, becomes obsessed with total extinction of all thoughts of food and all unnecessary eating. In such a case, which is abnormal: her normal pangs of hunger and occasional enjoyment of desserts, or her obsessive desire for perfect control of her appetite? It could be that for many boys, the guilt and anxiety they feel over their sexual desires and their occasional masturbation feed the drive to masturbate by making them feel more guilty and unacceptable.

There really is such a thing as compulsive masturbation. Stan has counseled several men who demonstrated true compulsive patterns, including one who masturbated at least three times, and up to six times, per day. Stan's feeling after working with several such men is that the problem was not so much the masturbation itself, but the deep personality problems they had, problems that would probably have resulted in some other addictive pattern of behavior if they had not happened to fix upon masturbation.

Masturbation is an act of homosexuality. We have encountered two forms of this argument. The first argues simply that masturbation is an act that homosexuals engage in and therefore must be wrong. The bad news for people who believe this argument is that people who are homosexual also kiss, hold hands, touch, and engage in a whole spectrum of sexual activities.

If heterosexuals are not supposed to do anything homosexuals do, then we heterosexuals are all in trouble.

The second version of this argument is a blatant example of convoluted reasoning: Masturbation is homosexual because when one masturbates, he is having sex with himself. Since each of us is the same gender as himself, then having sex with yourself is homosexual sex. Since homosexual sex is wrong, masturbation is wrong. This argument is so patently empty that we will go on to the next.

Masturbation is "unnatural." The traditional Roman Catholic view of masturbation as "unnatural" was based on the belief that "natural" sex occurred between a man and a woman and that each natural sexual act should have at least the possibility of procreating children. Since masturbation did not occur between a man and woman, it was often put in the same moral category as homosexual relations. This led to the curious tendency in the medieval penitential manuals for masturbation to be treated as a much more serious or mortal sin than was adultery or consorting with prostitutes, in that these sins were at least "natural." Something seems wrong with a view that treats masturbation as more heinous than adultery.

This argument also says that sex must have procreative potential to be moral, and since masturbation does not, it must be immoral. We would agree that sexual intercourse is meant to be intricately intertwined with our human potential for procreating children. But as we will argue in chapter 19, on contraception, this does not necessarily mean that every act of sexual intercourse or every sexual act (after all, kissing your spouse is a sexual act) needs to have the potential to beget children.

Masturbation is sexual immorality. As we noted in the last chapter, the Greek word *porneia* is often translated fornication or sexual immorality. Whatever *porneia* is, it is condemned in the Scriptures. The problem with saying that masturbation is one type of *porneia*, though, is that the precise meaning of the word is not clear. We must understand that minimally it means sexual intercourse outside of marriage. How much further it extends in its meaning is not clear. Many teens who go to summer camp feel immediately guilty about their experimentation with masturbation if the camp speaker singles out sexual immorality and impurity for condemnation. But does this guilt reaction necessarily mean that the guilt they feel is true guilt? Or are they merely being made to feel guilty for something that is morally neutral? After all, teens often feel generalized guilt about many things, and can easily be made to feel guilty about having any interest in the other sex at all. Our capacity to feel guilty is no perfect marker that we are truly guilty. Which leads rather naturally to the next argument.

Masturbation is not an act of faith. This argument goes as follows: There are clearly things that are right and virtuous, that God is proud of us doing. There are also acts that are wrong, that God condemns. And then there are acts in neither category: taking out the trash, paying a bill next month rather than this month, and so forth. The rule of conduct for the gray area, which some would call the arena of Christian freedom, is contained in Romans 14:23: "But the man who has doubts is condemned if he eats, because his eating is not from faith; and everything that does not come from faith is sin" (see also 14:14). All of our actions are meant to proceed from faith. How, the critic asks, can one consider masturbation to be an act of faith?

This is a powerful argument, and unlike the arguments to this point, we feel it contains a very important element of truth. But let us briefly explore two problems with it. First, as we stated above, our capacity to feel guilty is not a perfect index of right and wrong. Stan has counseled people from Christian homes who as adults struggle with profound guilt over many things that seem to require no such reaction. Whether it is guilt over saying no to demanding parents in order to give fully to one's spouse and children, the desire to be more creative in a marital sexual relationship, to be more comfortable with the naked body of a spouse, or to be able to express a strong opinion and disagree with a verbally abusive husband, there are many guilt reactions that seem misguided. A harsh application of this passage would say that the people who felt guilty for these things really were sinning, because they doubted what they felt led to do.

Second, this leaves us in a quandary about the objectivity of right and wrong. What if in response to this argument a teenager said, "Oh good! I feel no doubts at all about masturbation or oral sex, so I know that for me they are not a sin." Would we say the same thing to an adulterer who, after searing his conscience with repeated affairs (1 Timothy 4:2), said, "What I'm doing must be fine because I feel no doubts!" Certainly not! Scripture tells us clearly that the absence of guilt feelings by no means assures us that we are in the right. And reason guided by Scripture also tells us that people can feel lots of guilt for many things they have no scriptural reason to feel guilt about. The Holy Spirit does work through our consciences, but they are fallen instruments which themselves need to be redeemed through prayer and infusion of God's Word (1 Timothy 4:5).

Masturbation violates the intended meaning of sex. Our sexuality in general, and full sexual gratification particularly, is meant to be interpersonal, to be relational. It is meant to glue two people together, as we argued in chapter 10. Masturbation is solitary, and thus it must be seen as self-centered. And self-centered sex violates the intent of God that sex be loving, giving, and unifying. Therefore it is wrong. Further, when practiced regularly, masturbation may constitute training of oneself to be self-centered and thus less rather than more capable of truly giving to another.

This is a significant argument. But is it an argument that masturbation is immoral, or does it point rather to its incompleteness? Lewis Smedes

suggests that masturbation does fall short of what God inte
for our sexuality.[3] But it is part of our human condition to fa
fullness that God desires for us. Does the failure of the child t
full glory of our God-given rationality mean that the child's st
rationality is sinful? Does the husband's need to grow in his ability to love
his wife more sacrificially, or the new convert's need to manifest more of
the fruits of the Spirit, mean that his or her current state is *immoral*, or
is it simply incomplete? Smedes suggests that for most kids adolescent
masturbation is an incompleteness, a step of learning about oneself and of
handling the intense sexual urges of the teenage years. It is not all that God
wants for that child, but until he or she is married, it is a partial and neutral
experiencing of the gift of sexuality.

Masturbation involves lust. Jesus condemned lust (Matthew 5:28).
What are people doing when they masturbate but committing adultery in
their heart? Is the teenage boy masturbating to the fantasy of having sex with
a girl he is dating cultivating the purity of heart and intent that God desires?
Can the person fantasizing immoral encounters and staring at pictures in
pornographic magazines while masturbating be acting in faith? This is perhaps the most significant argument against the morality of masturbation.
But even here there are issues to discuss.

If one can trust the "research" on this issue, it appears that men almost
always use vivid and arousing sexual mental images to accompany their
masturbation. Women, on the other hand, do not do so as frequently. When
women masturbate, they often simply touch themselves because it feels
good. Much of a woman's fantasy, when she does fantasize, tends to be
vague thoughts of romance with the man she loves. Is a man's vivid fantasy
lust, but not a woman's?

Judging whether or not masturbation always involves lust forces us
back again to our definition of lust (chapter 15). If all sexual desire is
lust, then masturbation without lust would be a virtual impossibility. But if
one accepts a "tighter" or more restricted definition of lust, then it may be
possible to conceive of masturbation without lust. But even a fairly "tight"
definition of lust would still lead us to judge masturbation, especially as
practiced by most males, as often involving lust.

What to Tell Our Children

Can we be honest? We are confused about the morality of masturbation.
After musing about it for years, we can neither regard it as an unquestionably
and intrinsically evil act, nor as a blessing from God which we were meant
to enjoy with clear consciences. We would fall in the decisive third of the
Christianity Today group who said, "It all depends."

What does the morality of masturbation depend upon? The worst kinds
of masturbation would seem to us to be those that cultivate a heart of selfish

preoccupation with *my* pleasure, those that involve fantasy about clearly immoral and degrading acts with others, those that channel one's energies away from loving relationships with others, those that make one more rather than less preoccupied with sex, those that drive a wedge between the person and God by becoming a focus of guilt and shame. The least questionable kinds of masturbation would seem to be those that are a phase in adolescence rather than a life practice, those that do not use mental images of immoral acts, those that somehow contribute to the person maintaining his resolve to stay chaste, those that contribute to the person's positive appreciation of her body and sexuality as a gift from God, and those that help the person positively anticipate his eventual sexual union with a spouse in marriage.

It would seem that masturbation is not itself lust, but it certainly can involve lust. And we should actively urge our children not to cultivate a habit of lust.

Masturbation is not the fullness God desires. But perhaps in a sexually saturated and overstimulated world, it may be an expedient way for the teen to cope with his sexual urges along the way to becoming a person.

There is probably more suffering caused in Christian circles by over-reactions to masturbation than there is by the practice itself. Many people, men especially, who have grown up in the conservative Christian church have been deeply scarred and hurt by overly zealous crusades against masturbation. At summer camps, masturbation is too often the easiest subject on which the preacher can stir up guilt and thus generate more seemingly sincere conversions and rededications. It can take a long time to heal from such guilt, especially when one struggles for years about whether the guilt was legitimate in the first place.

Perhaps in trying to formulate one key message to give to our young adolescents, we can do no better than to quote James Dobson, who addressed this issue speaking to young teenagers: "It is my opinion that masturbation is not much of an issue with God. It's a normal part of adolescence, which involves no one else. It does not cause disease, it does not produce babies, and Jesus did not mention it in the Bible. I'm not telling you to masturbate, and I hope you won't feel the need for it. But if you do, it is my opinion that you should not struggle with guilt over it."[4]

EROTICA AND PORNOGRAPHY

Americans live in a society immersed in eroticism. Think back one hundred years, before the advent of television and movies, when photography was primitive and not easily distributed. In the premodern world, erotic images existed, as nude paintings and sexually explicit sculpture show, but they were typically uncommon. In contrast, today we are bombarded with sexual images on television, in movies, in glossy photographs in magazines, and so forth.

Not all images of the human body are erotic. Many cultures are less modest than our Christian subculture in America, but all cultures have modesty standards. Some cultures come quite close to approving almost total nudity and openness about such bodily functions as urination. But all cultures define certain parts of the body and certain actions as indiscreet, and it is the depiction of actions that go beyond those standards of modesty that often are seen as erotic.

It is common today to make a distinction between the erotic and the pornographic. We might best think of the erotic as that which is designed to stimulate sexual interest and excitement. The United States Supreme Court has defined pornography, on the other hand, as material that meets three standards: it has no artistic merit, appeals to a "prurient" (wanton or excessive) interest in sex, and violates community standards of decency. The material must meet all three standards to be classed as pornography, and all three standards are difficult to establish in a court of law. We might think of erotica as a very large circle, and pornography as a much smaller circle inside the larger circle; all pornography is erotica, but *legally* not all erotica is pornography. Many Christians may be surprised to learn that what they consider to be pornography, explicit pictures of nude bodies in *Playboy* or *Penthouse*, or even explicit pictures of sexual intercourse in "harder-core" magazines, is not legally pornography but rather erotica. The circle of material that can be classified legally as pornography has been shrinking steadily, while there has been an explosion of the availability of erotic materials.

In this book, we have used the term *pornography* to refer to all of the types of sexually explicit materials that most Christians would regard to be morally offensive. We are thus using the term in a way that lawyers and many sexual libertarians would view as too broad and repressive.

Most popular sex education books take a very neutral and permissive stance toward sexually explicit materials. For example, one popular book stated: "When parents come across this kind of thing, what should they do? Nothing. What harm can the pictures do if they are looked at in private?"[5] This is a good example of the privacy dimension of our modern sexual ethic (chapter 11). Sex, it is implied, can only be wrong when another person is directly harmed, while anything that occurs in private must be morally neutral. We feel this is utterly unacceptable for Christians, for reasons we will develop below.

Many parents are very naive about the kinds of sexual materials that are popularly available. When we think of pornography, we often think of the frontal nudity of *Playboy* pinups or "naughty" gas-station calendars of days gone by. But the material that is popularly available today goes beyond what many from earlier generations could even conceive. Depictions of such sexual acts as group sex, homosexual practices, rape, the infliction of pain and torture (especially on women), and the sexual victimization of children are all common.

And make no mistake—pornography is widely available to children. In our local schools, it is common for children as young as first grade to be exposed to pornography on the playgrounds as older kids bring the materials to school from home. The advent of cable and video players in our homes makes a wide array of sexually explicit movies and programs only a button-push away from our kids.

Is It Wrong?

We Christian parents should forbid our children from using pornography, and we should do our best to shape our children to utterly reject its usage when they are no longer under our control. We have several fundamental concerns:

First, pornography universally depicts immoral acts. There is no market for pictures and images of married couples lovingly meeting each other's needs in mutual tenderness and submission. Immoral and degrading sexual acts are presented in pornography in such a way as to make them seem thrilling and alluring. These immoral acts are powerfully imprinted on our minds. People appear to remember most vividly any images they see when they are emotionally aroused. Pornographic images arouse sexual desire, especially in men who are more visually oriented than women, and thus are vividly remembered. Kids digesting pornography are filling their minds with immorality, and the images can be indelible. At a time in life when it is vital to be filling the teenage mind with what is good and true and holy (Philippians 4:8-9), pornography programs it with what is evil and false and dirty.

Second, pornography presents people's bodies in ways that are likely to result in harmful comparisons with our married partners. Pornography presents idealized bodies doing fantasized acts under ideal conditions of lighting and makeup, with the resulting pictures touched up to remove any final flaws. How can a real marital relationship with a real person under the normal demanding and distracting conditions of life stand up to comparisons with such depictions? In reality, loving marital sex is better than pornographic sex, because it fulfills the intimacy goals that God built into us. But as couples are trying to develop their relationships, comparisons with idealized physical acts (that ignore real relationship) can be devastating. Taking these first two points together, we can say that pornography is likely to undermine a Christian view of marriage and of sex.

Third, pornography almost universally presents a degrading view of women. At the minimum, pornography presents women's bodies as passive objects of the sexual desire of men. Women's bodies are violently torn from the totality of who they are as a person, and made to stand apart as objects of lust. Pornography that presents women as the objects of violence, degradation, and torture are particularly repulsive. Given that so much pornography is of this kind, is it any wonder that scientific studies are suggesting a possible connection of the viewing of this type of pornography with the victimization of women? One study, for instance, found that men who viewed even a few hours of violent pornographic movies were more likely to believe statements like "Women who are raped really enjoy it" or " Many women secretly want to be raped" and were even more likely to agree with a statement saying that they would commit a rape if they were certain they would not be caught![6] It is likely that pornography contributes to the victimization of women.

What Should We Do?
First, we should anticipate that our children will be exposed to pornography, and we should attempt to inoculate them against this. In the spirit of chapter 11, we should help them avoid such contact by discussing the kinds of temptations that will come their way, and then helping them to build up some immunity to these temptations by developing solid reasons and strengths to avoid it. Perhaps a dialogue could go something like the following. This conversation should probably take place well before the teen years.

> **PARENT:** "Travis, have you ever heard the kids at school talking about looking at dirty magazines or movies that show people having sex?"
> **CHILD:** "Yeah, there are a couple of guys who have a lot of those magazines, and a lot of kids watch R-rated movies at home on cable. Some have even seen really dirty movies that their parents have on video."
> **PARENT:** "What do you think about that?" (a risky question that puts the teenager on the spot, because he knows the parents disapprove)
> **CHILD:** "Oh, I don't know; I don't think about it very much."
> **PARENT:** "Let me share some of my thoughts on stuff like that with you. I would really like to hear your thoughts and answer your questions if you have some. It is completely normal for men to be interested in women's bodies, and to find women sexually attractive. It's normal to really want to look and to feel excited. But I think pornography can't be right and it can't be good for you.
>
> "First, do you think sex was something that was meant to happen between strangers without real love, or between a husband and wife who truly love each other? (Married people, of course.)

I agree. Sex in marriage is great fun, *and* it helps your love grow stronger as you live out your lives together. But pornography usually depicts sex between people who really don't know each other, between people who aren't married. That's the way animals have sex; it's not what God meant for people. Pornography is also unrealistic; it shows people acting like they are really having a great time when the actors are probably lonely and unhappy people, and it shows women who do nothing with their time but make their bodies look good. What is even worse is that pornography usually makes the person watching interested in sex, especially in thinking in his mind about having sex with the woman he is looking at. Can you see how a kid who looks at pornography is being led to thinking about sex with a stranger, sex without love or commitment? If a young man sees a lot of pornography, he is filling his mind with pictures and desires for sex with strangers. He is also filling his mind with images of experiences he never has had, and that can make him more unhappy with where he is in life. Last, I think pornography degrades women."

CHILD: "What does that mean? My friends say it makes them look beautiful."

PARENT: "Maybe physically beautiful, but not beautiful as a person. A woman is beautiful only as a whole person when you appreciate all of her. When you focus only on her body parts and don't think of her the way God thinks of her, as a person with a body but also with a mind and emotions and dreams and thoughts and beliefs and relationships, when you make a picture of her that says she is there to be used as a thing to lust after for the men who buy the magazine or look at the movie, then you are making her into a thing, an object. And that, I believe, is wrong. For all these reasons and more, I urge you to resist the temptation to look at pornography. It will be hard when the guys say it is great and call you names if you don't. But by being strong, you will be pleasing God and making your chances better of having a beautiful and exciting and loving sexual relationship with your wife someday. And when they tell you that you're missing out, you'll know they are getting some thrills sinning now, but they are really hurting themselves and hurting God by what they are doing."

Second, we should do what we can to purify the environment our children live in. Cancel cable channels that broadcast questionable shows and movies. We also have to manage carefully their exposure to children's programming, as it is becoming increasingly common for very unsavory previews to be shown during commercial breaks in kids' shows. There are a number of books around that can give parents ideas about how to gain control of the television viewing habits of their children.[7]

We must be very careful of our response if we discover our child has or is using pornography. If this happens, we must not overreact and tear down our child's character. As in the previous dialogue, we must remember to affirm that curiosity and sexual interest are normal. We should make the issue the unacceptability of the pornography itself, of the values portrayed and the meaning of the messages presented. We can also deal with it as a matter of personal respect for the views of the parents.

If you as a parent are especially concerned about the problem of pornography and feel moved to do something to make it less available in your community, we would suggest that you obtain a copy of the 1986 *Final Report of the Attorney General's Commission on Pornography*, which contains a number of "Suggestions for Citizen and Community Action."[8] Even a brief discussion of this enormous issue is beyond our resources in this chapter.

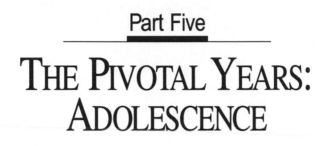

Part Five

THE PIVOTAL YEARS: ADOLESCENCE

17

Supporting the Adolescent

❖

I n this chapter, we will present a smorgasbord of ideas of how you can support your teenager in living a sexually pure life. For this chapter, we have in mind kids who have entered high school or begun dating, whichever comes first.

LESSONS FROM THE PREVENTION OF SMOKING

Recent research has suggested that certain types of programs have been effective in preventing kids from taking up smoking. Your kids have probably been through such programs in school, though you might not have been aware of the rigorous research behind these programs. Remember when your kids came home talking of graphic pictures of lungs black with tar, or wearing badges announcing that they were never going to smoke? They may have been part of a research study!

The most effective programs have tended to use certain types of interventions with children and adolescents.[1] We have written the whole book with this research in mind, but feel this chapter is the place to bring it all together.

Peer Pressure Resistance Training

Kids need confidence to be able to say no in a dating situation. As we said in chapters 4 and 12, being able to say no is a skill that has to be built up and encouraged, principally through practice. Do we want our kids to get that practice "on the job" (on a date trying to fend off an attack by their date) or would we prefer that they get some practice beforehand? We can't answer for you, but we would prefer the practice come before the on-the-job training. Psychologists and educators have developed techniques called "role playing" or "behavior skills training" to provide such training. These techniques basically amount to having kids watch others show them practical ways to handle tough situations, having them pretend they are in those tough situations and practicing their own responses, and getting some coaching on how they could do better on their responses.

Parents can do a lot to prepare their kids to resist peer pressure for sex. Most importantly, we can help them bring to adolescence a lifelong pattern of having been encouraged for speaking their minds and standing up for what they believe. Are we building up the strength of our kids as we lead them toward the teen years? Or are we chipping away at that strength by demeaning their ability to stand up for what they believe, criticizing them as "mouthy" or "uppity" when they assert themselves, and robbing them of any opportunity to think for themselves by always telling them what to do?

We feel that the actual process of practicing how to handle sexual advances and pressure is best handled in a peer context and not with parents. A church youth group would be an ideal place for this to occur. There are excellent resources out there to support such work in your church. David Lynn and Mike Yaconelli have put together some very fine exercises in resisting peer pressure in the context of a general youth curriculum on sexuality in *Teaching the Truth About Sex*.[2] Josh McDowell's "Why Wait?" curriculum includes a booklet, *How to Help Your Child Say "No" to Sexual Pressure*, that can be used in church youth groups to do peer resistance training.[3] Colleen Kelly Mast and her associates at Project Respect have produced impressive abstinence-oriented sex education materials for Catholic, Protestant, and nonreligious settings that include healthy exercises in resisting peer and media pressure to engage in premarital sex.[4] Despite their many other flaws, Planned Parenthood has some excellent material in booklet form about resisting peer pressure that can be obtained with a phone call to your local chapter. Perhaps you should be the one to encourage the development of such a program in your church. If your church cannot support your child well in this area, you should do your best to help. Here are some ideas:

Several elements are important in encouraging an adolescent to be able to say no.[5] First, encourage her to be able to simply say no and to keep repeating her commitment to no. She doesn't have to give reasons or justify her decisions to her date or anyone else. She can learn to say, "No, I don't do that. No, I am not going to change my mind and I don't have to give you a reason. No, I don't wish to discuss my reasons. My answer is no," and so forth.

Next, the young woman, instead of being a somewhat passive victim of peer pressure, can be encouraged to reverse the pressure. She can be taught to say things like, "Why do you keep pressuring me? Are you trying to make me do something against my will? Why do you keep pressuring me when I've told you no? Why do you think what you want is more important than what I want? Don't you think I have the right to say no? Don't you respect me enough to take a no as *no*?"

It can also be helpful to encourage teens to express their anger or frustration when they are pressured. "I'm getting angrier and angrier—you keep ignoring what I'm saying. You're trying to manipulate me and I don't like it and I am not going to do it! You keep pressuring me to do something that I have clearly said I don't want to do. That means you don't respect me and that makes me angry."

We must not suggest that our children simply stop at saying no, however. We must prepare them to rescue themselves from a bad situation. "That's it. I demand that you take me home right now. If you don't, I and my parents will make sure that your parents know just how you're acting." Help your daughter by giving her a threat she can use to regain control, such as, "If you do anything more, my father and mother will take me to the police station to file charges of criminal sexual assault against you. My father has sworn that anyone who pressures me to do what I don't want to do will go to jail!"

Information About Negative Consequences

Kids who get a rich amount of information about all of the bad things smoking can do to them are less likely to smoke. The more vibrant and powerful the information, the more powerful the effect; for instance, telling kids the bad things smoking does to your lungs is less effective than telling them and showing them clear pictures of lung damage, and pictures are probably less effective than bringing in a slice of "black-tar lung" to show them.

We will remind you below of the many negative consequences of sex outside of marriage. But don't just tell your kids about these consequences; help them to *see* them for themselves. Can your youth group host several unwed mothers to talk about the incredible changes and difficulty of their lives due to their unexpected motherhood? Can you find a Christian college student or young adult who was not sexually abstinent as a teenager and who can make a convincing case that he or she would have been better off to remain chaste, or perhaps use some of the good video material available on this topic?[6] Can the youth group host a talk by a person in his or her thirties who had hoped to have children but cannot because of the scarring of sexually transmitted diseases? What about a person dying of AIDS?

Teenagers can be affected by clear presentations of the negative results of sexual experimentation. We should help them by helping them to hear the truth.

Making a Public Commitment to Abstinence
The research has shown that kids who publicly announce to others that "I will never smoke" are less likely to take up smoking than kids who do not make such a public commitment. This is an interesting parallel to the practice in most of our Christian traditions of having new converts to the faith make a public proclamation of their new faith in Christ. We feel this principle may be of such importance that we have devoted the whole of the next chapter to it.

Correcting Misperceptions and Using Older Respected Peer Models
The smoking prevention research has shown that it helps to correct the inflated sense that many kids have that "everyone is smoking." One powerful way to do this is to show them living models whom they can respect who have made the choice not to smoke. Our problem in applying this principle to sex is that a whole lot more kids are having sex than are smoking. Sexual experimentation is continuing to go up; about two-thirds of high school upperclassmen can be accurately described as "sexually active."

It is vital for us to remember that for teens, as for adults, the cold statistics do not matter as much as the personal realities we surround ourselves with. For most of us, cold numbers like "fewer than 32 percent of adults take biblical authority seriously today" make little impact on us *if* we are surrounded by a few fellow believers who take biblical authority as seriously as we do. Three living people we respect who believe as we do can outweigh all the percentages and ratios in the world. After all, under pressure we can remember and be inspired by people much more than by numbers. The same is true in the area of sex: By surrounding them with people who believe as they do, we enable our teens not to feel alone in their pursuit of chastity. The statistics do matter; telling them that "If only 20 percent of teens remain chaste, that still means that 20 percent of 20 million, that is, 4 million teens, are fighting the same battle you are—you're in good company!" may make a big impact. But we would guess that abstract statistics can never have the impact of a peer group that is committed to the same standards as your child.

We should try to draw on older teens and young adults who can serve as role models for our teens. Speakers in youth groups, older teens who can disciple our children, movies that depict the meaningful pursuit of purity, all of these and more can be ways of giving our kids good models to follow and of reducing their feelings of being alone in their battles.

Discussing Family Influences

Kids in smoking prevention programs may come from homes where parents, siblings, and/or relatives smoke. In these programs, kids are encouraged to talk about how their own families may make it harder for them not to smoke, and what can be done to protect themselves from bad influences within their own family.

Any parent who cares enough about chastity to read this book is not likely to be a discouragement to his or her child trying to live an abstinent life. But there may be other influences that will make it tough on your kids. Families in which one of the parents does not believe in Christian sexual morality are common. If you are a single parent, how do your own dating standards or that of your ex-spouse stand as a model and encouragement for your teenager? Are there aunts and uncles or other members of the family whose example could erode the encouragement you are trying to give to your teen? These realities need to be discussed openly with the adolescent, along with ways to prevent these forces from undermining the foundation you have built as a parent.

Inoculation Against Negative Messages

Kids who learn early that tobacco companies want them to believe that smokers have more fun, are more suave, and are more beautiful, and learn that these messages are *utterly false*, are in a better position to resist those messages when they hear them. (See chapter 11 on inoculation.)

PROVIDING SUPPORT

During the adolescent years, parents are not as likely to feel that they are having fruitful times of teaching their teenager. We are more likely to be met with cool indifference or bored impatience. During this period, if we have built the proper foundation, our major role is to give strength to our child by being available and being a listening ear, an askable resource, an affirming voice, a source of affection, and a fair, firm, but compassionate limit-setter. The time has come for the teen to choose to live by the lessons we have taught. We help the teen make and live by those choices by providing the kind of supports we discussed as an element of character in chapters 3 and 4.

Affection is the cornerstone of our relationship with a teenager. However, expressing affection with teenagers can be a challenge. They are often disgusted by the idea of public displays of affection—forget a goodbye kiss at the curb in front of school! Even so, we must not be discouraged, and must continue to give them the love that we know they need. Be sure not to stop touching and being physically affectionate with your teens. Even when they are standoffish and difficult, a pat on the back, a shoulder rub, a quick hug, or a kiss on the cheek can all be vitally important.

As parents, we need to be constantly aware of what our kids really need—relatedness and significance, acceptance and purpose. We must continue to let them know how those needs can be met genuinely, rather than in a counterfeit fashion through sex. The parent can no longer fill up their needs—they are meant to go beyond the family to have their needs met now. But you can guide them as they try to get those needs met, and you can take the edge off of their needs enough to allow them to make good choices. As a full grocery shopper makes better decisions in the store than a famished one, so too your children will make better decisions if their needs are at least partially met by you than if they're famished. Your affection and acceptance, your encouragement about the significance of their life in God's eyes and yours, can send them into the world strong rather than weakened. If their need for love and affection, and for meaning and significance, are insufficiently met, those needs will be more likely to overwhelm their moral commitments.

We can help meet their needs for significance by being as lavish with *praise and encouragement* as possible. What can we find in their schoolwork to praise them for? Forget their grades! Sit down with them and read the essays they wrote for a test or the paper they composed and find things to praise about their insights and knowledge. Affirm the skills they are developing, whether they are in calculus class or auto mechanics. Praise their diligence in their part-time jobs. Praise any initiative or self-discipline they show. Affirm any signs of sensitivity to friends. As we do this, we will have to endure their teenage mood swings. We just have to tolerate and love them through those moods, continuing to find ways to praise them.

We must not give up on teaching our children, but now we must think much more about *teaching through our personal example* rather than lecturing. Whereas our teenagers may be unwilling to listen to us sermonize, they may be open to us as we share from personal experience. By sharing about our own triumphs and struggles in adolescence and young adulthood, we not only continue to instruct them about our views, but we also show them that we have struggled with similar issues, too. We know what it is like to have the feelings they are experiencing. We may also give them better skills in expressing their own struggles, as our talking gives them words to describe some of what they are going through. Can you tell them about times when you were lonely, pressured, tempted, content, in love, confused, or hurt? Showing that you have experienced some of what they are going through can build the bond between you.

In chapter 12 we discussed how teens' personal faith has a powerful influence on their sexual choices. We urge you again to do everything possible to *encourage their religious faith*. Pray for them diligently (as if you aren't already!). Continue to share about your own faith and walk with God in the home. Be willing to sacrifice time, energy, and money to boost their faith. Be a youth-group sponsor if needed, offer your home as a meeting place for the group, sacrifice to support your children's desire to go to a church camp or youth rally. Be as creative as you can in supporting their continuing development as Christians. By supporting their involvement in church, you are also helping them to form their peer group in a way likely to encourage their sexual purity.

Finally, we can support our adolescent by providing *reasonable but firm limits.* Family rules such as curfews, regular chores and family responsibilities, and restrictions on the kinds of activities he or she can be involved in are vital for the teenager. These supportive structures can give the teen a sense of safety. What makes our job as parents so difficult on this point is that our kids rarely praise us for providing such structures. Instead they fight against and complain about the limits. But it is one of the fundamental rules of parenting adolescents that such limits are good for them even if they don't know it! We should discuss with other parents what limits are reasonable. Limits also can provide "a way out" for our kid. Brenna found that one comforting thing her parents did during her adolescence was to have reasonable rules about her activities. And they explicitly told her that if she was ever in a situation where she was unsure or uncomfortable, that she would be wise to get out of that situation, using her parents' "unreasonable rules" as her alibi. She used this excuse on more than one occasion.

HOW ADOLESCENTS THINK ABOUT MORALITY

School-based sex education programs are failing. Roughly 80 percent of school districts in the United States offer some instruction on sex-related topics, mostly through classroom-based programs. Data from numerous sources suggest that these education programs do not lead to changes in adolescent sexual behavior; they do not reduce the frequency of "unsafe sexual intercourse or lower adolescent pregnancy rates."[7]

There are undoubtedly many reasons for this failure. Schools cannot be expected to reverse powerful social and moral changes in our country with a few hours of curriculum. The breakdown of the family will have a tremendous effect that no set of classes can heal. But a big part of the ineffectiveness of sex education is that it seems premised upon a profound overestimation of the moral reasoning ability of teenagers and a naive belief that sexual decisions are mostly made rationally. The common assumption is that teens can reason through sexual decision making on a purely rational basis if they have all the proper facts. Sex education in the public schools then, at its worst, throws an array of values and a smattering of facts at our kids, and then trusts their basic rationality in making the most informed reasonable decision based upon what they have heard. But teens often are not rational in their behavioral choices (adults often are not either). There is abundant research to suggest that teenagers are even less equipped than adults to reason well about difficult moral choices. An expert in adolescent sexual behavior was recently reported as concluding that "students didn't really change their behavior—even when they knew all the dangers."[8]

We would like to summarize briefly the evidence that such a simplistic trust in the rationality of adolescent decision making is misguided. If this is true, then the manner in which contemporary sex education is commonly taught could actually be destructive to adolescent moral reasoning.

Moral Development of the Teenager

Public school sex education is usually targeted at giving kids lots of facts and different values. Then teachers urge the kids to choose what they will do based on their evaluation of all they have heard *in light of certain universal values such as what is responsible, respectful, loving, or mature.* There is a small problem with this: The most widely accepted theory of moral development basically says that adolescents cannot think that way.

The moral development theory of Lawrence Kohlberg has been widely criticized and has many deficits, but it is still the most widely used theory.[9] Kohlberg suggests that we progress through a predictable series of styles of thinking about moral issues. At the most primitive childish level (stage 1), we have what might be called a punishment orientation to moral *rules.* Young children obey rules in order to avoid punishment. At this stage, if we ask a child why lying is bad, he or she is likely to respond, "Because Mommy will spank me if I lie." Children then progress to what is called a reward orientation (stage 2); they are likely to look at moral decisions as opportunities to be rewarded for good behavior. If asked why it is good not to hit other children, they are likely to talk about obtaining a reward or prize for being good.

Kohlberg's next stage is essentially that of being a "good boy or bad boy" (stage 3). The child at this stage conforms to moral *rules* in order to avoid the disapproval of other people. If asked why he or she shouldn't steal, the elementary school child is likely to say that nobody likes a thief and that nobody would be your friend if you engage in such behavior. If moral development continues, the person proceeds to an orientation of obedience to the rules of authority (parents, the state, or God) (stage 4). People are likely to justify their moral decisions by appealing to socially accepted rules and generally shared concepts of morality: "Premarital sex is bad because God and the Church say so."

Kohlberg proposes two additional stages. The fifth stage is a "social contract orientation" in which a person makes more individually based decisions rooted in the *principles* that *the person* feels are essential to living in community. Kohlberg proposes the highest, the sixth, stage of ethical reasoning to be that of "ethical principle." At the ethical principle stage, a person would internalize an abstract ethical *principle* such as justice, dignity, or equality, and make his or her own individual moral decisions on the basis of that principle regardless of what the community does.

Note first that stages 1 through 4 involve making moral decisions by rules. What changes with development is the reasoning that supports the rules. In the last two stages the rules disappear and are replaced by principles people embrace essentially on their own. In other words, the person makes up his or her own rules. Now, we think Kohlberg is profoundly wrong in many ways, and many of you may be objecting to this scheme as you read this. But assume Kohlberg was right. If he was right, *then sex education must be tailored to where kids are in their moral development.*

And therein lies the rub! Little evidence has emerged over time that stage 6 even exists, and it is abundantly clear that very few adults ever reach stage 5. Teenagers almost never reach stages 5 or 6. Paradoxically, however, most of the sex education that goes on in our public schools seems targeted at people in stages 5 or 6. Children are taught that there are no rules, no moral absolutes, with regard to sexuality, and that only general principles such as love, respect, and not hurting others should guide their decisions about sex. *In short, we are attempting to teach our children to reason morally in a fashion in which research has suggested that hardly anyone reasons.* If the majority of adults are at either stage 3 or stage 4, our sex education programs are doing terrific damage to our children by completely missing where they are in terms of their moral development.

To make matters worse, one of Kohlberg's most famous students found that adolescent moral reasoning is consistently less well developed in thinking about sex than in other areas of moral thinking.[10] In other words, adolescents reason at a more primitive and undeveloped way when thinking about sexuality than they do about such issues as honesty, violence, and so forth. Thus, the main effect of public sex education may be to erode our kid's confidence in moral rules about sex, but it may fail to replace those rules with anything that serves as a true moral guide for the child.

How Does Moral Thinking Relate to Moral Action?

A developmental psychologist recently reviewed the research on the relationship between moral judgment or reasoning (what people say about their thinking on morality) and moral action (how they act).[11] There was a very close relationship between how young children and mature adults talk about their moral decisions and what they actually do. But there was a much less powerful relationship between how adolescents talk and what they actually do. There is not a strong relationship between the moral talk and the moral walk of the teenager (ages twelve to seventeen). Why might this be? There are numerous possibilities.

First, adolescents may be so caught up in their developing capacities for thinking more freely and creatively about possibilities that their capacity to think far outstrips their wisdom and decision making. In other words, adolescents may be better at "playing mental games" than they are at making good decisions. For example, an adolescent girl going through a public school sex education class can grasp for the first time all the abstract possibilities of a sexual relationship that embodies "equality, mutuality, maturity, and respect" but be much less able to realistically judge the future consequences of her choices (pregnancy, sexually transmitted diseases, and emotional damage). Another possible reason for this finding may have to do with the way adolescents form their adult identities by distancing themselves from the beliefs and opinions their parents have expressed. While the teen is establishing her own identity, there may be a gap between what she says (which tends to be what she has been told) and what she chooses to do.

If there is a loose relationship between moral reasoning and moral action in adolescents, we cannot count on the enhanced moral reasoning which is supposedly facilitated by "values-neutral" public school education curricula to serve as a significant preventative force against teenage sexual experimentation. The forces that push in the direction of permissiveness are too powerful; only moral absolutes backed up by strength of character on the inside and supportive community standards on the outside can protect our children against the ravages of sexual permissiveness during adolescence.

Why Do Adolescents Take Risks?

Why do adolescents decide to engage in what seems to adults to be very risky behavior? A number of different hypotheses have been advanced.[12] One possibility is that adolescents lack information on the risks involved in the actions that they choose. Another is that the real problem is not in adolescent decision making but in their ability to resist peer pressure. Both of these hypotheses may be partially true.

But research has suggested that several other powerful factors encourage risk taking. First, it appears that adolescents do not make their decisions according to the same values that adults regard as important. A recent study provided a good illustration of this. A sizable sample of sexually active fourteen- to nineteen-year-olds was surveyed about why they would or would not use condoms. Adults might (reasonably) expect that adolescents would think about reducing the risk of teenage pregnancy and of spreading sexually transmitted diseases in choosing whether or not to use condoms. The researchers, however, found these reasons to have absolutely no effect on teenage condom use. Instead, the beliefs that were associated with condom use were that condoms are easy to use, that condoms are popular with peers, and that having condoms at hand facilitates spontaneous sex with a partner.[13] The teens were making decisions by different rules than the adults expected. This study would suggest that teens are not likely to use condoms for the reasons that Planned Parenthood promotes in secular sex education. We need to know and shape the values by which our kids make decisions.

Also, to make good decisions about risks, teens have to make good judgments about the chances of getting hurt. But they are weak here as well. They greatly underestimate the chances of their experiencing negative consequences to their risky decisions.[14] For example, college students underestimated the risks of being in a car accident after drinking heavily; the actual risk was twelve times that which the college students guessed.

Finally, there is evidence that adolescents have difficulty paying attention to possible consequences of their actions that are vague or that might occur in the distant future. The further away the consequence, the less likely adolescents are to take it into account. Adults have this problem as well, but it is exaggerated in teens. This pattern has its worst effects in the area of sex. All of the "benefits" of engaging in sexual activity (being "cool," physical pleasure, and so forth) are concrete, clear, and immediate, while all of the negatives (violating God's law, possible pregnancy, possible sexual disease, and so forth) are abstract, long-term, and only probable (but not certain). The negatives of using contraception are also immediate and concrete—awkwardness, discomfort, embarrassment. Immediate and concrete consequences are more powerful than long-range and "probable" results for all of us, but especially for adolescents. It is for this reason that researchers have questioned whether adolescents are really capable of being rational about their sexual choices at all.[15] If rationality involves, at a minimum, a careful balancing of long-term and short-term risks and rewards, adolescents are at a disadvantage in making rational decisions about their sexuality.

What Can We Parents Do to Improve Our Adolescents' Decision Making?

Because their thinking tends to be influenced most by visible examples, teenage friends who engage in sex without using birth control and who don't become pregnant are much more powerful influences than a hypothetical discussion in class about "the percentages of girls that become pregnant within a year of initiating sexual activity." We as parents and churches have to try to "even the score." We must strive to make the long-term and intangible consequences more obvious and powerful by showing those consequences to our children. One way to do this is to make sure they see examples of the difficulties and devastations of pregnancy and disease. Instead of shielding our children from seeing examples of pregnancy and disease, we should make sure they see such examples.

Another way to encourage greater teenage rationality is to walk your adolescent through the consequences of sexual activity and pregnancy. We can ask our child how his or her friends would respond if he or she got a sexual disease. We can follow this by these sorts of questions: "What would you look for to know that you had the disease? How would you make a doctor's appointment? How would you pay for the doctor's appointment? How would you eventually handle telling the person you were going to marry that you had had a sexual disease? How would you handle the possibility of never being able to have children from having the sexually transmitted disease?"

We can ask our kids some of the same questions about pregnancy.[16] We can say, "I want to help you think through what teen pregnancy would be like, so that you can understand the consequences for yourself and anyone else you know who happens to get pregnant." We can then follow with questions of how they think their life might change if they did get pregnant? We can add and flesh out their responses. We can ask, "How would having a baby affect your going out with your friends? How would it affect your finishing school? How much do you think it costs to raise a baby? What kind of job would you need to get in order to adequately care for your baby? If you had to work to support your baby, how would you be able to spend enough time with it to give it the love and care that it needs? How old do you think the baby would be when you will have graduated from college?" These and other questions like them can be a way of making the hypothetical quite concrete.

Finally, we must continue to emphasize the enduring value of God's rules for our lives and the lives of our children. Christians believe in a God who is perfect, loving, and just; a God who has chosen to reveal to us how we are meant to live. His laws are based on the true love and perfect justice that only He can perfectly embody. But we cannot throw out His laws and live by the abstract principles of love and justice; to do so is to trust too much in our own abilities and to set ourselves up as little gods. His laws can never be replaced by abstract principles.

> Blessed are they who keep his statutes
>> and seek him with all their heart.
> They do nothing wrong;
>> they walk in his ways.
> You have laid down precepts
>> that are to be fully obeyed. (Psalm 119:2-4)

> The law of the LORD is perfect,
>> reviving the soul.
> The statutes of the LORD are trustworthy,
>> making wise the simple. (Psalm 19:7)

18

The Commitment to Chastity

❖

Millions of dollars have been spent studying how to prevent children and teens from taking up cigarette smoking and the use of drugs. One effective method that has emerged in this scientific research time and again is having the child or teenager make a *public commitment* that he or she will not smoke or use drugs.[1] For example, schools commonly put on antismoking programs that conclude with kids publicly throwing a cigarette in the trash, signing a promise not to smoke, and making public promises that they will not hurt their own health by smoking. Kids who make such public commitments have lower rates of smoking than those who do not.

It is curious then that even though teen pregnancy and sexually transmitted diseases are just as great a health crisis as smoking, our public schools would never dream of encouraging kids to make public commitments to sexual virginity the way they try to encourage smoking virginity. But we must not be too quick to point an accusatory finger at the schools. Parents and churches are often so hesitant about talking about sex with our young people that we would not dream of encouraging such an explicit promise either.

Richard and Renee Durfield have popularized the idea of a "key talk" resulting in a pledge to stay chaste in their book *Raising Them Chaste: A Practical Strategy for Helping Your Teen Wait Till Marriage* (Bethany, 1991). The core of their idea is this: Following a discussion about sex and morality with a child, the parent asks the child to make a covenant, a solemn vow or promise, before the parent and God that the child will remain sexually pure until marriage. When the child agrees to make this covenant, the parent gives the child a token of their agreement, usually a ring or necklace fashioned after a key (to symbolize the "key to your heart"), which can serve as a constant reminder of the commitment the child has made.

This is an intriguing and potentially very powerful idea. The Durfields describe it as an extremely effective way to encourage your teen toward chastity. Let's examine in more detail their proposals for the "key talk" and then summarize some potential strengths and weaknesses of this approach.

THE BASIC "KEY TALK" PROCEDURE

The Durfields point out that children are ready for a key talk at different ages. Some children who are "early bloomers" might need to be talked to as early as age eleven, while "late bloomers" could probably wait until age fourteen or fifteen. To judge when a child is ready, we need to watch for physical signs of puberty as well as the telltale signs of growing interest in the opposite sex, either on the part of the child or the child's peer group.

They recommend that the key talk be preceded by the normal types of sex education that go on in a Christian family (there is not much guidance in their book about how this is to be done). The first step in the key talk process is for the parent to make an appointment with the child several weeks in advance in order to clear a substantial block of time and to communicate to the child the importance and solemnity of the occasion.

Parents should tell their child that the focus of the evening will be to talk about sex and sexuality. Children should be urged to think and pray in preparation for this talk. They are specifically encouraged to ask any questions they have about sex, because part of the goal of the talk is to answer such questions. The Durfields suggest that you attempt to build the child's anticipation of this talk as a special event by keeping a bit of an air of mystery around it.

Parents need to prepare for the talk in three principal ways. One is to make sure that you are emotionally, intellectually, and spiritually prepared to answer any question the child might come up with. Conceivably there could be questions to which you would have to tell a child, "Well, I'll have to get back to you on that one," but it is hoped that this will happen as infrequently as possible. Second, purchase the symbolic key jewelry (ring, bracelet, necklace) that you will give the child to mark or seal the commitment he or she makes. Finally, choose a public place to hold the key talk, like a nice restaurant, which will help to underscore the specialness of the event. Other possibilities for a place for the key talk include a weekend camping or canoeing trip or an overnight stay in a hotel.

The key talk is composed of the following basic elements. You begin with a relaxed and easygoing time just enjoying the company of your child. As naturally as possible, lead into a discussion, composed mostly of sharing by you, of the beauty and value of sexuality and the importance of each person preserving his or her virginity until marriage. Then invite the child to ask any and all questions about sexuality or married life, and attempt to answer these questions as best as possible. After that, discuss the meaning of covenants, drawing the child's attention to the way God's people in the Bible repeatedly made covenants with Him. Introduce the child to the fact that you are going to ask him or her to make a covenant with you and with God that very night that he or she will remain chaste until marriage. It is suggested that the child join with you in praying for the child's future marriage partner, for the growth and well-being of that unknown partner, and that the partner, too, will preserve his or her chastity until marriage. Then present the child with the key jewelry and explain its significance as a symbol of the child's willingness to covenant before God to stay chaste until marriage. Conclude with a formal signing of a written covenant wherein the child promises to stay chaste until marriage.

The Durfields recommend a number of other supportive strategies for parents to follow after the key talk. They strongly recommend praying regularly for your child's future spouse. They emphasize the need for parents to be available and present in the children's lives. They briefly discuss the importance of physical touch, of regular communication, and of parents making themselves understood clearly by the teenager. They encourage parents to develop empathy for the teenager, creatively remembering the pain and confusion of that age. They urge that parents stay active as discipliners and limit-setters as well as encouragers. They suggest "dating goals and guidelines," as we also suggest here. And they have guidelines for future and ongoing discussions with your adolescent.

Weaknesses of the "Key Talk" Approach

Perhaps the greatest weakness of this approach is its seeming emphasis on *one* solution to the premarital sex problem. With all the focus on the powerful key talk, there is a danger that parents will neglect the vital importance of the early years of laying the foundation for the child's godly understanding of his or her sexuality. For most parents, talking to their children about sex is an intimidating process, and it is too easy for many parents to put off the task of shaping their child's sexual character until later.

This also relates to a second concern, which is that the typical child needs a thorough groundwork to be laid for that child to ask intimate questions about sex and to share his or her doubts and concerns with the parent. If the parent has not laid the foundation of talking with the child before the key talk, where is the child's openness and directness for asking questions going to come from? If there is a long tradition of openness and honesty in asking questions about sexuality, at least one portion of the key talk, the question and answer period, seems less vital. So in general, we would argue that an emphasis on the key talk strategy can discourage ongoing communication with the parent.

Finally, the key talk method runs the risk of being artificial and heavy-handed. While this is not at all what the Durfields have in mind, let's think through a negative caricature of what the talk could become in a worst-case scenario. A child who has difficulty communicating with his parents and is beginning to sense the stirrings of adolescent rebelliousness in his heart agrees to go along with the invitation for a special talk about sex. The talk goes moderately well, but the teenager remains guarded and uncertain about the parent's objective. Let's assume that the child is not himself sexually active, but has heard stories circulating around school and listens attentively to television and the messages of rock music, and is not at all sure that he wants to make a definitive commitment to chastity. The parent "springs" the idea of a covenant on the child, dragging out the written chastity covenant form from the Durfields' book and the key jewelry symbol. The child begins to feel trapped: he's in a restaurant and can't get back home without a ride from the parent, doesn't want to kick up a fuss for fear of embarrassment (the ultimate horror for many adolescents), and is generally feeling like he has been hit by a steamroller. The parent, sensing some hesitancy and ambivalence from the child, comes on even stronger, begging the teenager to put aside his doubts and hesitations and make a commitment in the name of God.

One of two bad outcomes could occur. One is that the child angrily accuses the parent of manipulation and heavy-handedness and the evening ends as a complete disaster. This could drive a very deep wedge between parent and child that could be difficult to remove. The other possible outcome is that the child grudgingly makes the commitment that the parent requests, but in his heart feels that he has either lied to God and to the parent or has been trapped into a promise unfairly. Such feelings of resentment, pressure, and deception could speed the process of the child falling away from the parent and from God, in a way not dissimilar to when a teen responds to an altar call at church or to an impassioned plea for commitment at a summer camp, but later feels hypocritical and insincere in his actions because he feels he was more motivated by guilt, fatigue, or peer pressure than by the sincere call of God.

Strengths of the "Key Talk" Approach

We think this approach has three critical strengths. First, it appears generally true that one way of creating commitment is to make commitments. We believe that we are not supposed to wait until we feel absolute certainty in our hearts to make our commitments to God. We are to trust God, to have faith in God, and trust and faith both involve making commitments without absolute certainty. Our situation is rather like that of the father who cried out to our Lord, "I do believe; help me overcome my unbelief!" (Mark 9:24). We believe and are committed, but we never believe or are committed to the degree that we would like. Part of growing in belief and commitment is to vocalize our commitments, to take that step of faith of raising our hand or going to the altar or joining the church or agreeing to share what God has done in our lives. It's a bit like getting married. We marry someone because we're sure that person is the right one for us. But the person who waits for absolute, unwavering, ironclad certainty that he or she is marrying the right person is often the person who never marries. Part of the certainty that we have married the right person comes from making the commitment of marriage to each other and then sticking by it.

The key talk's strength is that it *challenges the child to make a commitment*. We are exhibiting a timidity that is unbecoming of our God if we seem to give our children the following message: "Well, God hopes and we hope that you will think about staying faithful, but we know that this is something about which you have to make up your mind on a daily basis, and some days you'll feel like being chaste and other days you won't feel like being chaste. It's certainly not something you can make up your mind about and live by for an extended period of time." When we marry, we make a commitment to stay sexually faithful to our spouses. There is something right about asking a child to make an explicit commitment to sexual chastity as an expression and outgrowth of the child's commitment to the Lord Jesus Christ.

Secondly, we applaud that this commitment is made in public and not in private. By public, we do not mean at a restaurant, but rather in the presence of another believer, though this need not be the parent. As we wrestled with the key talk approach, we realized that some of our doubts were the residual effects of a worldly view of sexuality that afflicts us all. We have already discussed how one of the most prevalent anti-Christian moral messages in our world today is the notion that sex is a private decision with only individual implications and dimensions. The reality is quite the reverse. The way we handle our sexuality has tremendous public ramifications. Just because we don't talk openly about sex in public doesn't mean that it's not a public phenomenon. We remember that part of the embarrassment of getting married was the knowledge that everyone who knew we were getting married, regardless of what else they knew about us, knew that we were going to have sexual intercourse that night. Our lives are bound together in communities, and what we do with our sexuality in those communities has a powerful effect. The choices our children make about their sexuality are intimately interwoven with all of their other choices of what they do with their lives. How they express their sexuality is intertwined with their public and private character. There is something right about the

Christian adolescent being called to make a public commitment to the sexual morality standard that God calls us to.

Third, we appreciate the Durfields' attention to symbolism as embodied in the key jewelry given to the child. Deuteronomy 6 calls parents to surround their children with tangible reminders of faith. Protestants have rightly been cautious about icons and other religious symbols that can become the focus of rather than facilitators of true religious devotion to Christ. But we Protestants have perhaps overshot a balanced position on this matter. God frequently dealt with people through symbols. Whether it is the primitive and brutal animal sacrifice covenant ceremony of Genesis 15 or the ecstatic symbolism of Christ on a white horse with a sword coming from His mouth in Revelation 19, God doesn't limit Himself to words. Christ Himself instructs us to regularly remember Him through the sacrament of the bread and the wine. With this in mind, the symbolism of giving a child a symbol of his or her chastity (whether in the form of a key or whatever) could be a powerful reminder for that child during times of temptation and doubt.

RECOMMENDATIONS REGARDING A COMMITMENT TALK

The strengths and potential benefits of asking our child to make a commitment to purity outweigh the dangers of doing so. Having a commitment talk with an adolescent can be a very helpful thing to do. But we recommend this with some cautions.

First, such a commitment talk must be seen as one more point in a long process of shaping our child's sexual character, a process that began in earliest childhood. Parents who neglect sexuality with their growing child and depend on a "one-shot" covenant talk to do the trick are likely to hurt rather than help the child.

Second, such a talk should occur only if the following conditions are met:

- There is a track record of openness and dialogue about the spiritual, moral, relational, and physical aspects of sexuality.
- The adolescent voices a genuine personal commitment to the Christian faith, one that goes beyond a passive submission to the parents' religious wishes.
- The parents feel sufficient readiness to go into such a conversation with the ability to back off if they sense hesitancy or ambiguity on the part of the child.

It may be that the parent is not the best person to have this commitment talk with the child. If your relationship is tense, and if there is not a history of openness in discussions about sexuality, it may be wise to choose another person. The scientific research on preventing smoking is helpful here too, because it shows that older respected "peer advisors" often have a very powerful effect in solidifying a child's resolve not to smoke. It doesn't have to be the parent the child makes the commitment with.

But it's one thing to trust an older peer to talk with our child about not smoking; it's quite another to trust that person to talk with our child about sex. What if that peer falls into sexual sin and turns up pregnant six months later? Perhaps a first option would be to consult with the youth minister or leader in your church and see if the church could host a special set of services or a retreat for youth that focuses specifically on sex, where the kids present are challenged to make a covenant of chastity. Having the child discuss sexuality and make a covenant in the presence of a youth leader may be an option as well. As a final option, a youth leader in your church could suggest an adolescent of the same sex three or four years older who could talk to your child and challenge her or him to make a covenant of chastity. If the older peer is admired and respected, this could be very powerful in the life of your child. Ideally, this person would have an ongoing relationship with your child, and would be carefully chosen for the stability of her or his commitment to Christ and to personal purity.

Third, we think it important that children not be put in a situation where they think they've been forced into agreement with the idea of the covenant. Social psychological research strongly suggests that when people adopt attitudes for strong *external* reasons, when they feel pushed or manipulated from the outside rather than choosing from their own insides, these attitudes or commitments tend to be easily shed or changed. For instance, research has shown that when people adopt attitudes under the inducement of financial reward ("I'll pay you twenty dollars to write a one paragraph essay in support of my political candidate"), the external pressure (the lure of the money) on the people actually robs them of an internal sense of commitment to the attitudes they are voicing. Think, for example, of how differently we feel about service on a church committee that we have freely chosen versus how we feel when we are pressured to serve.

For this reason, we feel that the covenant-making process should ideally occur in a different format than what the Durfields recommend. We recommend that the talk take place in a special but private context, not in a public place like a restaurant. On a camping trip, on a long walk, during a quiet evening at home when everyone else is elsewhere—all are good alternatives.

We suggest that the parent raise the idea of a covenant, expressing the wish that the child make such a covenant. *But* the parent should explicitly tell the child that it is the child's decision and that the parent would like the child *not* to make the covenant on the spot. Rather, the parent can urge the child to pray and reflect on the magnitude of his or her commitment for at least two days, and then report back to the parent if he or she has decided to make the covenant with God. We would urge that the covenant be described as a covenant between God and the adolescent himself or herself, with the parent serving only as a witness, rather than a covenant that the adolescent makes with God and the parent. This helps to communicate the proper reality, namely that the parent is to serve as a resource to the child but not as the person who "keeps the kid chaste" or who serves as a policeman over the child's sexual life. The child can be told that the parent will not inquire after the child's decision if he or she says nothing, but that the parent would like to share as a witness to help strengthen the child's resolve. For that reason, the parent hopes to hear from the child after two days what the child's decision is. In other words, the parent must not pester the child to make the covenant.

We would urge that the symbolic piece of jewelry be given to the child freely, with the child invited to wear the piece of jewelry *if* the child makes the covenant with God, but again the jewelry is not to be worn for at least two days, until the child makes the covenant in and of himself or herself.

We are a bit concerned about the idea of a written covenant. As we said above, it is our opinion that the most long-lasting and powerful decisions and commitments are internally motivated. There is a danger that a written covenant will come across as coercive and thus ultimately undermine the child's resolve; it could even become a point of resentment.

The commitment talk begins with a summary of why we believe sexual purity to be God's will for our child's life. Remember, repetition of key lessons about sexuality is vital! We will need to be able to tell our child exactly why we think God wants him or her to be chaste (see "The Heart of Christian Sexual Morality" in chapter 10). We should discuss with the child the coming struggles to stay pure, reminding the child both of the arguments others will use to encourage him or her to have sex and the pressures the child will feel to go along with the crowd. We should pay special attention to the emotional side of relationships, of how the desire to be physical goes naturally with caring for another person. We should be ready to answer, or find the answers to, any questions about the physical, emotional, relational, or spiritual aspects of sex.

The conclusion of the commitment talk, as we discussed it above, might go something like this:

"Beth, your dad and I have always told you how strongly we believe that it is God's will that you save your sexual purity for marriage. This talk isn't the beginning or the end of our talking about sex. Sexuality is an important part of life for everyone. But now that you are a young woman, now that you have started your period and are capable of having sexual intercourse and of becoming pregnant, now that thinking about and being interested in boys and dating are going to become an important part of your life in the next few years, you are at a point where you have to decide what sort of life you will live.

"Dad and I believe that what you will do with your body, who you will share yourself with and when, is not an accident that happens to you. It's a decision. And while the world will tell you that sex is just good fun or that you have to have sex to fit in, God's ideas are different. He wants you to stay pure for the sake of His glory, your future marriage, and your own safety and welfare.

"And so, I want to invite you to decide now what kind of life you will live sexually. And I invite you to make a commitment, a promise, to God and to some other person you respect. I would be glad to be that person. But I ask you not to make that decision and commitment now; it's too important to do on impulse. I ask you to really pray and think for the next two days what you really believe about sex and how you will live your life. Then I ask you to make a commitment to me based on what you decide. I won't pester you about this; if you don't come back to me I won't harass you. But this is too important a decision to make on a date or at a boy's house. Whatever you decide will shape your life forever. I pray you will make the right choice."

We feel that a process like this will help the child to internalize the covenant that he or she is making and maximize the impact of this technique.

19

Teaching Your Teenager About Contraception

❖

Hilga had a sinking feeling that she had botched it in teaching Becca about sex. She had told her daughter the basics, about menstruation and the "facts of life," but she had done so late. Becca had complained bitterly that she had heard it all already in school, and had acted embarrassed and ashamed to be talking about it at all with her mom. That had been three years ago. Since that time, Hilga had tried several times to inquire about Becca's relationships with boys, but had received evasive answers. What frightened Hilga most was that Becca never asked her any questions and never disclosed anything. She had not started really trying to tell her daughter about God's sexual rules until Becca was fourteen, and Becca had clearly acted like her mother was speaking Russian. Now, in the last six months, she felt a change in her daughter. Becca was clearly disenchanted with church and the youth group; was hanging out with a crowd of surly, haughty, and sneaky sixteen-year-olds; and was pushing her parents' limits with ever greater frequency and defiance. Hilga had just overheard Becca whispering to a friend out on the front porch that one of the girls in the group was going to have an abortion. "I really have no clear sense that Becca has any commitment to Christ or to God's standards for sex. What if it's Becca who's going to get an abortion in six months? What does God want me to do?"

What does today's teenager really need to know about sex? According to many experts, since most teens are "sexually active," what they need is to know how to stop feeling guilty or ashamed about their sexual activity, how not to catch one of the many sexually transmitted diseases of today (especially the HIV infection that leads to AIDS and death), how to prevent getting pregnant or causing a pregnancy, and how to get access to a safe legal abortion if they do get pregnant.[1]

The faithful Christian parent will have a different agenda entirely. We desire for our children to grow to be women or men of God, to know the fullness of God's mercy and grace, and to be consumed with a desire to be like Christ. In the sexual area, that means that they abstain from all forms of sexual impurity when they're not married, and prepare for a life of sexual enjoyment and union within marriage or for a possible life of healthy, disciplined, and fulfilled singleness.

If our goal is that our children abstain from sexual intercourse, why would we ever consider telling them about contraception? Is it right or wrong to teach our children about ways of preventing pregnancy and sexually transmitted diseases if they become "sexually active"?

Let us first briefly clarify what we mean by the terms *contraception* and *birth control*, and discuss the main methods of each. We will then examine the arguments on both sides of this thorny issue of whether Christian children should be told about contraception, and draw our best conclusions.

METHODS OF CONTRACEPTION AND BIRTH CONTROL

"Birth control" does not mean the same thing as "contraception." In many textbooks of human sexuality, the terms are treated as synonyms, but they are not. The term *birth control* refers to anything that prevents a live birth of a healthy human infant from occurring. By this standard, contraception is a form of birth control, but so is abortion, even in the eighth month. This is why public school sex education that teaches "birth control" is declared by researchers to be successful even when sexual activity rates and pregnancy rates go up—as long as birthrates go down due to increased abortion, you are still doing "birth control." Contraception, specifically, means literally to prevent conception from occurring. Though disease prevention is not the same thing as either birth control or contraception, we will be including disease prevention in our discussion of contraception.

Birth-control methods can basically be classified into three types. The methods that prevent conception (the joining of the egg and the sperm) are the only methods that can truly be called *contraceptive*. A second group of methods prevents implantation of the fertilized egg into the wall of the woman's uterus (which occurs hours or days after fertilization). The final group are those methods that interrupt or terminate the pregnancy and thus kill the developing fetus at some stage in its development.

Contraception

Contraceptive methods that block the fertilization of the egg by the sperm themselves fall into three major groupings. First, there are those methods that put a physical or chemical barrier between the sperm and the egg. A condom worn over the man's penis catches sperm (when the method works) and does not allow them to get near the woman's egg; it is a physical barrier. The diaphragm, cervical cap, and cervical sponge all put a physical barrier over the woman's cervix that does not allow the sperm to pass into the woman's uterus and Fallopian tubes where the egg could be fertilized. Spermicide foams kill the sperm, thus rendering them incapable of fertilizing the egg; it is a chemical barrier. The diaphragm and cervical cap are often used with spermicide foams, and cervical sponges contain spermicidal agents, thus imposing a double barrier.

It is vital to know that only the condom provides some protection for both partners against the transmission of diseases. Neither the "pill" nor the diaphragm, two popular methods for married couples, provide significant disease protection; they are contraceptives only. In the age of AIDS, parents have to worry not just about pregnancy, but also about sexually transmitted diseases (STDs). All of the STDs are serious, many can have very devastating consequences, and AIDS is deadly.

The second category of contraceptive methods that block fertilization are the oral contraceptives (the pill), the contraceptive implants that deliver the same hormones as the oral contraceptives but through implants in the skin (only Norplant® is being distributed in the United States at this writing), and the vaginal rings distribute ovulation-blocking hormones. There is some ambiguity as to exactly how these hormonally based contraceptive methods work. The consensus of medical opinion is that they block ovulation, so that a woman never releases a fertile egg while she is on these drugs. It is possible that these methods occasionally allow ovulation to occur, and thus, the woman's egg might be fertilized by the man's sperm even when she is taking these. It is thought that the artificial hormones may have the additional effect of preventing implantation in the uterus, so that the woman never becomes pregnant and never knows that she did release a mature egg.

The third group of methods of contraception that actually block fertilization are the surgical sterilization methods: vasectomy in the man and tubal ligation in the woman. Vasectomy surgically prevents live sperm from getting into the semen a man ejaculates during intercourse. He has a seemingly normal ejaculation, but if his semen were examined under a microscope, it would contain no sperm. A tubal ligation prevents a mature ovum from passing from the ovaries through the Fallopian tubes into the uterus. The tubal ligation basically severs both Fallopian tubes so that ova cannot get into the uterus, and the man's sperm cannot get out of the uterus.

Thus sperm and egg are prevented from joining together in both methods. It should be noted that the physical/chemical-barrier methods and the hormone-blocking methods are obviously reversible. Couples can get pregnant by stopping using those methods. The surgical methods are generally seen as irreversible.

Anti-Implantation Methods of Birth Control
The second category of birth-control methods are those that block the implantation of the fertilized egg in the uterus of the woman. Here the woman's egg may be fertilized by the man's sperm in the beginning of its journey down the woman's Fallopian tube, but then the zygote (the cluster of smaller cells that the fertilized egg has already become) is not implanted into the wall of the woman's womb, or uterus.

Two types of methods disrupt this natural implantation. The first is the various "morning-after pills," which are thought to render the woman's uterus "inhospitable" to the fertilized egg. The IUD (or intrauterine device) is the second. While neither of these methods involves any "direct" action to damage or kill the zygote, the methods do artificially cause what might be called a miscarriage for the woman. The zygote thus dies because it fails to implant.

There is substantial argument about the legitimacy of these anti-implantation methods in Christian circles. Because it is estimated that a significant percentage of all pregnancies naturally end in miscarriage anyway, with many occurring so early that the woman never even knows she was pregnant, some argue that these methods parallel natural development. Further, since the woman never knows for sure whether or not an egg was fertilized, a life conceived, she can take comfort in having made no deliberate choice to "end a pregnancy."

For those, however, who believe that life begins at conception, these methods are unacceptable. They constitute deliberate action that results in the death of any child who was conceived as a result of sexual intercourse. We personally regard these methods as being morally questionable at best for general use, especially given the availability of methods to prevent conception from occurring at all. For that reason, we classify them as birth control and will not discuss them further as morally acceptable options in this chapter. A number of Christians feel that these methods may be questionable in general usage, but that they are acceptable when a woman has been raped.

Abortive Methods of Birth Control
Finally, there is a range of abortion-inducing methods that will "terminate the pregnancy," the politically correct term for killing the living fetus inside the pregnant woman. Some of these are designed to work early and "indi-

rectly," forcing the uterus to reject the implanted and developing embryo. Others are designed to work later and more directly to destroy the life of the developing fetus. Because abortion is the deliberate sacrificing of a human life, we regard it as an immoral and unacceptable form of birth control. In the remainder of this chapter, we will not have the anti-implantation methods and abortive methods in mind. (Also see chapter 20.)

THE MORALITY OF CONTRACEPTION ITSELF

Before we can weigh other factors, we must first ask if contraception is itself moral.[2] If one believes that contraception itself is intrinsically immoral, as many Roman Catholics and some evangelicals and fundamentalists do, this is reason enough not to talk to children about this option. Most Protestants, including evangelicals and fundamentalists, do not appear to take this position. Let us take a brief look at the moral issues involved in judging the acceptability of contraception *within marriage*. This will serve as a foundation for thinking about contraception with teenage children.

Procreation and the Nature of Sexuality
We must carefully think through what place procreation, childbearing, has in sexual life and in the nature of sexuality. The traditional Roman Catholic view is that every sexual act is meant to have the potential to result in children; sexual intercourse by its very nature involves the potential for procreation. Any separation of the sex act from its potential to generate children is judged to be "unnatural" and a basic betrayal of God's intent for the nature of that sexual act.

A second, less severe view would argue that sexual relationships, marriages, should have the *potential* to result in children in general, but that it is too excessive to argue that every sexual act must have the potential to generate children. Some would take a third view that the potential for generating children is a purely optional part of marriage and the act of intercourse. Given the dense population of our world and the pressure that ever-increasing population is placing on our ability to meet human needs, they would argue that there is no reason to necessarily intertwine sexual expression with generating children.

You can see that the first view would make all contraception immoral, the third view would make contraception always acceptable, and the middle view would make contraception acceptable at times, depending on the motives of the couple and other factors. It would seem to us that the third view, that procreation is purely optional, separates intercourse too drastically from its natural potential to create children. The first view, the traditional Catholic view, may go too far in making the possibility of children a necessary part of every single sexual act in a marriage. So perhaps contraception can sometimes fit in with the general nature of our sexuality. Which leads us to the next issue.

Is Procreation a Command?

Another issue we must confront is whether it is God's will that married people always have unprotected intercourse and have however many children result. Mary Pride, in her book *The Way Home*, claims that God's statement to Adam and Eve to "be fruitful and multiply, and fill the earth" (Genesis 1:28, RSV) was a command. But many biblical scholars have suggested that this is a misrepresentation of the intent of Genesis 1:28. This statement appears to be a blessing, not a command. In Hebrew society, blessings were often stated in ways that in English culture sound like commands. For instance, Rebekah's family responded in the following way to her plans to go off and marry Isaac: "They blessed Rebekah, and said to her, 'Our sister, be the mother of thousands of ten thousands; and may your descendants possess the gate of those who hate them!'" (Genesis 24:60, RSV). Clearly, it is not their command that Rebekah have thousands and ten thousands of children, but it is their hope for her blessing stated in emphatic language.

We would argue that we are not commanded to procreate, but that the possibility of having children is an enormous blessing from God. Even if filling the earth were a command, one could quite ably argue that human beings have fulfilled this command to the extent that the earth can bear.

God's Sovereignty

The issue of contraception is another area where we confront a seeming conflict between God's sovereign will and our human capacity for choice. Could we, by using contraception, "frustrate" God's sovereign will that we conceive a child by a particular sexual act? But if God wants it to happen, can any human strategies frustrate God? This is a very complicated question with implications for all of our Christian lives.

Our sexual behavior may be an area where God has a specific intent and design, and will carry out His purposes regardless of what we do. It may be an area where He has an intent, but is willing, out of respect for our human freedom, to allow us to block what He intends and desires in our lives. Even further, our procreating of children may be an area where God's will is completely permissive; we may be allowed to have children if we choose to do so, and to choose the number and spacing/timing of their conceptions. These are deep issues each of us must grapple with. Each of us must decide if the use of contraceptives is more like Jonah running in the opposite direction in response to God's command, or rather like Paul's choosing escape from Damascus in a basket even though he had total faith that God could protect him (Acts 9:25).

Motives

Finally, in considering the morality of any use of birth control, we must think through our motives for using contraception. At one extreme is the couple in their midforties who have six children, and after serious deliberation and prayer have chosen not to take the increased risk of a problem pregnancy or child with physical deformities. After considerable prayer and reflection, they decide that God has given them all the children they should have, and so they prayerfully choose to begin using contraception. At the other extreme, we might have the couple who, out of a selfish commitment to a materialistic lifestyle and out of their own spiritual and emotional poverty, decide there is no room in their lives for children, children who are expensive, inconvenient, draining, unrewarding, and so forth. They thus choose to remain childless and use contraception for this reason. There are all sorts of potentially problematic reasons for using contraception, including overinvestment in career, negative attitudes toward children, and greed. There are also sinful reasons for choosing to have children as well, we would note.

We conclude from the above that contraception is itself, for the married couple, an acceptable option when used in response to prayerful consideration of God's call on your life as a couple and to sober self-examination of your motives for its use. But what about your children? Surely it's not a good thing for a teenager to conceive a child or to contract a sexually transmitted disease; what are the reasons against and for teaching an unmarried teenager about contraception?

THE CASE AGAINST TEACHING YOUR CHILD ABOUT CONTRACEPTION

In a recent *Focus on the Family* newsletter, Dr. James Dobson voiced utter opposition to teaching a teenager about contraceptive methods, particularly the use of condoms. He argued forcefully for how important abstinence from sex before marriage is, a point with which we are in total agreement. He talked in vibrant detail about how the campaign for "safe sex" is an illusion, because even the most effective contraceptive methods are not foolproof against deadly sexually transmitted diseases or pregnancy. He talked about the tragedy of our whole society underemphasizing abstinence. We concur completely with these concerns, especially as they are cautions about the confused and permissive attitudes that seem frequently expressed in public school sex education programs.

In fact, a prominent developmental psychologist has provided some support of Dr. Dobson's concerns about contraception instruction in the public schools, suggesting that teachers or counselors who provide adolescents with information on contraception in a public school context without

giving any moral messages are most likely conveying three powerful lessons: that the adult condones teenage sexual activity, that the adult quietly
approves the teen's use of contraception, and "that these methods are both
safe and effective."[3] Teachers and other authorities may say that these methods have failure rates and so forth, but adolescents believe them to be safe
and effective *simply because the authority figures endorse them.*

But Dr. Dobson also applied his concerns to the specific area of parental
communication with their teenagers. "But if you knew a teenager was going
to have intercourse, wouldn't you rather he use a condom?" In response to
this question, Dr. Dobson wrote in his February 13, 1992 newsletter:

> No, because that approach has an unintended consequence. The
> process of recommending condom usage to teenagers inevitably
> conveys five dangerous ideas:
> 1) That "safe" sex is achievable;
> 2) That everybody is doing it;
> 3) That responsible adults expect them to do it;
> 4) That it is a good thing;
> 5) That their peers *know* they *know* these things, breeding prom-
>   iscuity. Those are very dangerous messages to give our kids.

The core of his opposition to teaching kids about birth control is that
*instructing teenage children about condom or other contraceptive usage
undermines their commitment to abstinence.*[4] This is a powerful and important argument. There can be no doubt that it is horribly counterproductive
to tell our children that we don't want them to do a certain thing, and then
to tell them how they can bail themselves out of their difficulties if they
disobey us. We would never commend our child to study for a test, and
then teach her how to cheat to get a good grade in case she doesn't ever
get around to studying. We would never tell our teenager to get drunk, and
then tell him how to avoid getting caught by us and the police if he does
get drunk.

Debra Evans, author and childbirth educator, recently described her
own experience of going on the pill at age fifteen. She expressed a desire to
a high school counselor to begin taking oral contraceptives. The high school
counselor, without consulting her parents, acted quite aggressively to make
an appointment for her and take her to the doctor's office. As she began
taking the pill, she gained weight and developed other physical changes
that her mother noticed. When asked, she told her mother that she was
on the pill, and her mother acted in a basically supportive manner. "Over
the next three years, I avoided getting pregnant and claimed to be liberated
from traditional restraints, all the while naively thinking I was in control
of my own destiny. I refused to consider that I might be being 'used' by

the young men I was dating. I know better than that now."

Reflecting on her experience, Debra Evans now believes that being on the pill protected her from the ravages of unwanted pregnancy, but failed to protect her from the ravages of "the emotional and spiritual consequences of sin." She argues that putting a young woman on birth control can have devastating implications:

> Providing the pill (and other forms of contraception) to an unmarried woman does more than prevent her from getting pregnant: it may also erode her ability to say no to sex. It can make her more vulnerable to the pressures of a man in search of physical gratification. The potential for sexual abuse, fornication, sexual addictions, adultery, and perpetration of double standards grows instead of diminishes. The pill was not designed to treat or cure anything but only to make sex easy. Women come out losers. "Baby-proofing" them increases the odds that they are being sexually used by, and sexually using, men.[5]

In part, what Evans has said is that the fear of pregnancy and disease is a legitimate and vital barrier to immoral sexual intercourse. Eliminating those possibilities makes immorality more likely.

THE CASE FOR TEACHING YOUR CHILD
ABOUT CONTRACEPTION

Teenagers who are firm believers are less likely to engage in sexual experimentation than nonreligious teens. Some studies suggest that religious teens are about half as likely to have engaged in sexual intercourse. That's the good news, though we might wish it were even more positive—that Christian teens never engaged in premarital sex.

The bad news is that the same research also consistently shows that religious young people do engage in premarital sex (though less frequently), and that *when religious teens do engage in sex, they are LESS likely than their nonreligious peers to use effective contraceptive and disease-preventive methods.*[6] Thus, they are *more likely to get pregnant when they do have sex,* and are probably more likely to contract sexually transmitted diseases. And this finding makes sense. The adolescent who is most likely to use contraception is the one who has deliberately chosen to engage in sex, has thought through the consequences, does not feel a lot of emotional conflict or turmoil about that decision, has received prior education about contraception methods, has a network of friends also having sex who can serve as a resource pool for information (however defective), can talk explicitly with the romantic partner about what method to use, and who can also talk with parents who accept the adolescent's decision and encourage contraceptive use.

Christian teenagers who have sex are not in this category. Often they feel alienated from peers and parents. Often they have not received education about contraception. Often they are terribly conflicted with guilt over their actions, even to the point of convincing themselves that they had no choice in the matter (lust took over, or a demon took control of them, or they were forced, or whatever). They may swear to themselves that they will never do it again (even though they have been "doing it" with their partner for two months now and have not stopped going out with that person). In short, Christian teens will have a hard time deliberately, with premeditation, planning for their exploits by arranging for effective contraception. And because they don't intentionally plan to prevent either pregnancy or disease, they are more likely to experience both.

From the little we actually know, teen contraceptive use is horribly infrequent and ineffective anyway. The percentage of sexually active adolescents that consistently use condoms may actually be less than 10 percent. Perhaps even more amazingly, it has been estimated that perhaps over a quarter of all teenage females have engaged in the one behavior most likely to spread the AIDS virus, anal intercourse, and that only one-third of those who engage in this extremely risky activity use condoms.[7]

In light of this reality, the core argument *for* telling a teenage child about contraception is that all sins are not equal.[8] True, at one level, Christ taught that all sins are equally heinous in the sight of God. All sins, big or small, mark us as fallen and disqualify us from meriting or deserving God's love and acceptance. In this way, lust is equivalent to adultery and unrighteous anger is equivalent to murder (Matthew 5:21-30). Lust and rage, like adultery and murder, amply demonstrate how far we fall short of God's standard of righteousness and how much we need God's merciful forgiveness.

But only a fool would argue from this that it makes no difference whether we simply lust, or lust and also commit adultery, whether we simply get bitterly angry or also take a shotgun and blow someone's head off. In terms of how they affect other people, in terms of the damage they wreak on human beings and the world God made, sins definitely differ, with some worse than others.

And so it is with sexual sin. It is a serious matter, a terrible affliction, to struggle alone with lust. That person is defiling his or her own mind. But when that lust issues forth in actual physical immorality, another human being is being hurt as well, and the bodies of both persons are defiled. When the sexual partner is married, a third person is being ravaged—the innocent spouse. When multiple sexual partners are involved, the damage is spread further. When diseases are transmitted, even greater damage is done and the temple of the Holy Spirit, the human body, is further devastated. When the immorality results in a pregnancy which is brought to birth, that child may have to be raised by a single parent or be given away for adoption, either of which may turn out well but neither of which can be described as God's ideal will for that child. Finally, when fornication results in pregnancy and the child is aborted, as so commonly happens today, the sexual sin has borne the fruit of death—the very opposite result that the life-giving gift of sex is meant to produce. The effect of AIDS is the same.

If we cannot guarantee that our children will remain chaste, should we give them enough information to encourage them not to compound their sexual sins against their own bodies and that of their partner with even more grotesque sins against the other person's body (in the form of disease transmission) or against a yet-unborn child? This view would suggest that telling our children about contraception may be equivalent to telling teenagers not to drink alcohol, but if they choose to drink they must remember that God firmly condemns drunkenness, and if they ever do get drunk to please never drive so that they do not risk the even worse sin of killing someone else or even themselves.

One additional argument for teaching our children about contraception within the Christian family is that they are going to hear about these methods anyway. Only the child who is cloistered in a home school and not allowed to watch television or listen to popular radio, who stays out of gas-station bathrooms and is somehow separated from nonChristian acquaintances, is not going to hear about condoms and other contraceptive methods in our current society. If our kids are going to hear about it anyway, shouldn't they hear about it from the parent, so that the right perspective is put on the information?

Based on the above, we have concluded that we must tell our children about contraception. We don't regard contraception in itself to be immoral within marriage. The couple who has sex outside of marriage is engaging in fornication, a sinful act in the eyes of God. But if that couple fails to protect themselves and other innocent persons (a future spouse, an unborn child) by using contraception, that multiplies the damage they are causing. The arguments against explaining contraception are powerful; we must not give mixed messages, pretend to be "morally neutral," undermine our message of abstinence, or increase the likelihood of our children becoming sexual victims. We will discuss below how we will try to take the concern of Dr. Dobson and others into account in the way we advise that teens be told about contraception.

EXPLAINING CONTRACEPTION
IN THE CHRISTIAN FAMILY

The secular experts say that an important part of getting children to effectively use contraceptives is to reduce their sense of guilt and anxiety about their sexual behavior.[9] In other words, parents and educators should help kids to feel comfortable and good about their fornication. Many secular sex education programs are targeted at decreasing guilt at any cost, even if that cost is the loss of the religious faith of the teenager.

Can the Christian parent justify deliberately trying to reduce the guilt and anxiety teens might feel over their sexual experimentation? The answer is no. We cannot be party to eradicating guilt for the sake of the teen using more effective contraception. We know as Christians that our subjective feelings of guiltiness may have no necessary relation to our standing guilty before God; as the Apostle Paul said, "My conscience is clear, but that does not make me innocent. It is the Lord who judges me" (1 Corinthians 4:4). We or our children may convince ourselves that what we are doing is acceptable, but we deceive ourselves if we go against God's revealed Law. Christian parents regard premarital sexual intercourse to be sin, and how can we be party to assisting a child to feel less guilty about sin? We cannot. And so a part of our paradox is how to faithfully proclaim God's standards, and to talk about contraception without eroding the value of those standards.

Christian parents, unfortunately, take the risk that their messages about abstinence and restraint will fail in influencing their children to not engage in premarital sex, but will succeed at making them feel extremely guilty about their sexual choices. This guilt, which we would regard as true guilt, could have the practical effect of preventing them from ever admitting to themselves that they have departed from the ways of their parents. If they do not, with premeditation, admit to themselves and/or to their sexual partner that they are deliberately choosing to be sexually active, this will serve to prevent them from making the choice to get information about contraceptives and to use them appropriately.

We cannot take the world's way out of this dilemma, which is to throw away our standards, assume that teens are going to be sexually active, and encourage them to feel good about using contraceptives. We must continue to hold up God's ideal. But we can inform them about contraceptive methods, and tell them that we pray they will never use the information until they are married, except perhaps to counsel a friend who may be acting foolishly by engaging in unprotected sex. We can challenge them to courageously decide what they are going to do with their lives. We can challenge them that if they decide to go against God's standards, and we pray that they don't, that they use an effective contraceptive method so that a disease is not transmitted and/or an innocent child is not conceived. What, then, is the essential information we should convey to our children about contraception?

Myths to Dispel
In talking with teens about contraception, it is important to confront the

many absolutely erroneous myths that circulate among young people about pregnancy. These myths include:

- You can't get pregnant or contract a disease the first time you have intercourse.
- You can't get pregnant or contract a disease unless you have an orgasm.
- The woman can't get pregnant if she is having her period.
- You can't get pregnant in certain positions (such as having sex standing up, in a sitting position, or with the woman on top).
- The woman can't get pregnant if she urinates right after sexual intercourse.
- You can prevent pregnancy and disease with a homemade condom made of such materials as Saran Wrap or a baggie.
- Douching with any number of substances (soda pop, baking soda, and so forth) will prevent pregnancy and disease.
- Withdrawal of the boy's penis before he has orgasm will prevent pregnancy.

Pregnancy Without Intercourse
Teens need to know that it is possible for a girl to get pregnant *even if intercourse never occurs at all.* The male ejaculating anywhere near the woman's vagina can result in sperm entering her body by coming in contact with her vaginal lubrication. At the risk of sounding sacrilegious, many family-planning clinics and gynecologists have reported "immaculate conceptions" where the girl's intact hymen clearly demonstrates she has not had intercourse, but she is undeniably pregnant. The possibility of pregnancy exists every time a teenage (or any age) couple engage in any kind of heavy petting where the boy ejaculates and the girl is aroused to the point that her vagina lubricates. For instance, some couples engage in mutual touching of each other's genitals with clothes mostly or totally off. When the boy ejaculates in the vicinity of the girl's crotch, any contact of his semen with her vaginal moistness can allow his sperm to begin the journey inward, resulting in conception. That is all it takes!

Contraceptive and Disease-Prevention Methods Fail More for Teens
One of the elements that must be factored into parental decision making about teaching teens about contraception is the reality that *all contraceptives appear to have higher failure rates when used by teenagers.* Even Planned Parenthood acknowledges that effective use of contraceptive methods needs to be a habit cultivated in a stable relationship for birth-control methods to work. They also acknowledge that such habits and patterns are difficult to develop in the unstable, transitory relationships that tend

to be the staple of teenage romances. The research studies of the Planned Parenthood organization itself indicate that typical teenagers don't use birth control the first time they have sex, that the average girl who is sexually active engages in sex for about six months before she begins to use contraception, and that the average girl is sexually active for up to one year before she ever visits a doctor or family-planning clinic.[10]

Even the contraceptive method that is regarded as "most foolproof," the pill, has a higher failure rate with teenagers. In 1973, the major journal of Planned Parenthood itself published a study showing that teenage women who regularly use the pill tend to have a pregnancy rate about 400 percent higher than that of older women using the pill.[11] A study published in 1986 looked at a group of teenage girls who would be expected to have highly effective use of the pill (an advantaged, suburban group), and found that almost 20 percent reported at least one pregnancy during the first year of use.[12] This is a staggering rate of pregnancy, almost ten times that reported by adult women!

Condoms also appear to fail more often for teens than for adults. It is well known that the two greatest causes for the failure of condoms in preventing pregnancy, and presumably in preventing sexually transmitted diseases, are improper use and breakage during use. One common example of improper use is the male not putting on the condom until the couple is already engaging in sexual intercourse and he feels himself near orgasm. This can fail in preventing pregnancy because the man will emit tiny droplets of fluids from his penis well before orgasm, droplets that can contain live sperm that can impregnate the woman. Condoms fail in preventing disease because they do nothing to stop him from getting a disease from her, and any secretions his penis releases during unprotected intercourse can transmit disease.

Most adult married couples require a time of adjustment to learn to use a condom properly, a luxury that the teenage couple struggling with guilt and in a hurry does not have. Condom breakage is also more likely to occur among teen users. To work well, condoms need to be handled with care, put on correctly, removed carefully after intercourse to not allow the escape of semen, used with an artificial lubricant such as K-Y Jelly to reduce the amount of friction they are subjected to in intercourse, and protected in proper storage. Condoms are more likely to be handled inappropriately, stored inappropriately, or used without an artificial lubricant that helps to prevent breakage by teens.

With all their flaws, condoms do lower the occurrence of pregnancy and decrease the spread of diseases, including the HIV (or AIDS) virus. Even in the gay community, the widened use of condoms combined with more reliance on lower-risk sexual practices (for example, mutual masturbation rather than unprotected anal sex) has slowed down, at least temporarily, the spread of AIDS. So, condoms work—they make it less likely a child will get pregnant or get a disease. And condoms don't work—many people still get pregnant and get diseases using them.

There Is No Reliable Protection Against Disease or Pregnancy

To repeat the words of James Dobson, *there is no "safe sex."* No method utterly prevents all pregnancies, and no method utterly stops the spread of sexually transmitted diseases.

But while there is no safe sex, there is "safer sex." Flawed as the use of contraceptives is, especially the use of condoms, any use does help to lower the chances of pregnancy. The use of condoms does decrease the disease rate.

One of our most powerful messages to our kids must be that premarital sex *is not worth the risk of disease or pregnancy.* This is not the moral core of God's view of sexuality; the dangers of sex are not the main reason God says "no!" But the dangers of sex are helpful reminders of the eternal validity of God's laws.

Just one of the decisions we have to make in talking about this subject with our kids is how much detail we are willing to go into about how contraceptive methods work. Are we willing to show children how a condom rolls on the penis (school programs have had kids practice rolling them onto bananas)? Are we willing to practice walking into a drugstore and requesting a condom (another frequent school activity)? Do we give them the phone numbers and addresses of a gynecologist or "family-planning" clinic? Do we suggest certain books where they can get contraceptive information if they should desire it? These are very hard questions. When do we cross over the line from telling them not to destroy their lives if they decide to sin, and begin to make it easier for them to sin and tell them we don't really expect them to live rightly after all? Each parent must answer these tough questions for himself or herself.

Turn "Accidents" to Choices

Despite the protests of adolescent boys, human beings are not lower animals enslaved by their raging hormones. Neither are we psychologically programmed robots. Children need to be told that apart from rape, sexual acts do not just "happen." The adolescent who protests, "I don't know what came over me," is denying responsibility for his or her actions.

Human beings make choices. Parents need to help their children understand that, well before they go out on a date, they have made up their minds about the kinds of things they will and will not do. It is the teenage boy who is open to the possibility of intercourse who engages in wild petting in an empty apartment and happens to have a condom in his wallet; it is the teenage girl who is open to the possibility of intercourse who drinks heavily with a boy with a reputation as a Don Juan.

We as parents must put the responsibility for choice squarely where it belongs—on our teenagers. We are not their bodyguards; we cannot make every decision for them. We must challenge them to face the enormity of their human responsibility. Except for rape, intercourse is not something that will "happen" to them; rather, they may choose as responsible persons to follow God's path or they may choose to go their own way, to be their own god. In the sexual area of their lives, they face just one of the many instances where they, like Adam and Eve, have to choose obedience or disobedience. They will either pursue the light, or they will be walking into darkness.

A SAMPLE "MONOLOGUE" ABOUT CONTRACEPTION

"Nancy, today I want to tell you a bit about contraception. What I have to say will not take long, but it is something that I really don't want to talk about and that makes it hard. I don't want to talk about it because I pray that you won't need to know about this for yourself until you are married. Maybe you will be able to help someone else with what I have to say, but I say it for your benefit.

"We have told you what we believe is God's view of sexuality and of sexual intercourse. Your female body, your ability to feel love and desire for a boy, your ability to have intercourse, to feel the pleasures of sex, and to carry and give birth to a child, are all wonderful gifts from God. He wants you to use them well. Intercourse is made for marriage, as an act that will 'glue' you to your husband, making the two of you one. Saving sex for marriage gives glory to God, builds your character, and lays the foundation for a better marriage than you might otherwise have.

"Sadly, not all teenagers follow God's way in this matter. By the time you are a senior, probably more than half of the girls in your grade at school will have had sexual intercourse; some only once, some quite often. Some will have been pregnant and had abortions, some will have had children. Some Christian friends will fall into sexual sin as well.

"I pray that will not be the story for you. Sex before marriage dishonors God and risks disease and pregnancy. You are gambling with your life and the lives of others when you have sex outside of the bounds God intends, outside of marriage.

"In light of that, I have two things to tell you. First, *sex never just happens*—people decide to have sex. You must have the honesty and courage to be straight with yourself; are you living your life God's way, or are you choosing to reject God's way for your own way? I pray you choose God's way, but either way is a choice. It doesn't just happen. And I know you *can* choose and live by the right way. I'm thankful you have told me that you choose God's way, that you will stay a virgin until marriage. I pray you continue firm in that commitment.

"Second, if you do choose to sin, if you do choose to reject God's way and go the way that our society says is the way, *I pray that you will choose to protect yourself and others against pregnancy and disease*. It would be a sin that would bring tears to God's eyes for you to reject His sexual rules. Imagine how much worse it would be not only to do that, but also to get pregnant and thus hurt an innocent child, or to contract a disease that can haunt you for years, maybe even kill you. Using a condom and the pill do not make sex before marriage right, but they can prevent some horribly wrong things that could happen from happening.

"Honey, I want you to know that you don't have to live a life of sexual sin. God wants more for you than that. He wants you pure. But if you choose not to be pure for God's sake and because it is right, then I pray that you will have the honesty to face your decision, and the intelligence not to hurt yourself even more profoundly by not protecting yourself.

"I want to tell you a little bit about contraception. I pray the only use you will make of this information before marriage will be to help a friend who is choosing the wrong path. I won't go into all the details of how to use the pill or a condom. A woman has to get the pill from a doctor who can tell her how to use it. It works only if she takes it every single day, and it takes time before it works. Anyone can get condoms at any drugstore, but they have to be used right or they don't work. Using a condom the wrong way is the same as not using one at all. Don't believe all the myths you may hear about how to keep from getting pregnant. Many kids who use the condom and the pill still wind up pregnant or with diseases. Kids who have sex and don't use both are even much more likely to wind up pregnant or with a disease.

"I pray you will follow God's laws because they are good and right. If you decide to have sex anyway, tell me, and I'll try to change your mind, and if I can't, I'll direct you to someone who can give you the information you need to lower your chances of getting pregnant or a disease. You can lower the chances, but sex will never be safe. God didn't make it to be safe, not even in marriage. But in marriage, you experience it the way God intended, and have a soul mate to share the risks and the joys with."

·

20

Date Rape, Cohabitation, Abortion, Homosexuality, and Redemption

❖

I n this final chapter on shaping your child's sexual character, we will discuss preventing and dealing with four topics that are particularly fearsome to many Christian parents: date rape, cohabitation, abortion, and homosexuality. We will close the chapter with a general discussion of how to be redemptive if your child goes astray.

DATE RAPE

The majority of rapes do not occur in the way so many of us imagine—a violent ambush committed by a total stranger with a weapon. Instead, most rapes occur on dates, and most rapists are known by their victims. Estimates of the frequency of date rape based on surveys of college women range from about 4 percent to 20 percent of women having been raped on a date.[1] Our daughters are much more at risk when they date than when they go about the rest of their lives. Increasingly today, boys are getting pressure from girls, but since pressure and coercion is mainly a problem for women, we will use female examples here.

We need to take steps to prevent this from happening. Sadly, not all of the messages our girls receive in the Christian community are helpful in protecting them against unwanted sexual experiences. Some conservative Christians teach that girls were made to satisfy the male's powerful sexual urges. Implicitly or explicitly, girls exposed to these conservative Christian teachings often come to believe that a man's sexual drive is uncontrollable or nearly uncontrollable, leading them to think that they are being cruel and destructive by saying no to a boy. This teaching fails to offer the balancing view that it is *wives* who were made to satisfy *their husbands'* sexual needs, and the husbands the wives', and *not* that any woman is made to meet the needs of a man she is dating. Also, girls are not harming boys by remaining chaste and denying them sex. The male sex drive is controllable. Finally, the emphasis on female submission in some churches can become twisted in the minds of young women to mean that they must be docile and acquiescing even when being victimized. This is very unhealthy and wrong.

A woman's first defense against date rape is to communicate clearly about her sexual limits and standards. We covered this theme in chapter 14. Second, a woman must be prepared to say no with every ounce of forcefulness. We discussed this in chapter 17. In addition to being prepared to repulse pressure with her words and even threaten police prosecution and public humiliation of the boy, young women should also be prepared to fight back physically if words are not enough. While physical resistance is often not advised when the rapist is a stranger with a weapon, in date-rape situations a gouging of his eye or breaking of his finger can cool off physical pressures. Girls are often afraid of physical violence, but the pain of a physical blow or two fades much more quickly than the emotional and physical pain of a rape. She should strike and yell "Fire!" if anyone can hear, or strike and yell "I'll keep fighting and you will go to jail if you touch me!" if no one can hear her.

Next, to prevent date rape a woman should be able to recognize when she is in danger, be able to trust her instincts, and to act decisively to get out of danger. Women who have been victims of date rape are often described as naive. Discussing this can quickly sound like blaming the victim for what happened, and we do not wish to do that. But no one should ever be able to describe our daughters as naive—the best cure for naiveté is information. We need to train girls to look for danger signals and high-risk situations. Among the factors that predict rape occurring is one that is perhaps the most chilling—simple *opportunity*. Some men who would otherwise have no predisposition to rape will simply seize on the opportunity to coerce sex. Therefore, women should stay out of situations where there is the opportunity for the man to get away with rape—they should not agree to go to isolated places or enter any situation where there is no accountability and no escape route.

Two kinds of factors about people are predictive of a higher risk of date rape: characteristics of the woman herself and characteristics of the man she is dating. One study suggested that the following "risk factors" or characteristics of a young woman made it more likely that she would experience forced sex: (1) having parents who drink heavily, are alcoholics, or use drugs; (2) having a physical, emotional, or mental handicap;

(3) having lived separate from both of her parents before age sixteen (such as having lived with a grandparent or in a foster home); and (4) having lived in childhood poverty.[2] These factors seem to add up to a description of a young woman who has very few supports and many needs, a woman who could be victimized by a man with very little possibility of his getting punished for what he did. A woman is in danger if she comes across to men as a victim. If we parents provide the supports our daughters need, and shape their character to be strong and confident, and if they specifically know how to conduct themselves to stay within their limits and protect themselves, they will be much less likely to become a victim.

There seem to be only two predictors that indicate if a man is likely to be the kind who would attempt a date rape: domineering and aggressive attitudes toward women, and use of alcohol or drugs on dates. Girls need to listen carefully to the reputations of boys at school; they should do some homework on the person who has asked them out. Is he respectful, polite, and sober? Avoid "risky" young men like the plague! And exit quickly if alcohol or drug use begins.

What if a date rape occurs? Though we pray this does not happen, we must be prepared for action. Our first concern must be for the well-being of our daughter. We must attend immediately to her physical and emotional needs. We must also have a concern about punishment of the man who forced himself upon her and preventing him from victimizing other women. The hours after a rape can take a terrible toll on a young woman, especially if she reports the rape to the police and has to endure questioning. The best course of action would probably be something like the following. The woman should not wash or clean up in any way, as this destroys evidence for prosecution of the rapist. She or her parents should call the police and have them meet her at her medical clinic or hospital emergency room. She will be able to decide whether or not to press charges later—she can talk to the police immediately and not press charges, but if she does not talk to the police and later does decide to press charges she is much less likely to be successful in having the man convicted. So it is best to talk to the police immediately, even if later she decides not to prosecute. In the clinic or emergency room she should get a complete physical exam; the attending physician should take physical samples that will stand as evidence later. She should answer the questions that doctors or police ask her as directly as she can. A parent can be her advocate and support during this process, and should protect her from insensitive, demeaning, or inappropriate questions. She will probably be offered a "morning-after birth control pill," which will make implantation of an egg fertilized as a result of the rape unlikely. We discussed this method of birth control in chapter 19, and the young woman and her parents may be forced to make an agonizing and major moral decision in a very short and difficult time—such a pill must be taken within seventy-two hours of intercourse or so to be effective, but is more effective if taken sooner. And remember—in the long run, she will have to be tested for sexually transmitted diseases, especially AIDS.

During this time, make use of the support of a rape-crisis team or counselor. At the same time, you must be aware that the advice you will get is never neutral—police may be supportive or they may have other "more serious crimes" they are concerned with, rape-crisis counselors may be pushing for prosecution, a pregnancy-clinic counselor may be stridently proabortion or stridently prolife. Pray that in the midst of chaos you will receive God's own counsel.

COHABITATION

In adolescence, it is important to help your teenagers think through and make commitments about the important life decisions they will make after high school. One of these is the decision of how they will prepare for marriage; namely, will they "live together," or cohabit, with the person they feel they want to marry? Or will they live apart and hopefully stay chaste until marriage?

Cohabitation, "living together," or "trial marriage" has become extremely common in modern American society. Cohabitation is estimated to have increased over 600 percent since the 1960s. What was once a shameful and hidden practice is now widely accepted. One recent study found that just over half of college freshmen agreed that "a couple should live together before marriage."[3]

Cohabitation is actually recommended by secular authorities. It is seen as a way to try out a relationship in order to make a better decision about marriage. Speaking to college students in a textbook, the premier "sexologists" in the world say: "One way of assessing someone's marriage potential is to stay in a long term relationship . . . by living together, a route chosen by about one quarter of United States undergraduates in the 1980s. . . . While sex is not the most important ingredient in most marriages, it does help to know if you and your spouse-to-be are sexually compatible or have considerable difficulty getting things together sexually."[4]

This is bad advice morally and scientifically. As Christians, we believe that sexual intercourse outside of marriage is wrong, and since very few cohabiting couples live together under a vow of celibacy, cohabitation is a context for the abuse of God's beautiful gift of sexual intercourse. We believe such a deliberate choice of a sinful lifestyle must drive a wedge in the couple's relationship to God, and must also grieve a loving Lord who wants better for the couple.

This is not good advice scientifically either. We have been amazed at the way some secular writers bend the truth here. For example, "To date, there is no evidence that living together sets the stage for unhappy marriages or divorce."[5] The only problem with this summary is that it is utterly false. Study after scientific study over the last fifteen years has shown that cohabiting actually increases one's future chances of getting divorced, and also decreases the stability and satisfaction of one's marriage. Estimates of how much cohabitation before marriage increases the chances of the subsequent marriage ending in divorce range from 30 percent to 80 percent increased likelihood of divorce.[6]

Social scientists are not sure why cohabitation has this effect. Some actually speculate that people who accommodate themselves to sex outside of marriage before they are married (premarital sex) are more likely to have sex outside of the marriage during the marriage (adultery), which can break the marriage. Others argue that people who choose to cohabit probably believe less strongly in the importance of marriage if the first place, and hence are more likely to divorce. Finally, we would add the hypothesis that sexual union and loving commitment together are meant to naturally build on each other in marriage to create greater love and loyalty. But in cohabitation the opposite takes place—the couple is engaging in sexual union while they work actively to forestall their commitment. In essence, they engage in an act of union physically while training their hearts not to be united or committed. Any commitment to marriage made later would have to be greatly weakened by their earlier choices.

As parents, we should make practical use of this information about the effects of cohabitation. We should appeal to the common desires that we share as human beings with our children and draw their attention to the long-term consequences of cohabitation. We should ask our children, "What kind of life do you want to have? Do you eventually want to have a stable home with one partner that you want to share your life with? Do you want to be able to share your soul with one person whom you will be able to love all your life and grow old with? Do you want to be able to jointly share the task of raising children and building a home together?" If these things do represent what our children want, we can then present a reminder that cohabitation makes them less likely to achieve these goals and is against God's will. Going against God's will by cohabiting pushes people further away from what they truly want, which is to be able to build a successful and long-lasting marriage.

ABORTION

We take a firmly conservative stance on the topic of abortion. While recognizing that there may be some room for individual moral choice in such tragic and rare cases as rape, incest, and medical threat to the life of the pregnant woman, we feel that the *vast* majority of abortions must be viewed as wrong.

We are preventing abortion when we contribute to our child's commitment to sexual abstinence. Every teenager who remains abstinent means one less unintended pregnancy that could end in the death of the fetus. But we should also directly teach our children that abortion is wrong. Christian parents must teach their children to value life as sacred, and to repudiate a pragmatic and relativistic ethic that can so casually disregard the value of the life of the developing child in the mother's womb; we should teach them to be horrified by such logic as, "Well, having a baby now would really crimp my lifestyle and put me behind in the career advancement plans I had laid out for myself." Parents should not, however, so emphasize this foundation that they minimize the complexities of the issue *or* destroy the possibility of their child coming to the parents as a resource should the child become pregnant. If parents come across as screaming extremists on the issue to their children, the kids will most likely not come to them if they do become pregnant. Parents need to develop in their child empathy for the plight of the pregnant unwed mother, including an understanding of the tremendous difficulties involved both in keeping a baby and in giving one up for adoption. Developing such understanding and empathy can serve well to strengthen the resolve of the child to stay a virgin until marriage.

HOMOSEXUALITY

If it is indeed possible to prevent a homosexual orientation from developing, the major portion of that preventative work undoubtedly occurs in the early years of childhood, before age eight or so (as discussed in chapter 9). But this does not mean that the adolescent years are irrelevant. Even if a young person has some leanings in the direction of homosexual desire, it is quite possible that the adolescent years are critical to that person "finalizing" his or her sexual identity as heterosexual or homosexual. Prominent psychoanalyst Robert Friedman suggested, for example, that "the final sexual orientation may not consolidate until after puberty."[7]

And we must remember that we live in a society that thinks in absolute black-white terms about sexual orientation: a person is either gay or straight, and if you have sexual feelings for the same sex, you are gay. But this is not a good description of reality. Some people have very exclusive feelings about what arouses them sexually, while others experience a mixture of feelings. Also, we are not static creatures who are frozen in place sexually; our feelings change and refocus as we grow.

Homosexual thoughts and impulses are a normal part of adolescence for many people who are *not* "gay" as we understand it. Teenage sexual interest can be so powerful that teens find themselves reacting to any sexual stimulus; a very normal teenage boy may be secretly horrified to find himself aroused when he hears a description of oral sex between two men. The teen years are also a time of intense sexual curiosity, and so a teen may be confused by her own fascination about hearing of homosexual practice. We are very complex creatures!

Many public schools, however, under the relentless pressure of gay-pride and gay-rights groups, are moving toward having "gay-awareness groups" on campus that encourage early identification and acceptance of one's "gay identity." The great danger here is of a premature leap into an identity that does not really fit our children. And yet it is realistic to think that some teens do already have a fairly stable orientation toward the same sex by midadolescence, and we should not minimize the pain that these people feel. To find oneself to be so different from most other teens, at a time when we crave nothing more than to be like everyone else and be accepted, is a kind of pain that many of us have never experienced.

We would remind parents first that probably the central psychological building block of sexual identity and sexual orientation is your child's identification with the same-sex parent or other-parent figure. We have talked repeatedly about how a close relationship between parent and child is a strong predictor of the child staying sexually abstinent. We think it likely that the same thing is true about sexual orientation. A child who enters adolescence confused about his or her sexual identity is most likely to resolve that confusion positively if he or she has a close and loving relationship with the same-sex parent or with someone who is like a parent to him or her (a grandparent, relative, older brother or sister, youth minister, scoutmaster, teacher, and so forth). Adolescence is no time to let down on the work of relationship building!

The other-sex parent, the mother of a boy or father of a girl, should also be very careful of the messages she or he gives about the child's developing manhood or womanhood. Our teens need us to radiate an excitement and joy about the transformation they are going through, not condemnation and rejection. Many of us have "unfinished business" from the past that can contaminate our dealings with our children. Do we hear ourselves saying, "Well, that's just like any of the brainless men I've known who think with their hormones rather than their brains and don't have any human feelings," or "I'm glad you aren't turning out like those fluffy, weepy airheads who chase and hang on the guys"? Our kids need more from us than that.

It is vital for a father with his son, and a mother with her daughter, to talk about how confusing sexual feelings can be and how common sexual feelings are for persons of the same sex. Whether it is a girl who feels powerful feelings of closeness and longing when she hugs her best friend, or a boy getting an unwanted erection in the locker room when he is sneaking curious looks at how other boys' genitals are developing, our children must be helped to see these confusing feelings as normal and no cause for alarm. Perhaps a father could say something like the following to his son:

"Lee, you are going into what is the hardest time of life for many people. I found junior high and early high school to be very difficult. You're changing so fast, you sort of want to stay the same but you sort of want to grow up, and sometimes it just seems that nothing is right. We have already talked about how powerful your sexual feelings can be; sometimes it seems like you think about sex a lot, and you get erections that are embarrassing, and on and on. It's tough. One of the things that can be most confusing is having sexual feelings that seem weird, that you don't want to have. I want you to know that it's normal to have such feelings. I remember other guys talking about sex in a way that was dirty and gross, but I felt turned on by what they said. I remember wanting to look at other boys in the locker room because I was curious, and it was kind of exciting too, but I heard other kids being called a 'fag'—I didn't know what that was back then, but I knew it wasn't a good thing to be, given how other kids made fun of anyone with that label. And I remember the first time I heard about homosexuals having sex, I was repulsed, but again curious and half excited by hearing about it, and I remember thinking, 'Is there something horribly wrong with me that I think this way?' I want you to know that you will have many strange feelings that you won't be able to explain and that won't make sense. But I want you to trust that you're okay; what you are going through is what I went through and what most men go through. I want you also to thank God that you have a brain and a will; you don't have to act on any of the feelings you have. And decisions you make will help to shape the feelings you have—the more you trust in God and act rightly, the way God wants you to act, the more your feelings will go in the right direction. And I want you to know that you can talk to me about anything. Is there anything you want to talk about now?"

Parents should not panic or make much about a child who seems uninterested in the other sex or who doesn't fit the gender stereotypes. The vast majority of people who don't fit those stereotypes turn out well. We have one friend who has given his life to painting and the visual arts and who was almost tortured in adolescence by other kids who were convinced that since he was introverted, gentle, sensitive, artistic, unaggressive, and highly verbal he had to be gay. What was particularly damaging was that he picked up clearly from his parents that they also suspected something was wrong with him. Kids should not be hauled off to a psychiatrist because they don't want to play football, try out for cheerleader, or date. As parents, we must trust and love and affirm them, and not undermine their confidence by catastrophizing prematurely.

A teenager may trust his parents enough to come and express concerns that he is homosexual. If this happens, we should first be very careful to distinguish between homosexual experimentation and homosexual orientation. Our society is in a rush to identify homosexual orientation and affirm it. But many kids feel homosexual feelings and many experiment with homosexual behavior, all without ever becoming homosexual people! You should pray for wisdom to discern whether your child simply needs to be affirmed that he is okay (as well as urged not to engage in any further experimentation!) or whether you should seek professional counsel of some kind.

If you do choose to get professional consultation for yourself as you deal with your child, or for your child himself, you must carefully screen whom you see. The gay and lesbian groups in most major mental-health organizations have come to exert tremendous power, and the "official" position of all the major organizations today is that homosexual orientation is normal, something to be embraced, affirmed, and celebrated. Yet a very sizable group within each major profession still regard homosexual orientation as undesirable. You should ask the respected professionals you are referred to three critical questions: Are they Christians themselves, or at least respectful and accepting of your Christian beliefs, so that counseling will not undermine the faith of your family? Do they regard homosexuality as a normal and acceptable variation of human sexual practice? If not, do they have any professional training and experience in dealing with matters of homosexual desire and interest? One final caution: While you will hope to find a professional who can answer these questions in a way that fits with your beliefs, *do not confuse Christian morality and religious belief with professional competence.* We are concerned that there are some doctrinally conservative Christian "counselors" out there who substitute orthodox belief *in place of* professional competence, rather than as a complement to it. We hope you will be able to find someone who combines both qualities.

Finally, do not believe the popular line that healing is impossible for the homosexual, that there is no changing this orientation. We know personally several "healed" homosexuals; we know healing is possible through God's grace, with possible help from a competent professional. But it also seems true that healing in the form of complete resolution of homosexual feelings and complete conversion to heterosexuality is difficult to impossible for some others. The situation is rather like what we face in dealing with physical disease; our God is a God of healing power, but that healing power is not always extended in the way we might desire. Some give glory to God in their healing, while others can give glory to God in the way that His strength is shown through their weakness. We must remember that God's grace is sufficient for all human weakness, and that people whose homosexual inclinations are not healed have the same calling as Christian singles: they are called by God to live a celibate life of loving service to God and to His Body.

REDEMPTION

Bad things happen in good families. Good things happen in bad families. Kids may turn in the right direction despite our weaknesses and failings as parents, and kids may turn in the wrong direction despite our wonderful efforts to the contrary. Our kids may become sexually active, even promiscuous; they may get pregnant or get someone pregnant; and they may get an abortion or abortions. Let us discuss the foundation for dealing with the wrong choices of our children.

The heart of the gospel is the good news that, although we are alienated from God and cannot make ourselves right with Him, God Himself, through the forgiveness made possible by His Son Jesus Christ, can make us right and can bring us into a relationship of love with Himself.

God can make anything right. We want to offer this as our last key principle in shaping our child's sexual character:

PRINCIPLE 12: Our God can heal and redeem us from anything; no human actions are beyond the reach of His redeeming intent and capability. We must teach our children how to recover from mistakes and wrong choices by the Christian disciplines of confession, repentance, forgiveness, and reconciliation.

There are two beautiful passages in the Old Testament that illustrate this truth. Exodus 15:22-26 tells how the Israelites, only three days after their dramatic rescue by God from their enslavement to Pharaoh in Egypt, find only a pool of bitter water in the desert. Almost comically, they begin to grumble about God's provision. The Lord shows Moses a tree, which Moses uproots and casts into the bitter pool. The water immediately becomes sweet, and the Lord declares, "I am the LORD, who heals you." The transforming tree seems to symbolize the cross of Christ, which when cast into the midst of the most bitter waters can make anything sweet.

The book of Joel prophesies God's judgment on His people for their sins. A plague of locusts that strips their fields and leaves them starving is God's symbol for His judgment. The people will be disciplined, chastised for their faithlessness and sinfulness. But if the people turn again from their sin to the Lord in confession and repentance, God promises to pour out His blessings on them. In Joel 2:25-27 He says,

"I will repay you for the years the locusts have eaten— . . .
You will have plenty to eat, until you are full,
    and you will praise the name of the LORD your God. . . .
Then you will know that I am in Israel,
    that I am the LORD your God,

and there is no other;
never again will my people be ashamed."

Along with Romans 8:28 and many other passages in the Scriptures, these verses comfort us that God can heal and redeem anything if only we will turn to Him as our Healer and Redeemer.

Note that none of these passages says anything about God taking away the consequences of our acts or extricating us from our circumstances, or of God's discipline being comfortable and convenient. The life of a teenage daughter who bears and keeps a child to raise is changed forever; so are the lives of her parents. The woman who gets an abortion will carry that act in her body and soul for the rest of her life. Like David, who was forgiven for his adultery (2 Samuel 11) but whose life of faith, and especially the faith of his sons, was never the same; or like Moses, whose act of disobedience to God (Numbers 20:6-12) was forgiven but who was still never allowed to see the Promised Land because of that disobedience (Deuteronomy 34); so also we may be forgiven and even healed, but we may still have to bear for life the heavy consequences of our choices and of the things others do to us. "You were to Israel a forgiving God, though you punished their misdeeds" (Psalm 99:8).

God can heal a girl who is raped, but her life is forever different. Like Job, who was tested and sifted by Satan and changed forever, but who experienced God's blessings and redemption in this life; or like the saints through the ages who endured horrible persecution and received God's strength to endure, but had to wait until the next life to see the final redemption of their sufferings (for example, Revelation 2:8-11); so too we have to trust that when horrible things happen to us, God is at work to redeem and heal, even when we must wait to receive the final fruits of that redemption until we pass from this life.

One of our heaviest responsibilities as parents is to live out these realities in our families. In chapter 3 we discussed parenting as the creation of a family environment in which our children will see the truths of God laid out in flesh before them. Parenting is a form of incarnation—God's work of incarnation did not stop with Christ, but continues as God inhabits His people the Church through the work of the Holy Spirit. Incarnation continues as husbands and wives act out the divine drama of the relationship of Christ and His Church in their marriages. And incarnation continues yet again as parents act out the divine drama of God's parenting of His children—a disciplining, teaching, pursuing, loving fathering of His children.

As we deal with the mistaken or wrong choices of our children, with their weaknesses and defects of character, and with the consequences that fall from them, we must remember that we are to manifest God's very character in dealing with them. We have done our best to lay a grou... work for them to feel a loving, tenacious acceptance that is rooted in God's stubborn love. When they fall or are injured, then is our time to live out that tenacious acceptance in their lives. We continue to discipline and instruct, but all discipline is rooted in a stubborn and unyielding love.

We are to forgive as God Himself forgives. Often, our children's actions hurt them *and* us; the most dramatic example of this is the parent who unexpectedly becomes a grandparent out of season. Such an event can forever change the course of family and career life. We often also take our child's successes and failures as vindications or judgments of our worth as parents. One of our fears as parents in writing this book has been the haunting question of what will become of *our* children; we feel these pressures too. These factors can make it difficult to forgive our kids, as we feel that their wrong choices have hurt us as well as them. But forgiveness is our responsibility and privilege as Christians.

We should also model godly repentance for our kids. We should have an entire life history of this coming into adolescence, a life pattern of confessing to our children when we have wronged them, of seeking their forgiveness, and of truly turning over a new leaf as true repentance demands. When our children fall, we should compose ourselves and devote time to prayer and reflection. We should ask God to give us insight into our role in this, honestly ask God to show us where we let our children down, where our weaknesses as parents might have affected them. At the same time, we should ask God to preserve us from taking blame that is not ours. God views our teenagers as responsible moral agents, and so should we. Pray that as we talk with our children about their behavior, we will evidence a spirit of love, grace, forgiveness, and strength.

There are no formulas for dealing with the family crises that come when children go astray. At those times, we must be guided by God Himself, by His Word in the Scriptures, by His Body the Church, and by a love that only He can give.

So the foundation for our dealing with all of the problems that can happen with our kids is the gospel itself—our confidence that our God can heal and redeem anything, and that we as parents can find the strength in Him to embody His very character in dealing with them.

21

at If I Get Started Late?

✦

We began to write this chapter under the working title of "What If I Get Started Too Late?" It didn't take us long to realize that there is no such thing as "too" late. Earlier is better. But any sex education that we give to our kids is a gift; any communication on this delicate topic will be an improvement over no communication whatsoever. And you are reading this book because you love your child enough to want to give him or her such a gift.

It's never too late to instruct your child about sexuality and to try to shape his or her character. Further, the way of understanding your child's character that we developed in chapters 3 and 4 applies as well to two-year-olds as to twenty-year-olds. The principles of sex education we have assembled apply to persons of age five or fifteen or fifty-five. The moral foundations for the Christian ethic discussed in chapters 5, 6, and 10 apply to persons of all ages. You will be better equipped after reading this book to understand your child's character wherever your child is right now, to understand how your child's character might yet be molded, to understand what kinds of messages and efforts might be most meaningful, and to understand in depth the Christian morality we are trying to impart.

If you're starting late, at least you're starting. Remember, our God is a God who wants to start a good work in us and keep at it until it's done (Philippians 1:6). God is willing to start His good work any time we are ready. Earlier would always have been better, but don't be discouraged, now is a wonderful time to start in God's view.

CONCRETE SUGGESTIONS FOR PARENTS WHO START LATE

Since we urge that you start very early, "late" could mean starting at age seven, or at age seventeen. Whether it is seven or seventeen makes a considerable difference, but we will try to share in general what you might do if you are starting late.

First, we urge, however old your child is, start sex education *now*! Give yourself a crash course with this or other books, and dive in. Don't put it off for more preparation or out of a fatal sense of having already waited too long. That would be defeatist thinking. *Any* discussion you can have with your child that follows the guidelines we have discussed in this book will bear some fruit. *Any* discussion that you can have with your child will be a victory of some sort. Start now.

Next, review the twelve core principles of shaping your child's sexual character that are spread throughout this book. These principles are:

PRINCIPLE 1: Sexual education is the shaping of character. (Introduction)

PRINCIPLE 2: Parents *are* the principle sex educators; you will either have an anemic, unintentional, mixed-up and hence negative impact, or a powerful, deliberate, clear and positive impact. (Chapter 2)

PRINCIPLE 3: Stories are as powerful or more powerful than principles or "logic" as a teaching tool. (Chapter 3)

PRINCIPLE 4: The best teaching of a child occurs at "teachable moments" when discussion and instruction mesh naturally with the events and needs of daily life. One of the best goals for parents to strive for is to become an "askable" parent whom kids can come to with questions. (Chapter 6)

PRINCIPLE 5: First messages are the most potent; it is far more powerful to form a child's view of sexuality from scratch than it is to correct the distortions they will pick up in the world. (Chapter 7)

PRINCIPLE 6: Accurate and explicit messages are far better than cryptic, vague ones. (Chapter 10)

PRINCIPLE 7: Positive messages are more potent than negative messages. (Chapter 10)

PRINCIPLE 8: We can "inoculate" our children against negative influences. (Chapter 11)

PRINCIPLE 9: The closer and more positive the relationship between parent and child, the greater the parent's influence upon the behavior of the child. (Chapter 12)

PRINCIPLE 10: Repetition is critical; the most important messages about sexuality rarely "get through" on the first try. (Chapter 13)

PRINCIPLE 11: Sexuality is not the most important thing in life. We must strive to put sexuality into its proper perspective. (Chapter 14)

PRINCIPLE 12: Our God can heal and redeem anything; no human actions are beyond the reach of His redeeming intent and capability. We must teach our children how to recover from mistakes and wrong choices by the Christian disciplines of confession, repentance, forgiveness, and reconciliation. (Chapter 20)

Every one of these principles is as relevant to sex education that starts at twelve as it is to that which starts at two. We can inoculate our kids against negative messages at any age, but the later we start, the greater the head start the media moguls and advertisers have on us. Stories are powerful at any age, but our stories are more powerful if they are early stories rather than late ones. The best sex education occurs at teachable moments, but we will have more teachable moments if we have a strong track record in talking with our kids. A close relationship with your child will exert real influence on him or her, but the earlier you work on that kind of relationship the more likely you are to meet with success.

If you are starting the process of shaping your child's sexual character later than you would wish, we urge you to creatively make use of these principles. We hope that the examples of how they have been implemented at each age level will provide you with ideas of how to put these into action.

Third, we urge that you make an honest assessment of the kind of relationship you have with your child. In addition to everything else you do on sex education itself, you *must work diligently on the quality of your relationship with your child.* Build on the strengths of your relationship. Don't become bogged down in the negative! There must be strengths of your relationship, so use them! Use them as the cornerstone upon which to build a new and improved building. Do you enjoy sports or music or hobbies together? Are there certain topics you are both interested in and can talk about? Do you share similar temperaments and understand each other emotionally? Are you able to help with homework? Whatever the area of strength, use it as a launching pad to build a better relationship. Bookstores are filled with useful books about communicating with your child regardless of age. Pour energy into making your relationship with your child stronger.

Fourth, we urge that you also try to make an honest assessment of your child's faith in Christ. The presence of a firm personal faith in Christ when your child hits the teenage years will have a powerful effect on your child's sexual choices. Have you done everything you can to encourage your child's faith? Remember that "doing everything you can do" doesn't mean smothering your child with Bible lessons, scripture memorization, Christian music blaring at all hours, and church every evening of the week. Faith is best caught, not taught. Your child can catch faith from you, if your faith is alive enough to be a "communicable disease." Without preaching or nagging, share about your belief in God and about God, and talk naturally about the connections between your faith and your daily choices, your work, your ethical beliefs, and your love for your child. Your child can also catch faith from a community of faith, whether Christian friends at school, the church youth group, the church in general, or the quiet witness of one neighbor. Pray that your child might grow into a sincere and deep faith in Christ.

Next, we would urge that you seek to have a balanced view of your children's character, both of their strengths and weaknesses. Reread chapter 4 with your children specifically in mind. Think about their basic needs for relatedness and significance, both how well they seem to be met and how aware they are of what those needs really are. Think about their core beliefs, about how well they understand Christian morality and how well they view themselves to be creatures and creations of God. Think about the values they seem to be beginning to live by, and about the values you passed on to them over the past years. What values did they catch from you? Think about the skills they have developed and failed to develop. And think about the supports you are able to provide for them. We would urge you to think strategically about what aspects of their character, their sexual character, you can still influence. Where do you still have an opportunity to have an impact upon them?

If you are starting late in this whole process, it is probably due in part to your uncomfortable feelings about this whole topic. We hope that reading this book has made you decidedly less uncomfortable. We would encourage you to share honestly with your children your hesitancies in communicating about sex, and that you then confess to them your embarrassment for getting this late start. Parents should not always try to be strong before their children. A parent who is uncomfortable communicating about sex, but goes ahead anyway despite obvious distress, is moving ahead in the task of sex education *and* is communicating to the child that he or she cares so deeply about the child that he or she is willing to endure embarrassment and discomfort for the child's sake. That is a sacrifice of love which can bear fruit.

Remember to maintain a balanced focus as you talk about sex. Talk about the biological realities, but also to talk about the moral realities, the relational realities, and the emotional realities. We hope our selection of topics through this book will be a good guide for you as you strive for this balance.

Finally, we urge you to pray. We obviously hope that not just parents starting late, but all parents, will be praying diligently and specifically for their children. We can pray for the general welfare of our children, and for their particular concerns, on a day-to-day basis. But it may also be helpful to pray in disciplined ways for specific developments in their lives. For instance, we might pray through the Ephesians 6:10-17 list of the armor of God, beseeching God that our kids might be so equipped. We can pray similarly through the Galatians 5:22-23 fruit of the Spirit, or the Matthew 5:1-12 beatitudes of our Lord, or through Christ's parables, or through the letters from John's revelation that Christ dictated to the seven churches (Revelation 2-3), and so forth.

Such prayer can have a profound impact in a number of ways. First, and obviously, God works through prayer. We don't know why or how, but our God has chosen to work through the vehicle of the prayers of His people. Our prayers may be a critical element in God's direct intervention with our kids. Second, God may Himself stir us up as Christian parents as we pray for our kids. Praying for the fruit of the Spirit or the armor of God to be manifest in the lives of our kids may be a stimulus for us to be more attentive to how we might teach and encourage our children to better receive those gifts from God. Finally, if we actually pray with our children out loud for these things to happen, we are sharing powerfully with them our hopes and values for their lives, and that may itself have a powerful effect.

You might also consider, as your child begins to date, praying with your child for his or her future spouse. Pray for the growth, protection, and sexual integrity of that person. Again, God works through prayer, and our prayers may be critical in the life of this as yet unknown person. Also, this may help your child understand at yet a deeper level how enormous the decisions are that he or she is making during adolescence. To protect against our children taking such prayers as pressure to take dating very seriously, find a spouse, and rush into getting married, we should offer such prayers only occasionally, and should also make prayer for their dating relationships (that they would have fun, learn about the other sex and a wider array of people, be protected, and so forth) and for their friendships a regular part of our prayer life individually and together with them.

We hope these suggestions for the parent who is starting late are helpful. Wherever your starting point is, START NOW! God will, we trust, honor your efforts. After all, he is a God of new beginnings, a God who puts the past behind and causes us to move forward into new adventures!

22

What Is True Purity?

✛

P arenting is rather like all of the Christian life. It is a life of striving and of rest.

The Christian life is a life of striving. We are to run the race (1 Corinthians 9:24), press on toward the goal (Philippians 3:7-16), work out our salvation in fear and trembling (Philippians 2:12), press on to maturity (Hebrews 6:1), enter through the narrow gate (Matthew 7:13), and bear our cross and follow Christ (Matthew 10:38). But it is also a life of rest. We are to trust in the Lord (Proverbs 3:5-6), wait upon Him (Psalm 27:14), take up the easy yoke (Matthew 11:29-30), abide in Christ (John 15:4) and in His Word (8:31), and enter into His rest (Hebrews 4:10-11).

Strive and rest. Even strive to rest. This is a deep paradox of the Christian life. And it gives rise to a deep continuing theological debate, the debate around understanding the relationship between law and grace.

Parenting embodies this paradox as well. This book has been almost completely preoccupied with only one side of this paradox. We have urged you to strive with all your energy and creativity, to strive to shape your child's sexual character.

Many of us are in danger of not striving enough. Maybe we simply don't know where to start or what to do. Many of us have lost our vision of marriage and family as a *vocation*, as a life work that is well worth our investment of our whole selves.

But we would guess that anyone who has read this whole book has done so because he or she is willing to work and is searching for ways to do that work better. Some of us need to remember that life in Christ, and that includes parenting in Christ, is also a rest from striving. And so, we close this book with an invitation to rest, to trust God. And perhaps nothing provides us more of an opportunity to rest than to reflect on the deepest meaning of true purity.

The sexual behavior of our children matters to God, who loves them dearly. You hope with all your heart that they will live a chaste and pure life, and this is a hope that God shares with you. But true purity, understood properly, is something that is done *to* all of us, both our children and us, and not something our efforts, even guided and empowered by the Holy Spirit, can accomplish. This is because true purity is to be washed in the blood of the Lamb. We urge you to meditate on biblical passages that state this truth most clearly: Titus 2:14; Hebrews 9:14, 10:22; 1 John 1:7; Revelation 7:14.

We are right to hope that our children will live sexually pure lives. Living such lives will bring glory to God and save them (and us) from much pain and distress. But like the righteousness of the Pharisees, right living may do more to instill a sense of arrogance and self-righteousness than to draw the person toward God. Often in the midst of brokenness we turn to God for healing and cleansing. That is how it was for the Christians in ancient Corinth. The Apostle Paul exhorted them:

> Do you not know that the wicked will not inherit the kingdom of God? . . . Neither the sexually immoral nor idolaters nor adulterers nor male prostitutes nor homosexual offenders nor thieves nor the greedy nor drunkards nor slanderers nor swindlers will inherit the kingdom of God. And that is what some of you were. But you were washed, you were sanctified, you were justified in the name of the Lord Jesus Christ and by the Spirit of our God.
> (1 Corinthians 6:9-11)

"And that is what some of you were." God can redeem anyone from anything. God can transform anyone into His own child. We can take our best shot as parents at shaping our children's sexual character and yet rest in trust of God because we realize that no matter what choices our kids make, God can always redeem them. No matter how pure and upright their lives may be, they will be in need of cleansing with the blood of the Lamb. No matter how awful and devastating their choices may be, they can be cleansed by the work of God and achieve the true purity that only He can offer. Our ultimate hope for the true purity of our children does not lie in our efforts as parents, but in the work of Christ in their lives.

May God be with us in our parenting efforts. May the Creator God who made us all sexual beings give us wisdom as we teach our children of the magnitude of His good gift. May Jesus Christ, the source of all that is pure, give us discernment and persuasiveness as we teach the Christian view of sexual ethics and give us great effectiveness as we shape our children's character to His greater glory. May the Holy Spirit fill us with the deepest and most vibrant love imaginable for our children, even the very love that the Father has for all His children.

Notes

❖

INTRODUCTION

1. Andrew Greeley, *Faithful Attraction* (New York: Tor Books, 1991).
2. Slight rewording of the concluding sentences of Sharon Sheehan's "Another Kind of Sex Education," *Newsweek*, July 13, 1992, pages 10-11.

CHAPTER 1: THE BATTLE WE ARE LOSING

1. *Morbidity and Mortality Weekly Report*, vol. 40, nos. 51 and 52, U.S. Department of Health and Human Services, Public Health Service, Centers for Disease Control, January 2, 1992, pages 885-888.
2. "Teenagers and AIDS," *Newsweek*, August 3, 1992, page 46.
3. W. Masters et al., *Human Sexuality*, 4th ed. (Glenview, IL: Scott, Foresman and Company, 1992), page 233ff.
4. Masters, page 233ff.
5. These statistics were published by the Alan Guttmacher Institute, which is the research arm of the Planned Parenthood Federation of America, in *Family Planning Perspectives*, March/April 1989 and May/June 1990.
6. *Family Planning Perspectives*, July/August 1988.
7. J. Brooks-Gunn et al., "Preventing HIV Infection and AIDS in Children and Adolescents," *American Psychologist* 43 (1988), pages 958-964.
8. Brooks-Gunn, pages 958-964.
9. "Teenagers and AIDS," page 45.
10. *Drug Use Among American High School Seniors, College Students and Young Adults, 1975–1990*, DHHS Publication (ADM) 91-1813 (Rockville, MD: National Institute on Drug Abuse), pages 5-15.
11. All research from this section summarized from Masters, chapter 18.
12. A. Greeley et al., "Americans and Their Sexual Partners," *Society* 27, no. 5, pages 36-42.
13. *Abortion and Moral Beliefs: A Survey of American Opinion* (Chicago: Americans United for Life, 1991). This survey was conducted by the Gallup organization and dated February 28, 1991.

14. J. Maxwell, "Media: The New Hollywood Watchdogs," *Christianity Today*, April 27, 1992, pages 38-40.

15. See M. Medved, *Hollywood vs. America: Popular Culture and the War Against Traditional Values* (New York: HarperCollins, 1992).

16. Masters, page 668.

17. L. Kirkendall and R. Libby, "Sex Education in the Future," *Journal of Sex Education and Therapy* 11, no. 1, pages 64-67.

18. Masters, page 256.

19. Masters, page 396.

20. J. Hyde, *Understanding Human Sexuality*, 3d ed. (New York: McGraw-Hill, 1986).

21. C. Byer and L. Shainberg, *Dimensions of Human Sexuality*, 3d ed. (Dubuque, IA: William C. Brown, 1991), page 355.

22. D. Baumrind, "Adolescent Sexuality: Comment on Williams' and Silka's Comments on Baumrind," *American Psychologist* 37, no. 12 (1982), pages 1402-1403.

23. J. Olsen and S. Weed, "Effects of Family Planning Programs for Teenagers on Adolescent Birth and Pregnancy Rates," *Family Perspective* 20, no. 3 (1986), page 167. See also pages 153-193.

24. J. Flora and C. Thoresen, "Reducing the Risk of AIDS in Adolescents," *American Psychologist* 43 (1988), page 967. See also pages 965-970.

25. One of the more exhaustive presentations of a whole array of negative findings regarding sex education programs is compiled in J. McDowell, *The Myths of Sex Education* (San Bernardino, CA: Here's Life, 1990).

26. P. Benson, *A Troubled Journey: A Portrait of Sixth-Twelfth Grade Youths* (Minneapolis: Lutheran Brotherhood, 1990).

27. C. Hayes, ed., "Determinants of Adolescent Sexual Behavior and Decision Making," in *Risking the Future: Adolescent Sexuality, Pregnancy, and Childbearing* (Washington: National Academy Press, 1987), pages 99-100.

28. J. Robson, *Valuing Your Sexuality* (St. Louis: Concordia, 1989). Balanced, morally conservative, and targeted at encouraging coordinated church/home presentations with seventh and eighth graders, this program calls for parents to be involved and is abstinence-oriented. Adapted from the widely used abstinence-oriented public school curriculum, *Sex Respect* by Colleen Mast (1986).

29. For example, D. Lynn and M. Yaconelli, *Teaching the Truth About Sex: Biblical Sex Education for Today's Youth* (Grand Rapids: Zondervan, 1990).

30. For example, J. Forliti, *Valuing Values: Reverence for Life and Family II (Sexuality Education in the Catholic Tradition)* (Dubuque, IA: Brown ROA, 1986); this curriculum is balanced, Catholic (the Virgin Mary as a model, etc.), targeted at coordinated church/home presentations with seventh and eighth graders, emphasizes parental involvement, and is abstinence oriented. Also, *New Creation: A Catholic Program for Catechesis in Sexuality* (Dubuque, IA: Brown ROA, 1985) presents a graded introduction to sexuality with materials for students in grades one, two, four, five, and eight, with transparencies, audio and video, and leader/parent materials.

31. Hayes, pages 103-104.
32. J. Wallerstein and S. Blakeslee, *Second Chances: Men, Women and Children a Decade After Divorce* (New York: Tickner & Fields, 1989). See also Hayes, page 104.
33. Tim Stafford, "The Next Sexual Revolution," *Christianity Today*, March 9, 1992, pages 28-29.
34. A. Greeley, *Faithful Attraction: Discovering Intimacy, Love and Fidelity in American Marriage* (New York: Tor Books, 1991). This book reports results from two major studies of marriage sponsored by the magazine *Psychology Today* and conducted by the Gallup organization, along with findings from numerous other resources, including the results of the annual General Society Survey conducted by the National Opinion Research Center.
35. Greeley, *Faithful Attraction*, page 250.

CHAPTER 2: KNOWING YOUR STRENGTHS AND WEAKNESSES

1. D. Baumrind, "Parenting Styles and Adolescent Development," in J. Brooks-Gunn, R. Lerner, and A. C. Petersen, ed., *The Encyclopedia of Adolescence* (New York: Garland Press, 1991).
2. This is a lot like Kevin Huggins's concept of "incarnational parenting." See K. Huggins, *Parenting Adolescents* (Colorado Springs: NavPress, 1989).

CHAPTER 3: CHRISTIAN PARENTING AS CHARACTER FORMATION

1. Summarized by P. Vitz, "The Use of Stories in Moral Development: New Psychological Reasons for an Old Educational Method," *American Psychologist* 45 (1990), pages 709-720.
2. We have found J. Cook and K. Comina, *The Family Bible Companion* (Downers Grove, IL: InterVarsity, 1991), to be very worthwhile for this purpose.
3. Possible resources in this task would include a recent book by William Kirkpatrick, *Why Johnny Can't Tell Right from Wrong* (Simon & Schuster, 1992), which discusses the value of stories but also contains a great list of "great moral literature" for kids. Also, we have found James Trelease, *The New Read-Aloud Handbook* (Viking/Penguin, 1989) and John and Kathryn Lindskoog, *How to Grow a Young Reader: A Parent's Guide to Books for Kids* (Harold Shaw, 1989) to be helpful.
4. We are here using a collage of ideas from various personality theorists in this "working theory of character." William Glasser, among others, proposed understanding basic human needs as proposed here, though we are using the terminology of the early work of Larry Crabb. Of all psychologies, modern object-relations theory has a rich understanding of the relational needs we discuss, while Adler and the existential psychologies have rich understandings of our human needs for purpose and meaning. Alfred Adler, all of the humanistic psychologies, and the modern cognitive psychologies all embrace the idea of our fundamental purposes being pivotal. The idea of the importance of basic beliefs is common to Alfred Adler and the con-

temporary cognitive psychologies. The emphasis on cognitive and behavior skills, and of understanding the impact of the social environment, are unique strengths of the cognitive-behavioral psychologies. Family systems psychology enriches the understanding of the impact of the family environment. For more, see S. Jones and R. Butman's *Modern Psychotherapies: A Comprehensive Christian Appraisal* (Downers Grove, IL: InterVarsity Press, 1991).

CHAPTER 4: UNDERSTANDING YOUR CHILD'S SEXUAL CHARACTER

1. C. Hayes, ed., "Determinants of Adolescent Sexual Behavior and Decision Making," in *Risking the Future: Adolescent Sexuality, Pregnancy, and Childbearing* (Washington: National Academy Press, 1987), pages 100-101.
2. A number of different writers have pointed this out clearly in recent times, including: L. Crabb, *Inside Out* (Colorado Springs: NavPress, 1988); S. Arterburn and J. Felton, *Toxic Faith* (Ann Arbor, MI: Servant, 1991); and C. Thurman, *The Lies We Believe* (Nashville: Nelson, 1989).
3. An excellent book on raising responsible children is F. Cline and J. Fay *Parenting with Love and Logic* (Colorado Springs: NavPress, 1990).
4. Peter Kreeft has argued that suffering brings us to understand that the goal of our lives is not to live a happy life, but rather to live a good life. Part of the mystery of understanding pain comes from the realization that God is not in the business of making any of us happy. Happiness can be a wonderful byproduct of a good life, but we have bigger purposes to serve than simply becoming happy. Our lives are a training ground for the development of goodness. See P. Kreeft, *Making Sense Out of Suffering* (Ann Arbor, MI: Servant, 1986).
5. Hayes, page 105. Also F. DiBlasoi and B. Benda, "Adolescent Sexual Behavior: Multivariate Analysis of a Social Learning Model," *Journal of Adolescent Research* 5 (1987), pages 449-466.
6. P. Benson, *A Troubled Journey: A Portrait of Sixth-Twelfth Grade Youths* (Minneapolis: Lutheran Brotherhood, 1990).

CHAPTER 5: THE BIBLICAL FOUNDATION FOR SEXUALITY EDUCATION

1. One example of this tendency might be seen in the widely read, ancient devotional classic *The Imitation of Christ* by Thomas a' Kempis, trans. Leo Sherley-Price (New York: Dorset Press, 1952), pages 171-172: "Grant me this great grace, so necessary to my salvation, that I may conquer the base elements of my nature, that drag me down into sin and perdition. Within my being I can feel the power of sin contending against the rule of my mind, leading me away an obedient slave to all kinds of sensuality." Here the life of the mind is pitted against bodily existence (sensuality).
2. It is important to note that Scripture gives us no organized and extensive theology of sexuality. Most of the biblical passages about our sexuality either mention sexuality in passing as an illustration of some deeper point or are addressing some moral problem and laying down an ethical guideline for believers. Sexuality was not a major preoccupation of the biblical authors,

so assertions about our "theology of sexuality" must always remain a bit tentative.

3. Madeleine L'Engle, *The Irrational Season* (New York: Seabury Press, 1977), page 15. Used by permission from HarperCollins Publishers.

4. See A. Kosnick et al., *Human Sexuality: New Directions in American Catholic Thought* (New York: Doubleday, 1977), chapter 4, for an intriguing discussion of this.

5. The reader should note that a number of modern translations of the Bible are moving away from using the term *flesh* because of precisely the confusion we are addressing here—that the body is some sort of special locus of sin. Thus, while the term *flesh* is commonly used for a variety of meanings in the *New American Standard* and *King James* versions, the term *sinful nature* is used for the same Greek and Hebrew words in the *New International Version*.

6. The kinds of issues that we will be summarizing in our discussions of child development can be examined further by looking at any major text in child development. Two of the best representatives of these kinds of work include P. Mussen et al., *Child Development and Personality*, 7th ed. (New York: Harper and Row, 1990); or C. Schuster and S. Ashburn, *The Process of Human Development: A Holistic Life-Span Approach*, 2d ed. (Boston: Little, Brown, 1986).

7. J. Heiman, "Orgasmic Disorders in Women," in S. Leiblum and R. Rosen, ed., *Principles and Practice of Sex Therapy*, 2d ed. (New York: Guilford, 1989), page 55.

8. For example, a popular nonreligious "family book" on sexuality defines a family as "Two or more people who, regardless of gender, age (although one must be legally an adult), or marital status, elect to live together in commitment and trust in order to care for and about each other." M. Calderone and E. Johnson, *The Family Book About Sexuality*, rev. ed. (New York: Harper & Row, 1989), page 123.

CHAPTER 6: TEACHING THE GOODNESS OF OUR BODIES

1. S. Gordon and J. Gordon, *Raising a Child Conservatively in a Sexually Permissive World* (New York: Simon and Schuster, 1983). This is an excellent book, but the "conservativism" of the authors is a relative matter. They do not support promiscuity, but ultimately the book lacks any religious base and any compelling moral foundation in support of chastity.

CHAPTER 7: HANDLING SEXUAL CURIOSITY AND SEXUAL PLAY

1. See K. Wright, "Evolution of the Big O," *Discover*, June 1992, pages 53-58.

2. Once upon a time, it was said with some confidence that, of all female animal species, only human females experienced orgasm. The best current research, however, suggests that in some primate species and a few nonprimates, females do exhibit intensely pleasurable responses to sexual stimulation and from external observation seem to experience something like

orgasm. See Wright, pages 53-58.

3. M. Calderone and E. Johnson, *The Family Book About Sexuality*, rev. ed. (New York: Harper & Row, 1989), page 25.

CHAPTER 8: PREVENTING AND OVERCOMING SEXUAL MOLESTATION

1. Finkelhor (1984) as reported in Masters, et al., *Human Sexuality*, 4th ed. (Glenview, IL: Scott, Foresman and Company, 1992), pages 458-459.
2. M. Calderone and J. Ramey, *Talking with Your Child About Sex* (New York: Random House, 1982), page 59.

CHAPTER 9: GENDER IDENTIFICATION AND SEXUAL ORIENTATION

1. See the discussion in J. Joseph Nicolosi, *Reparative Therapy of Male Homosexuality: A New Clinical Approach* (New York: Jason Aronson, 1991), pages 32ff.
2. See S. Jones, "Doesn't Modern Science Teach That Persons of Homosexual Orientation Are Born That Way?" This was part of the minority response to the majority report of the Special Commission on Human Sexuality of the United Presbyterian Church (USA) prepared for the 203rd General Assembly, which was entitled *Keeping Body and Soul Together*. Available from the Office of the General Assembly, PCUSA, 100 Witherspoon St., Louisville, KY.
3. See Jones and Nicolosi.
4. Ross Campbell's *How to Really Love Your Child* (Wheaton, IL: Victor, 1983) is still the classic discussion of concrete ways to communicate love to young children and to have a balanced approach to discipline, in our opinion.

CHAPTER 10: "WHAT IS SEX? WHY IS IT WRONG?"

1. Carolyn Nystrom, *Before I Was Born*, illustrated by Dwight Walles (Westchester, IL: Crossway, 1984); sadly, out of print. Used by permission of the author.
2. L. Smedes, *Sex for Christians* (Grand Rapids: Eerdmans, 1976), page 129 (emphasis added). For a more "scholarly" discussion of these issues, see S. Grenz, *Sexual Ethics* (Dallas: Word, 1990).
3. A. Greeley, *Faithful Attraction* (New York: Tor Books, 1991), chapter 17. This effect is not overpowering, but is quite significant.

CHAPTER 11: INOCULATING YOUR KIDS

1. Planned Parenthood Federation of America, *How to Talk With Your Child About Sexuality* (New York: Doubleday, 1986), page 59.
2. Planned Parenthood, page 98.
3. See the summary of D. Myers, *Social Psychology*, 3d ed. (New York: McGraw-Hill, 1990), pages 261-265.
4. Myers, page 262.

5. Tim Stafford, *The Sexual Christian* (Wheaton, IL: Christianity Today/Victor, 1989).

6. W. Masters et al., *Human Sexuality*, 4th ed. (Glenview, IL: Scott, Foresman and Company, 1992), page 306.

7. Planned Parenthood, pages 98-99.

8. Planned Parenthood, pages 104-105.

9. Planned Parenthood, page 104.

10. C. Heyward, *Touching Our Strength: The Erotic as Power and the Love of God* (San Francisco: Harper, 1989); J. Nelson, *Embodiment: An Approach to Sexuality and Christian Theology* (Minneapolis: Augsburg, 1978).

11. By virtue of their role as authorities, adolescents expect adults to disapprove of premarital sexual intercourse by adolescents. Non-reaction by adults under conditions of expected disapproval is interpreted by adolescents as approval." D. Baumrind, "Adolescent Sexuality: Comment on Williams' and Silka's Comments on Baumrind," *American Psychologist* 37, no. 12, page 1402.

CHAPTER 12: LAYING THE GROUNDWORK FOR ADOLESCENCE

1. B. Benda and F. Diblasio, "Comparison of Four Theories of Adolescent Sexual Exploration," *Deviant Behavior: An Interdisciplinary Journal* 12, pages 235-257. Benda and DiBlasio survey this research. One of the best single studies is R. Jessor et al., "Time of First Intercourse: A Prospective Study," *Journal of Personality and Social Psychology* 44 (1983), pages 608-626.

2. Benda and Diblasio, pages 235-257.

3. C. Hayes, ed., "Determinants of Adolescent Sexual Behavior and Decision Making," in *Risking the Future: Adolescent Sexuality, Pregnancy, and Childbearing* (Washington: National Academy Press, 1987).

4. R. Jessor and S. Jessor, *Problem Behavior and Psychosocial Development: A Longitudinal Study of Youth* (New York: Academic Press, 1977).

5. Developmental psychologists have shown that being able to understand how a geometric form (such as a domino) looks to another observer who is looking at it from a different perspective is a capacity that naturally develops in the young child around age four or five. They have also shown, however, that children can be taught to perceive things from the other person's perspective. In other words, the capacity to see things from other perspectives can be facilitated or frustrated. We believe that this has direct applicability to the area of emotions.

CHAPTER 13: PREPARING FOR THE PHYSICAL CHANGES OF PUBERTY

1. C. Hayes, ed., "Determinants of Adolescent Sexual Behavior and Decision Making," in *Risking the Future: Adolescent Sexuality, Pregnancy, and Childbearing* (Washington: National Academy Press, 1987).

CHAPTER 14: PREPARING FOR DATING

1. C. Hayes, ed., "Determinants of Adolescent Sexual Behavior and Decision

Making," in *Risking the Future: Adolescent Sexuality, Pregnancy, and Childbearing* (Washington: National Academy Press, 1987), page 103.

2. Planned Parenthood Federation of America, *How to Talk with Your Child About Sexuality* (New York: Doubleday, 1986), page 11.

3. "Teenagers and AIDS," *Newsweek*, August 3, 1992, page 46.

4. We have lost the documentation of this particular study.

5. C.S. Lewis, *Mere Christianity* (New York: Macmillan, 1943), page 99.

6. James Dobson, *Preparing for Adolescence* (Ventura, CA: Regal, 1989), pages 91ff.

7. J. McDowell and D. Day, *Why Wait?* (San Bernardino, CA: Here's Life, 1987).

8. S. Jessor and R. Jessor, *Problem Behavior and Psychosocial Development* (New York: Academic Press, 1977).

CHAPTER 15: DEVELOPING MORAL DISCERNMENT ABOUT PETTING

1. J. Jaffe et al., "Anal Intercourse and Knowledge of AIDS Among Minority Group Adolescents," *Journal of Pediatrics* 112 (1988), pages 1005-1007.

2. S. Newcomer and J. Udry, "Oral Sex in an Adolescent Population," *Archives of Sexual Behavior* 14 (1985), pages 41-46.

CHAPTER 16: SOLITARY SEX: MASTURBATION AND PORNOGRAPHY

1. *Christianity Today*, October 2, 1987, page 33.

2. J. Johnson, "Toward a Biblical Approach to Masturbation," *Journal of Psychology and Theology* 10 (1982), pages 137-146.

3. Lewis Smedes, *Sex for Christians* (Grand Rapids: Eerdmans, 1976).

4. J. Dobson, *Preparing for Adolescence* (Ventura, CA: Regal, 1989), pages 83-84.

5. M. Calderone and E. Johnson, *The Family Book About Sexuality*, rev. ed. (New York: Harper & Row, 1989), page 142.

6. E. Donnerstein, "Massive Exposure to Sexual Violence and Desensitization to Violence and Rape," unpublished paper summarized in W. Masters et al., *Human Sexuality*, 4th ed. (Glenview, IL: Scott, Foresman and Company, 1992), page 352.

7. For instance, A. Jurs, *Becoming Unglued: A Guide to Help Children Develop Positive TV Habits* (San Marcos, CA: Robert Eerdmann, 1992).

8. *Final Report of the Attorney General's Commission on Pornography* (1986). Originally published by the U.S. Department of Justice; republished with a new introduction by Rutledge Hill Press and distributed by Word Books and Focus on the Family.

CHAPTER 17: SUPPORTING THE ADOLESCENT

1. We are here following the summary of the research by Flora and Thoresen who stated, "Programs demonstrating these results generally have these components in common: (a) Peer pressure resistance training, through the use

of role playing and behavior skills training, (b) Information on immediate physiological effects of smoking, (c) Making a public commitment to behave in particular ways, (d) Altering misperceptions about smoking prevalence, (e) Discussing family influences, (f) Inoculations against mass media on smoking and (g) Use of high status peer leaders." J. Flora and C. Thoresen, "Reducing the Risk of AIDS in Adolescents," *American Psychologist* 43, no. 11 (1988), page 967. The idea of applying the smoking prevention research to teen sexuality is theirs, and is not original to us. Flora and Thoresen, however, apply prevention ideas more to increasing condom usage than abstinence.

2. David Lynn and Mike Yaconelli, *Teaching the Truth About Sex: Biblical Sex Education for Today's Youth* (Grand Rapids: Zondervan, 1990).

3. Available from P.O. Box 1000, Dallas, TX 75221.

4. Available from P.O. Box 97, Golf, IL 60029.

5. These points are taken from M. Howard, *How to Help Your Teenager Postpone Sexual Involvement* (New York: Continuum, 1989), pages 82-83.

6. Among others, Focus on the Family is coming out with a line of curriculum and video support materials that may be ideal for this purpose.

7. J. Flora and C. Thoresen, page 967. Two conservative Christian critiques of public sex education are D. Richards, *Has Sex Education Failed Our Children?* (Colorado Springs: Focus on the Family, 1990) and J. McDowell, *The Myths of Sex Education* (San Bernardino, CA: Here's Life, 1990). For other references on the failure of sex education, see the relevant references in chapter 1.

8. "Teenagers and AIDS," *Newsweek*, August 3, 1992, page 46.

9. See, for example, P. Mussen et al., *Child Development and Personality*, 7th ed. (New York: Harper and Row, 1990).

10. C. Gilligan, "Sexual Dilemmas at the High School Level," in M. Calderone, ed., *Sexuality and Human Values: The Personal Dimension of Sexual Experience* (New York: Association Press, 1974), pages 98-110.

11. T. Buchanan, "Age Related Difference in the Moral Judgment—Moral Action Relation: A Meta-analytic Review," unpublished manuscript under review for publication, University of New Hampshire, Durham, New Hampshire.

12. L. Furby and R. Beyth-Marom, "Risk Taking in Adolescence: A Decision-Making Perspective," *Developmental Review* 12, 1992, pages 1-44.

13. Furby and Beyth-Marom, page 7.

14. Furby and Beyth-Marom, page 8.

15. G. Loewenstein and F. Furstenberg, "Is Teenage Sexual Behavior Rational?" *Journal of Applied Social Psychology* 21 (1991), pages 957-986.

16. This was discussed in a very excellent fashion in the book by M. Howard, *How to Help Your Teenager Postpone Sexual Involvement* (New York: Continuum, 1989), pages 15-22.

CHAPTER 18: THE COMMITMENT TO CHASTITY

1. See a good summary of this research in J. Flora and C. Thoresen, "Reducing

the Risk of AIDS in Adolescents," *American Psychologist* 43, no. 11 (1988), page 967.

CHAPTER 19: TEACHING YOUR TEENAGER ABOUT CONTRACEPTION

1. A prominent psychologist typifies this view in urging that "protection programs might be developed to help adolescents accept their sexuality (i.e., a 'liberal' attitude towards sexuality, sex education programs, contraceptive service)." N.D. Repucci, "Prevention and Ecology: Teen-age Pregnancy, Child Sexual Abuse, and Organized Youth Sports," *American Journal of Community Psychology* 15 (1987), page 5. See also pages 1-22.
2. For an introduction to the issues involved in this debate, an interested reader could seek out the *Christianity Today Special Issue*, which dealt with birth control, November 11, 1991.
3. D. Baumrind, "Adolescent Sexuality: Comment on Williams' and Silka's Comments on Baumrind," *American Psychologist* 37, no. 12 (1982), page 1402.
4. See also pages 52-53 of D. Richard, *Has Sex Education Failed Our Teenagers: A Research Report* (Colorado Springs: Focus on the Family, 1990) for a strong set of criticisms of the inclusion of any instruction on contraceptives in sex education.
5. D. Evans, "The Price of the Pill," *Christianity Today*, November 11, 1991, pages 39-40.
6. M. Studer and A. Thornton, "Adolescent Religiosity and Contraceptive Usage," *Journal of Marriage and the Family* 49 (1987), pages 117-128; D. Morrison, "Adolescent Contraceptive Behavior: A Review," *Psychological Bulletin* 98, 1985, pages 538-568.
7. W. Masters et al., *Human Sexuality*, 4th ed. (Glenview, IL: Scott, Foresman and Company, 1992), page 230.
8. The reader interested in a historical background for this perspective might want to read the *Westminster Longer Catechism*, questions 150 and 151.
9. J. Beck and D. Davies, "Teen Contraception: A Review of Perspectives on Compliance," *Archives of Sexual Behavior* 16 (1987), pages 337-368.
10. Planned Parenthood Federation of America, *How to Talk with Your Child About Sexuality* (New York: Doubleday, 1986), page 83.
11. N. Ryder, "Contraceptive Failure in the United States," *Family Planning Perspectives*, Summer 1973, pages 133-142.
12. M. Fisher et al., "Comparative Analysis of the Effectiveness of the Diaphragm and Birth Control Pill During the First Year of Use Among Suburban Adolescents," *Journal of Adolescent Health Care* (1987), pages 393-395.

CHAPTER 20: DATE RAPE, COHABITATION, ABORTION, HOMOSEXUALITY

1. W. Masters, et al., *Human Sexuality*, 4th ed. (New York: HarperCollins, 1992), pages 444ff.
2. K. Moore et al., "Nonvoluntary Sexual Activity Among Adolescents,"

Family Planning Perspectives 21 (1989), pages 110-114.

3. A. Astin et al., *The American Freshman: National Norms for Fall 1989* (Los Angeles: American Council on Education and UCLA, 1989).

4. Masters, page 306.

5. S. Gordon and J. Gordon, *Raising a Child Conservatively in a Sexually Permissive World* (New York: Simon and Schuster, 1983), page 107.

6. T. Balakrishan et al., "A Hazard Model Analysis of the Covariates of Marriage Dissolution in Canada," *Demography* 24 (1987), pages 395-406; N. Bennett et al., "Commitment and the Modern Union: Assessing the Link Between Premarital Cohabitation and Subsequent Marital Stability," *American Sociological Review* 53, pages 127-138; L. Bumpass and J. Sweet, "National Estimates of Cohabitation," *Demography* 26 (1989), pages 615-625.

7. R. Friedman, "The Psychoanalytical Model of Male Homosexuality: A Historical and Theoretical Critique," *The Psychoanalytical Review* 73, no. 3 (1986), page 85.

Authors

✤

Stanton L. Jones, Ph.D., is professor and chairperson of the Department of Psychology at Wheaton College, where he has been directing the development of the college's doctoral program in clinical psychology. He coauthored *Modern Psychotherapies: A Comprehensive Christian Appraisal* with Richard E. Butman, and edited *Psychology and the Christian Faith: An Introductory Reader*. He has contributed a number of articles to professional journals and to magazines such as *Christianity Today*.

Brenna B. Jones is a mother whose goals have focused on the nurture and formation of the character of her children. Her undergraduate studies were in landscape architecture at Texas A & M University. She has served as a leader in a Bible study ministry with women for a number of years.

Brenna and Stan are active in a church ministry to engaged couples. They make their home in Wheaton, Illinios, where they parent three children: Jenny, Brandon, and Lindsay.